The Language of Modern Drama

Gareth Lloyd Evans

Dent, London, Melbourne and Toronto

Rowman and Littlefield, Totowa, N.J.

© Gareth Lloyd Evans, 1977
All rights reserved
Printed in Great Britain by
Biddles Ltd, Guildford, Surrey
and bound at the
Aldine Press, Letchworth, Herts
for
J. M. Dent & Sons Ltd
Aldine House, Albemarle Street, London
First published in the U.K. (Everyman's University Library) 1977

First published in the United States
by Rowman and Littlefield, Totowa, N.J. 1977

This book if bound as a paperback is subject to the condition that it may not be issued
on loan or otherwise except in its original binding

This book is set in 11 on 12 point VIP Bembo

Dent edition
Hardback ISBN 0 460 10900 6
Paperback ISBN 0 460 11900 1

Rowman and Littlefield edition
Hardback ISBN 0-87471-990-0

British Library Cataloguing in Publication Data
Evans, Gareth Lloyd
    The language of modern drama. (Everyman's university library).
    Bibl. — Index.
    ISBN 0-460-10900-6
    ISBN 0-460-11900-1 Pbk
    1. Title 2. Series
    822'.9'1209   PR739.L3
    English drama — 20th century — History and criticism
    American drama — 20th century — History and criticism

The Language of Modern Drama

Contents

Preface

Publishers count themselves wise, and probably are, in their stern exhortations to authors never to reveal in preface or introduction what their book is not about. In ringing terms they should accentuate the positive, not advertise the negative.

I intend to break this tacit rule for a number of reasons. First, because the title of the book might be taken as promising a full and comprehensive historical study of the subject. Second, because I am anxious not to raise expectations which will not be fulfilled—which the book does not intend to fulfil. And, third, because I have an unbreakable if expedient faith in the notion that a compounding of negatives will eventually create a positive.

The implications of the title of this book constitute the most important reasons for expressing its intended scope in negative terms. The day of the encyclopaedic treatment of the arts is with us. The use of the temporal terms 'twentieth century' and 'modern', with their still haunting reverberations from the credit titles of the great days of Hollywood, suggests epic or serial vision and scope. My use of the term is not intended to have any sense of inflation, but, simply descriptively, to indicate that all the drama discussed in any detail was written by authors whose major work appeared in this century.

But the word 'drama' itself gives an impression of wide concern. My use of the word in the title is not intended to imply that all the century's major dramatists, nor by any means all the plays of those who do appear, are discussed. Moreover it is confined to works by British and American dramatists. An apparently more accurate phrase, like 'some dramatists', seems to me evasive. In any case, the use of the word 'drama' is intended not only to indicate the area of study but to focus the attention on the complexities of the word itself—part of the book's intention is to explore what is meant by 'drama'.

And, finally, in this parade of negatives, the word 'language' is crucial. The triumph of the encyclopaedist is matched only by that of the ubiquitous linguists. The fastidious ministrations to language of the old Grammarians and style-samplers have given place to the immense and often fierce lab-work of the linguists. To mention the word 'language' today (certainly in academic circles) is to call up a kind of study which, to most men of mere literature, is incomprehensible. This book is not, in any sense, a linguistic study, though it may have its own opacities. Its use of the word 'language' is to do with the way creative artists employ words creatively—in dialogue, stage-directions and related functions. It is also used in its now common sense to mean 'that which communicates'—as in, for example, 'the language of mime'. I try to place my main emphasis on the relationship that should exist between the verbal language of the dramatist and that non-verbal form—the language of theatre itself —with its vocabulary of lighting, sets, props, etc.

The authors and the plays discussed have been chosen in order to try and demonstrate their uses and abuses, their forms and formlessnesses, their subtleties and their crudities of language. Although, because of the selective nature of this book, no deliberate attempt has been made to accept the evidence of a mere one or two plays in order to make definitive critical assessments, I have not tried to avoid the expression of critical comment. It is impossible to study the very chambers of the heart of drama—its language—without coming to some opinion about the state of the rest of the body.

Underlying my decision to write this book are two motivations which, for me, have the force of beliefs. One—that the twentieth century has produced some of the most distinguished and varied examples of dramatic language in the history of drama. Two, that this same century, in its later decades, in drama, literature, education—the media of communication—has seen a decay in the use of language of alarming proportions.

So, on the one hand, the book is motivated by the rich fascination of the subject and, on the other, by what may seem, at times, to be a fierce despair. In neither respect, I hope, has my judgment entirely fled to brutish extremes.

There are many people to thank. Every book I write on drama contains my direct or implicit gratitude to the so-called 'common players'. It is only the actors and actresses who, ultimately, can prove the glorious efficacy of true dramatic language.

Again, every book on the subject I have attempted owes a debt to my mentor, colleague and friend, Allardyce Nicoll, recently dead. I have tried always to follow his advice—the best any scholar (or, indeed, anyone bent on proof and persuasion) can be given. He said, 'One of the dangers of research is that you discover what you set out to find.' He himself never urged mere opinion as fact, or theory as evidence, or enthusiasm as proof, though he employed all in judicious balance. I cannot emulate him though I have tried to. I hope my failings will not vex his ghost.

I cannot thank my wife in so many words. She will best understand that my depth of gratitude for her wise and loving encouragement is beyond expression.

Sometimes in the theatre when, for reasons that are rarely explained, the curtain (or its non-apparent alternative) is late rising, we while away the time by reading the credits on the theatre programme—cigarettes by Puffer, musical instruments by Blower, lighting by Power. They are the usually unheeded essentials. For years I have relied upon typing by Mrs Judi Payne. She has never been less than marvellously efficient, patient and swift. I hope she will accept my thanks for a very much needed and appreciated essential.

Gareth Lloyd Evans

Stratford upon Avon, 1977

Introduction

As the lights dim in a theatre auditorium before the beginning of a performance, the audience is being prepared to enter into another world. Often it seems to have the lineaments of their own familiar everyday world and the creatures they meet in it seem to have a distinct resemblance to themselves or to people they know—in which case the experience has at least the comfort of familiarity. But sometimes, of course, the revealed world of the stage is quite strange, requiring some mental adjustment to accept it, and some intellectual effort to understand it. More disturbingly, what we hear and see of its citizens is radically unlike anything we have known before. In this case the emotions of expectation, even fear, may be stirred.

Yet, putting aside the stranger areas of those theatre experiences which even in form and communication are remote from our everyday world—like ballet, dance, music, mime —all the rest have one single unmistakable common denominator. However familiar or unfamiliar the world of a tragedy, comedy, farce or melodrama may be, everything that we experience has its source, in the long run, in words. Even in contemporary theatre where, sometimes to our chagrin, dramatists seem somewhat parsimonious or eccentric or out-of-sorts about words, their creative presence is absolute. The famous Pinter pauses could not happen unless they were bracketed by words. Samuel Beckett's disturbing safaris into non-verbal territory have meaning only because we know that the verbal exists; more important Beckett's meaning depends on his own awareness that we are bound to make a tacit

connection between his dramatic silences and the language
that we know could fill them.

This book is written out of a conviction that there is a place
for any kind of drama that is created with honesty and artistic
responsibility. But it has been written with an equally strong
belief that, in the last third of the twentieth century, one of the
most important of these forms is in serious danger of being
relegated to a minor position. Forms and modes, in everything, rise and fall, come and go, but in this case the falling
away has a general as well as a specific significance. The case in
point is verbal drama.

The association of drama and verbal communication has a
very long, distinctive and distinguished history. Greek,
Roman, Elizabethan and late nineteenth- and twentieth-
century drama alone exemplify this—and there are, obviously, other examples which could be called upon. The fecundity
of this association—if that needed any proof—is amply shown
by a mere (and far from complete) catalogue of names—
Euripides, Aeschylus, Aristophanes, Marlowe, Shakespeare,
Jonson, Lope da Vega, Moliere, Congreve, Wilde, Ibsen, Shaw,
O'Neill, Eliot, Pinter.

The relationship, then, of drama with man's unique attribute—the ability to communicate in words both spoken and
written—is strong and deep. Moreover, the relationship has
never dismissively precluded the use of other forms of communication in the theatre—dance and music in the Elizabethan
age, the masque in the Jacobean period and, subsequently,
mime, ballet and film. There has been an equally fecund
history of happy marriage of words with other forms of
expression, notably in opera.

But, in the Western world, not until the latter third of the
twentieth century has there been so much apparent evidence
that verbal drama both in its own terms and in consort with
other forms of expression is in jeopardy. It seems ready to be
overcome by forces which regard it as outmoded, even
restrictive:

> . . . it is essential to put an end to the subjugation of the theatre
> to the text, and to recover the notion of a kind of unique
> language half-way between gesture and thought.[1]

Artaud's pronouncement has been echoed and re-echoed in the century since he made it and a good deal of contemporary drama (both good and bad) has tried to put it into practice.

Yet the effects of the decay of language are far from being confined to drama as a performed art:

> 'A discussion of Shakespeare's language and style can be a valuable and a delightful lesson for senior pupils: but it is a lesson that has nothing to do with the drama, and certainly nothing to do with a dramatic reading' . . . the report warns that there are dull passages in the great plays which the teacher had 'better omit', just as there are minor plays which are quite unsuitable for pupils to study.

The passage quoted is from a commentary in *Drama in Education* published in 1972. The passage is itself quoting from a report of 1919 for the Board of Education on the teaching of English in England. By the 1970s what is expressed and, even more, what is implied here has become received gospel for a growing majority of teachers of English and drama. The value of the word in the 1919 report is being 'allowed' with more than a hint of intellectual snobbery; the relevance of the verbal texture of a play to its dramatic qualities is positively denied. The committee which produced the report included Henry Newbolt, Arthur Quiller Couch, Caroline Spurgeon and John Dover Wilson.

By far the greatest influence on the huge growth of the importance placed on drama as an educative force has been made by agencies who, often with a fierce sincerity, seem to equate verbal activity with psychological restrictiveness, verbal facility with intellectuality and nothing else, and the study of the verbal as an emblem of an élitist approach to education. An emphasis is now placed on the proposition that non-verbal communication (and that can only mean aural, physical or extra-sensory) offers a far greater range and flexibility of expression.

It is, of course, certain, that communication by physical movement and by sound alone without verbal shape is common to the animal world, and it may well emerge that extra-sensory communication is also used by some or all species. But no one can tell the extent to which, or whether the use of, these methods gives the animal world a greater, more subtle, more flexible range of expression. What is clear is that the use of words has given to man exclusively an astonishing range, both intellectually and emotionally. At the same time, however much man, as artist, has refined and subtilized physical expression and aural communication he has fallen far short of the grace and apparent swiftness of apprehension of the animal world. More than this, there is little if any evidence that the animal kingdom is capable of even the most minimal form of reasoning—one of man's most precious attributes, and significantly one whose presence is demonstrated by a power over words. There seems little evidence to suggest that man, even though he does and should pursue the mysteries of the non-verbal, is in a position where he can, with safety, relinquish his gift of words.

Words must be cared for but those who care may well feel that there is no need for a book to celebrate that care, particularly one on the words of dramatists—upon which a good deal has been written. Yet it is astonishing that there has been relatively little study of the unique way in which the dramatist uses words. He is so often regarded as a spinner of tales, a weaver of characters, a mongerer of words much as a novelist or poet or journalist is. He has often and is now habitually taken to be the man who provides the mere raw material out of which others—the actor and the director—do the real dramatic creating. This book is written in the conviction that one of the ways a caring for words can be demonstrated is by examining the uniqueness of the way dramatists use them—in fact, have to use them, if they are to create true drama.

It would be taxing, however, to expect a theatre audience to be sternly aware of this unique force as they sit in the darkening auditorium Not only would it be taxing, it would be downright offputting. Yet the fact remains that all that they see ultimately depends on words. Take, for instance, what we call 'character'; most theatregoers would associate character not so much with words as with 'someone'. For them, that 'someone' is an amalgam of the actor and the part he is playing. No one goes to the theatre simply to see Olivier, or, conversely, simply to see Hamlet. They go to see Olivier/Hamlet. Indeed, for many theatregoers a rhythmical transposition is taking place as they watch Olivier playing Hamlet playing Olivier playing Hamlet—and so on like the Chinese box. But the blunt, and what should be the obvious, truth is that Olivier could not play Hamlet until, first, he had read and learnt his lines and, second, the dramatist, by verbal selection, had given him all that he needed to create what was required. The greatest actor can do nothing to create character until he has become engaged with words. What, in the exigencies of rehearsal, the egotism of temperament, or the whim of a director, he adds as he goes along is his alone (and the result should be his responsibility or the director's). But it should be remembered that even additions cannot be made unless the foundation exists.

But the potency of words in the creation of character alone is more subtle than what has been thus far described. If we accept that a single character takes life only when the actor has engaged himself with the playwright's words, it must follow that the relationships between several characters, as they are developed by actors, have their bases in words. If all we knew of Hamlet was a succession of soliloquies spoken most wonderfully we might be grateful but hardly inclined to believe that we had had an experience of completely dramatic and human proportions. It is when characters like Polonius utter words like, 'What is't you read, my Lord?' and receive the reply, 'Words, words, words' that the stuff of drama begins to be woven, because the words are providing not merely question and answer but attitude and relationship.

How often, in far less profound plays than *Hamlet,* do we find characters who so to speak 'hang about' in the plays in which they appear. They are the waifs and strays of drama. They are seen standing unhappily around, frequently with a glass in their hands (excessive use of alcoholic containers is often a symptom of faulty dramatic conception); they make occasional gestures, they smile, they leer, they say, 'I'd better go, then', or, 'I knew he'd come back—now my job is done.' Sometimes, however, they reappear, like Marley's ghost, but with far less justification. We are inclined to refer to them as 'pasteboard characters'. If we are of an academic turn of mind we point to them significantly as examples of the playwright's 'inability to create minor characters'. Whatever language we adopt, what we are really saying is that, in some way, the words out of which a believable character is supposed to emerge are being inefficiently used. The actor called upon to use them in order to create the performance may huff and puff and bellow and blow in an attempt to fill an empty vessel, but unless the playwright has distilled the true and potent essence in his words, the vessel cannot be anything but empty.

But it is not character alone which owes its existence to the power of words. The plot, the theme, the locations, also, ultimately, derive from them.

Where theme is concerned—that is, what the play is concerned with and which can be abstracted from it, described and discussed in non-dramatic terms, such as the theme of ambition in *Macbeth,* of jealousy in *Othello*—it is not difficult to see the role of the verbal. How else could a playwright express what he wishes to express except through the selection and placing of ideas and attitudes verbally in the play? Action, of course, has some part to play in this, but it is subservient to the verbal—indeed the motivation behind action cannot be comprehensively explained and expressed except in verbal terms.

Where plot and location are concerned, the association with words is less easy to see and perhaps, for some theatregoers, pointless to consider. We think of plot in mechanical terms, as if it is something rather ingeniously constructed by some kind of mental meccano, into which words and characters are fitted—if the construction is correct, the fit will be neat and pleasing. Indeed some plays seem to be constructed by such a method. But good and great plays are not. The true dramatist does not work in a dissociated sense conceiving of separate elements like plot, character, language, theme, locations, and then do what he hopes is a cunning job of construction. The true dramatist fulfils E. M. Forster's profound dictum (as applicable to art as to society)—'Only connect'. The connection between what the simple hack conceives of as separate elements to be jobbed together begins, in the true dramatist, with the initial conception, in the first spinning of the imagination.

In the true dramatist, then, what the characters 'are', what they do, are an inseparable part of what happens (that is, plot).

To imagine Macbeth turning up in the romantic complications of *Twelfth Night* is as ludicrous as to envisage Viola as the fourth witch. Language dictates the reality of character and character is conjugated with plot.

Location and its associated elements—stage-furniture and movement within the stated confines of the play's world—would seem to have little to do with words. But any intelligent theatregoer's experience can confute this. How often, despite the prodigious efforts of the stage-carpenter, the lighting-engineer, the scenic-painter, quite apart from the sometimes alarmed and always alarming sacrifices of the theatre financier, do we find ourselves in an audience looking at something that has signally failed to 'be' (in terms of place) what the play is asking for. Correct detail, scale, colour, material, mean nothing unless the location is 'right' for both actor and audience. Place has to fit a character as exactly as a costume should. Frequently we find, as we stare at a set that is dead despite all the ministrations of mechanics, that our ears have suddenly enabled us to imagine it alive—for a character has spoken something that identifies him with place—the particular place we should be seeing. The playwright's words, through the character's mouth, into our ears, have made us see what should be seen—and, moreover, we see it in terms of the character who is resident in the location.

In Pinter's *The Caretaker*,[2] the incessant dripping of the rain water filling the bucket that hangs from the ceiling not only sums up the sinister desolation of the attic, but the inevitable resignation which characterizes the presentation of Mick. He, when asked by Aston, the tramp, what he will do when the bucket is full, replies that he will empty it. We feel he will be emptying it for ever.

The importance of words in this matter of location, stage-furniture, movement, is graphically evidenced by the fact that the natural and mature playwright will require a minimum of stage-directions (unless, like Shaw, he puts them in for reasons often quite unconnected with the communication of the play on stage). The true playwright incorporates his stage-directions in his text. We need no director, no flying set, no cyclorama, to tell us where we are here:

> This castle hath a pleasant seat; the air
> Nimbly and sweetly recommends itself
> Unto our gentle senses.[3]

But, more subtly, the very same place can be made to change its 'mood' depending on who is describing it, and under what circumstances:

> The raven himself is hoarse
> That croaks the fatal entrance of Duncan
> Under my battlements.[4]

'Locale' is in a sense at the mercy of character, which itself is the progeny of language.

Again, no actor should need telling by a director what his body movements should be while these words are being spoken—for these words are directing the body's movements:

> Thou sure and firm set earth
> Hear not my steps, which way they walk, for fear
> The very stones prate of my whereabouts,
> And take the present horror from the time,
> Which now suits with it.[5]

Or, again, how can the organic and crucial necessity of words in dramatic realization be minimized or denied when we notice how a stage object can take on almost the function of an extra character as the words which, so to say, 'surround' it, give it much more than a local habitation and a name? They give it, in fact, what for the audience becomes an almost breathtaking attachment to mood, theme and character.

In Pinter's *The Homecoming*,[6] an inanimate piece of stage-furniture becomes a kind of Pandarus to finalize the lust that develops between Ruth and Lenny. Ruth, indeed, in her hot pursuit, identifies Lenny with the glass of water she has offered him. If he takes it, she will take him. Sipping the water, opening the mouth, holding the glass, become intensely dramatic sexual actions.

That inanimate piece of stage furniture becomes a kind of Pandarus—but only because the words dictating the movements cause it to be thus.

Any assertion of the pre-eminence of words in the total entity of what we call a play seems to run the risk of urging the obvious. But this may perhaps be excused on a number of counts. First, because the evidence is that, in a significant area of theatre today, the pre-eminence is, in theory and practice, discounted. In an even larger area of educational theory and practice the whole range of what we call communication by language is besieged by methods of teaching and attitudes which place more stress on 'freedom' of expression than on either accuracy or felicity. Second, because in the late twentieth-century theatre where the autocracy of the director is either tacitly implied or absolutely explicit, matters pertaining to the playwright are likely to be overlooked or overborne. There is a certain mordant truth in the cynical definition of the playwright given by a modern director—'A playwright is a man who writes a masterpiece, leaves it at the stage-door and goes home and commits suicide.' There can be little doubt that the verbal playwright, with notable exceptions, in the old accepted sense of the word is coming to occupy more and more a shadowy place in the world of theatre. An assertion of his traditional role as the 'onlie begetter' may not come amiss—particularly to a younger generation. Third, in a society in which many people believe that verbal standards of communication are being eroded, an assertion of the extraordinary power, beauty and utility of words when used in a controlled way cannot, surely, be misplaced. When a writer asks this question:

> Are we passing out of an historical era of verbal primacy, out of the classic period of literate expression into a phase of decayed language, of 'post-linguistic' forms and, perhaps, of partial silence?[7]

—we should ask what evidence there is of this in our drama.

An assertion of the importance of words to the playwright presupposes first, that he uses them in a way which is unique, if only because he is asking them to do so much; second, that the nature of that uniqueness can be demonstrated, if not fully realized, even without the benefit of experiencing his work on a stage; third, that while there may be strong resemblances between his use of them and that of a poet or novelist, these should never be regarded as evidence that exactly the same critical procedures can be used in analysing and discussing a play as are employed for a poem or a novel. For decades the study of mediaeval dramas was dogged and their quality entirely devalued by a critical process which saw their verbal content as bad verse rather than as (often) splendid dramatic dialogue.

The playwright is often identified in critical works as someone who has 'dramatic instinct'. But the phrase is used so imprecisely as to be sometimes valueless. Another phrase—'dramatic quality'—is often used (frequently with similar imprecision) to designate those qualities in a play-text which make it suitable for stage performance—but at times it is used as if it were some kind of fertilizer added to a plant to produce a larger, more richly coloured result. Both phrases are, in fact, used sometimes as a kind of shifty convenience which pays lip-service to a realization that there must be some difference between a play and other verbal forms. Surprisingly, the precise nature of the difference has rarely been investigated in any detail.

This book is specifically concerned with some of the areas that have been outlined above. It briefly discusses the notions of 'drama' and 'the dramatist' but the main part will be concerned with demonstrating how a number of twentieth-century playwrights have employed and are employing words. Throughout the book there is intended to be an implied context—that of theatre itself. In the larger portion this implication will become more explicit as specific plays are discussed. The reader is invited, therefore, to dim the lights in the auditorium of his head and to listen and to see in his mind's eye as well as, it is hoped, both reading and reflecting.

Part I
The Language of Drama and Theatre

1 The Word and the Play

There are so many self-evident things to be said about language that we are often in danger of taking them, and language itself, for granted. It is always here, it won't go away—there is no need to worry about it.

It is, of course, self-evident that language is, both in written and spoken forms, an astonishingly subtle and flexible means of communication. The language used, as Eliot says, by 'the lean solicitor' in his documents is of a very different order both in structure, intention and effect, from that used by the novelist who 'is making an imitation, an imitation of the life of man on earth. He is making, it might be said, a working model of life as he sees it.' The language of the poet is very different from that of the critic; we could never confuse the work of the man who comes to you 'with a tale which holdeth children from play, and old men from the chimney corner' with that of

Those half-learned witlings, numerous in our isle,
As half-formed insects on the banks of Nile.

The language of any dramatist who has not shunted the verbal into some deracinated siding should be obviously different from that of the novelist, the poet and the critic in that it is written to be expressed in a public environment. It shares this application with preaching, oratory and other public forms of verbal communication. The nature of the connection between the dramatist's language and that of the others is beguilingly indicated in the fact that when we want to express the nature and (often) the success of the preacher or the orator we will naturally speak of his 'dramatic' qualities. Even Eliot's

1

lean and desiccated solicitor, when he steps into a public court and becomes advocate, often becomes a 'dramatic' tiger and is applauded for it.

Clearly, there must be some quality or qualities in the language of drama shared with other public acts which has the effect of being 'dramatic', and which, therefore, ought to be identifiable. In attempting to identify it we should not forget that novels can often be described as possessing a 'dramatic' quality, that certain kinds of poetry, even those intended for the solitary private reader, can claim the same description: *Paradise Lost,* for instance, is certainly very 'dramatic'—it thrills the spirit.

But the force of a play—as of a sermon or a political speech—seems the more potent because it is spoken aloud by real people. The dramatic quality in a play must be something that is capable of communication by skilled human beings—that is, the actors. We should not forget that the most successful preachers have also been most skilled manipulators of the art of acting—though few of them, especially the Welsh (those protean parchs) would admit it. As to politicians, no one who witnessed on film or television the sensational, but controlled histrionics of Kruschev when, in a session of the United Nations, he removed his shoe and banged the table with it, is under any illusions that the politician supreme is the actor supreme. After his performance was over, Kruschev retired for drinks with those to whom his shoe-banging was directed.

But the language of a play is distinguished from that of orator and preacher in that it is designed to enable the actors who speak it to 'impersonate' a character—to 'be' somebody else, fictionally. Part of the unique potency of the language of a play lies in its ability to enable an actor to assume another (fictional) persona and, importantly, to convince an audience that what they are hearing is how the impersonated character would speak in the given circumstances. The language of drama is doing its job properly and excitingly when it is convincing the audience that what is being heard is actual, is true, for the duration of the play.

We instinctively recognize true dramatic language, certainly when we hear it but also (if we have a receptive inner

2

ear) when we read it, although most people don't read plays. They want to listen to actors, not to the unvisualized imponderables of the inner ear. If the actor is doing his job aright—that is, if he has correctly 'read' the notation of the play's language—we instinctively know, as we listen to him, that this is the real thing.

We are moving somewhat away from the orator and preacher at this point. Although they use the actor's skill, they do it alone; although they, like the actor, may very well be attempting to create a special role while they thunder and orotundate, we all know, all along, whom we are listening to—their attempts at 'impersonation' do not invite our 'willing suspension of disbelief '—in fact, usually, when we listen to a politician, even a skilled one, we are invaded by a feeling that oscillates between admiration and incredulity.

The language of a play, on the page, has, like music, to be 'interpreted' by actors and directors before it is deemed to be in the correct condition for us to experience it. In many cases (immediately to mind springs the case of Joan Littlewood's ministrations to Shelagh Delaney's original text of *A Taste of Honey* or Elia Kazan's to Tennessee Williams's *Cat on a Hot Tin Roof*[1]) the play as a written entity is considerably changed in the course of preparation and rehearsal of the first production. The language of drama is at the mercy of the interpreter in a much more comprehensive way than the language of the musical score. This is because the language of drama *seems* to be common property because words are common to us all, while musical notation is not. We, and certainly the interpreters, start off in our appraisal of a play with the decided conceit of assuming we know the meanings of the words—we do not believe that we have to learn a special notation, and therefore we assume a familiarity which can breed many contempts. Apart from this, so far as the late twentieth century is concerned, the power of the interpreting director is very much greater than that of the musical conductor.

In the latter part of the twentieth century we have become conditioned to the notion that a director of a play is, in effect (sometimes absolutely), the most important element in the process of its communication on stage. The actors' names still have a magical effect upon us, as do their individual skills and

3

qualities, but at times even they seem to have to step back-stage, 'corpsed' into shadows by the spotlight that falls on, say, the name Tyrone Guthrie, Papp, Kazan, Peter Brook or Peter Hall. It is, however, a salutary thought (and it ought to be) that in the late sixteenth and early seventeenth cen-turies—the era of the greatest flowering of both drama and theatre—such admirable men would never have been heard of or would have been called Peter Quince and expected to toe the line—Bottom the actor's line.

The twentieth century has seen the triumph of another language—the language of theatre—a concomitant, but a major partner, to the language of drama. The language of theatre, in which the power of the director is invested, is now a vast apparatus identified separately from the language of drama. It is at the command of the director who can, at will, use its energy in the production of a play. The energy, it must be emphasized, is at the command of the director's will, not the actor's, not the playwright's. It is the director who calls upon the oratory of sets, lights, costumes, sound effects, to do their work.

Equally as profound in its effects on the playwright's work as the exercise of control over the language of theatre is the director's freedom to interpret the play. Together the manipu-lation of theatre-language—lighting, sound, sets, costumes—and the ingenuity of interpretation, can sometimes produce an end-product vastly different from the playwright's concep-tions. The word 'interpretation' is, nowadays, much overused and frequently abused. It is the motto of the scholar who seeks to describe some newly discovered aspect of a play's meaning or, in minutiae, some line, or phrase, or word. It is the darling of actors to describe what they call their 'approach' to the task of preparation of a role.

The actor's use of the word 'interpretation' is usually closest to that of the director. It is characterized by an instinctive perception or attitude towards the problems of embodying the character in performance—and this is sometimes achieved at the expense of a more scholarly way. Intuition is not always the scholar's strong suit, but he will always hedge his bets on any imaginative gambling with the apparently 'fail-safe' sys-tem of rational deduction. The actor is far more prepared, as is

4

the director, to abandon at the drop of a hat the scholarly method, largely because of a widespread belief that the method will inhibit an emotional flow—as philosophy is said to clip an angel's wings.

The director, today, often seems to use a hazy combination of intuitive and non-intuitive method in his interpretative work. The 'research' (another overused word) undertaken by some modern directors prior to rehearsal is sometimes deep, comprehensive and perceptive. But, in the long run, the results of this research are (and, to an extent, have to be) subsumed by subjective responses to the play. It is the nature of these responses, the amount of freedom or licence it involves, and the extent of its effect on the dramatist's creation that justifies discussion of interpretation and the role of the director.

This justification can be intensified simply by providing two examples of the extremes to which directorial power can go. The first example sounds like a joke, but it is as true as it is trite and ludicrous: a well-known director faced with a distinguished company at the first read-through for a production of *Othello*, addressed the assembly with the words—'Now, boys and girls, this is a sexy play. I want you to give it all you've got.' The second example is more serious, and comes from Jan Kott, the influential Polish director who described *A Midsummer Night's Dream* in these words: '*The Dream* is the most erotic of Shakespeare's plays. In no other tragedy or comedy of his, except *Troilus and Cressida*, is the eroticism expressed so brutally.'[2] The first point is arguable—some of Shakespeare's other plays could well claim more eroticism. But quite apart from the confusion raised as to whether we are to take *Troilus and Cressida* as comedy, tragedy, or neither, the second point is an astonishing claim about the brutality of the eroticism in *The Dream*. This might easily be ignored were it not for Kott's influence and were it not that here we have a clear example of the language of the play (since it is expression he is concerned with) being overborne by the director.

The subordination of the dramatist's text to the director's will is an unmistakable feature of the way of the theatre world in the latter part of this century. The process is, to a degree, the result of historical factors. In the great periods of dramatic

5

activity—in Greece and Elizabethan England—the dramatist was so close, in a workaday sense, to the actual final communication of his play that the idea that a play was something written and then irrevocably handed over from dramatist to director neither could nor did exist. Any changes in the play which happened (and it is certain that they did) during preparation and rehearsal must almost inevitably have involved the dramatist to a degree which today would normally be deemed surprisingly unusual.

Since the seventeenth century in England there has been a continuing process in which the dramatist's status as part of the entity of theatre has been eroded. In a way, it is true to say that over the centuries drama itself has been made 'respectable' by being given the accolade of literary work and, gradually, the benediction of becoming a subject for academic study; it has, perforce, entered the groves of Academe. Now, not only are the classic plays studied, but when a new writer produces four or five plays, articles, even books, are written about him; he enters a pantheon which is constantly being kept up to date.

The process of setting drama up as a separate entity from theatre pleases the scholar and the literary-minded, and it offends the director and the histrionically orientated. The mutual suspicion of stage and study, still glowering in our society, is a result of this separation. The director feels, not without justification, that drama belongs to the theatre. In his attempts to ensure this, and in the frequent absence of an intimate relationship between dramatist and production, he may often go too far in his efforts to make a play part of theatre: it is here that the language of drama tends to be overwhelmed by the language of theatre. All ages have had their cries from the heart when men of literature have contemplated what, to them, have seemed the awful depredations of theatre on drama, as, for instance, this from the early nineteenth century:

> Of all the works in literature, it certainly is at present the most heart-rending . . . the managers only seek to fill their houses, and don't care a curse for all the dramatists that ever lived. There is a rage for fire, and water, and horses got abroad . . . literary men see the trouble which attends [writing plays], the bending and cringing to performers—the chicanery of mana-

gers . . . and content themselves with the quiet fame of a 'closet writer'.[3]

But no age has so comprehensively and brashly accepted the hegemony of the language of theatre, as our own, and thereby accepted that 'the medium is the message'.

It would be futile to believe that a play achieves its full and correct and natural communication while it still lies silent on the page, any more than a piece of music does before it is brought to life by musicians. But, more and more today, there is a tendency to believe that the director and the actors together alone give a play its theatrical qualities—those qualities which allow it to leap from page to stage. The crux is well expressed in these words of Arthur Symons:

> The question is this: whether the theatre is the invention of the dramatist, and of use only in so far as it interprets his creative work; or whether the dramatist is the invention of the theatre, which has made him for its own ends, and will be able, when it has wholly achieved its mechanism, to dispense with him altogether, except perhaps as a kind of prompter.[4]

But that the alternative expressed above which concerns the existence of the dramatist is the more crucial is starkly borne out by the words of one of the twentieth century's most distinguished directors, Peter Brook:

> Now the lukewarm virtues of good craftsmanship, sound construction, effective curtains, crisp dialogue, have all been thoroughly debunked.[5]

And that what this says has immense implications the same writer makes abundantly clear: 'It is a strange role, that of the director: he does not ask to be God and yet his role implies it.'[6]

While we have to accept the futility of an over-protective attitude towards the play-text and the unreasonableness of denying the director his predisposition to use the language of theatre, we have equally to beware of demoting the dramatist and reducing his text to a blueprint. If we think of a musical performance we must readily concede that the violinist, even the humble triangle-tapper, is literally providing the arpeggios and the pings which penetrate our ears. Yet, we have to remember that the notation of music, to anyone who can read it, enables him to hear the arpeggios and pings in his head. Why else do people buy scores and, with eyes set with a midnight look, play the music in their heads? This is naturally accepted. If, however, one were to suggest that, to a degree, the same is true of a play-text, there would be much head-shaking. But in that case why, so often, are directors who receive new plays through the post, often unsolicited, obviously capable of knowing, after only a few pages of reading, whether a text is viable for stage-production? It is because they must be able to hear the play's arpeggios and pings—and see them, too!

For a play to be fully realized it requires four essentials—a dramatist to write it, a space to enact it, actors to embody it, and an audience to experience it. It is very noticeable that, reduced to essentials, some of the conditions we accept as natural to the communication of a play are not absolutely necessary. It is particularly surprising that a director is not an unarguable requirement—God is expendable. As to the language of theatre, as we know it, little of it is essential; natural lighting can suffice, complicated sets and costumes are a luxury. A true play is capable of theatrical communication without the sophistications of theatre-language. If we think of plays that require little or nothing of modern theatrical ministrations a list can easily be made which covers the centuries and the twentieth century will be conspicuously represented—the anonymous *Everyman*, most of Shakespeare's plays, Shaw's, Eliot's, Pinter's, the almost specific 'placelessness' of Wilder's *Our Town*. The choice is casually made, but the implication is plain—much of the language of theatre is not required, because the language of drama already includes it. This is equally true of setting. It is a truism to be reminded of Shakespeare's verbal scene-painting and location-pointing in the body of his text, but there is no doubt that many of Shakespeare's plays require no set, but only space. Visual illusion on the comprehensive scale the modern theatre is able to provide is unnecessary—if the dramatist has allowed for its 'representation' in verbal terms.

The visual opulence of the late nineteenth century and the visual ubiquity to be found in the twentieth century have of course contributed to audiences' experiences of plays in the theatre. Theatre history, however, tends to show that that experience is often unnecessary to the play itself, and derives from the language of the theatre. Indeed the more the language of theatre is, or needs to be, employed the less effective is the language of the play itself. Sometimes the language of theatre is a cover-up. The more dramatically comprehensive and sensitive the language of drama the less necessity for the intervention of anything else. There is a good, if somewhat self-conscious demonstration of this in Thornton Wilder's play *Our Town*. This was welcomed as being innovatory when it was first produced, and gained the Pulitzer prize in 1938. It is located, but not 'set', in Grover's Corner, which, because it becomes a microcosm of anywhere that decent ordinary folk live, requires no specific set. The choric-like figure who conducts us on our tour through the play's humanity supplies, by verbal means, all that is needed.

This play also demonstrates that another theatrical convention—sophisticated costume—is not an absolute requirement. Indeed, although costume is required far less often than it is customarily used, there is and always has been a very strong urge in people to relate the dramatic and the theatrical with 'dressing up'; to dress up seems a more natural concomitant to enacting a play than a set.

We must not, incontinently, throw costume out of the window, but it still remains true that, in absolute theatrical terms, it is of less consequence than is often tacitly maintained. It is interesting, indeed, that the phrase 'costume drama' can be used, almost in a pejorative sense, to indicate a play which puts excessive reliance on the magic of merely 'dressing up'.

The specialness of a play then is something that has to be sought for beneath the additions and excrescences and decorations that (often with a great access of pleasure) have been laid upon it. This specialness lies in its containing, within itself, in its notation, most, if not all, that is required for the actor to awaken it. It is a sleeping beauty. There is nothing mysterious about this. One is not claiming or requiring huge and subtle characteristics; one is simply saying that the inertia of a play-text is like the inertia of a plane on the ground. The pilot doesn't build it before he flies it. He responds to what is within its mechanism to make it fly.

9

Drama, as we see, shares certain qualities with other verbal forms—like oratory and preaching. The most potent common factor is designated but not clearly defined by the word 'dramatic'. Like so many words, it can be all things to all men—there is little that is self-evident about the meaning of the word, and it is not difficult to find examples which show how impossible it is to pin it down to any one specific definition. It is used, for example, to express an experience of almost incredible surprise. No one could give you this particular kind of dramatic moment more sensationally than the traditional Welsh preacher—alas, a dying breed. One day, in a chapel in Anglesey, such a preacher had reached the top of his vocal bent with his head thrown back and his voice tenored like angels. Suddenly the flow of Welsh stopped, and, in a most startling parenthesis, he shouted, 'See, where Christ's blood streams in the firmament.' We were jolted, then riveted, then he allowed us to find ourselves, and proceeded in Welsh. This was, indeed, a dramatic moment—the moment when the totally unexpected was totally surprising. Such drama is found in Faustus's sudden cry, 'O lente, lente, currite, noctis equi'; it must have occurred, too, on that incredible night when Irving in his role of Mathias heard the bells ringing for the first time.

'Dramatic' is also true of yet another experience which the Welsh preacher was capable of creating. The Welsh word 'hwyl' is almost untranslatable. It specifically describes the process in which the old-fashioned Welsh preacher allows his voice gradually to rise to a tremendous pitch and height and then, after an unbearable pause, there is a slow declension down to the merest whisper. It is like an orgasm's effect and it is dramatic. It gains its effect by contrast—between the surge of activity, the passion, the upward aspiration, and then the slackening, the quietude, the disposition to inertia—all passion spent. This is the drama of contrast.

The orator (again something of a dying breed, although politics, from time to time, still spawns such creatures) can use the dramatic in both the senses just described—surprise and contrast. This is usually calculated and employed to win an audience less by reason than by a kind of emotional hypnosis (like Hitler). But the orator—more usually in an atmosphere which is not over-emotionally charged—can use yet another species of the dramatic. This is where there is a relentless build-up to a result—the result itself need be neither unforeseeable nor violent. The drama rests in the immaculate logic of movement from point to point of an argument, or the stacking up of situations and psychological attitudes and postures, in a process which has an obviously architectonic quality. It is a kind of wit, in that mental processes rather than emotional flows are very much in evidence in the language in which this is expressed. There is an element of 'thrill' for the audience in contemplating the theorem completing itself—the inevitable progression with QED written at the end. To mention American 'courthouse' dramas and films is easy enough, and they are often extremely effective in their demonstrations. But this kind of dramatic effect is often found in unexpected places. Eliot's *Murder in the Cathedral* has a very firm logic of intellectual movement in its language. This does not, at any given moment in the play, shock you with surprise or engage you with contrast, but there is, particularly up to and including Becket's Easter sermon, that relentless and gradual tightening of dramatic effect for us in the audience as we listen and watch inevitability reach for its culmination.

Again, 'dramatic' is frequently brought to the service of description to denote the effect which the author's words make, and are calculated to make, on us. The effect is not violent shock, great surprise, contrast, neither is it architectonic, nor rational, but something to do with the uniqueness of a verbal texture. W. B. Yeats took a passage from Pater's critical work—*Studies in the Renaissance*—and printed it as verse in his own *Oxford Anthology of English Poetry*. By breaking up the lines to create a more obviously tight form, he brought out a 'dramatic' quality—simply because his version pointed up relationships between words in the verbal texture.

We can also observe this drama of verbal texture in Arthur Miller's *The Death of a Salesman*. It rests in its rhythmical quality, in the repetition of certain phrases such as, 'He is liked, but not well liked.' This drama of verbal texture thrills by a kind of stealth, insidiously drawing attention to some kind of ritual enshrined within the words.

When the 'heavy' walked into a stage drawing-room in a nineteenth-century melodrama, the audience instinctively

11

realized that the most 'dramatic' character in the play had arrived. The association of character with 'dramatic' is made by audiences perhaps far more often than either they themselves or critical commentators realize. In this usage of the word 'dramatic' we have to be careful to distinguish between two distinct nuances of meaning and effect. The association of character (the fictional embodiment) with 'dramatic', usually assumes that the character will be involved in surprising incidents, situations of great portentousness, decisions of unusual severity or magnitude—one might almost say that this is the drama of status. But mixed in with this is the fact that such characters are usually only undertaken by actors who are capable of giving them full vent—in other words what are called 'dramatic' actors are to be reserved for 'dramatic' characterization. Even now, in this relatively sophisticated age of theatregoing, audiences have a natural sense of thespian hierarchy—the top-rank star (the heavy) is he who plays the lead; the popular, reliable second-ranker is he who supports the lead; and then there are the others.

The drama of status, then, is one which encompasses both the importance of the character to be embodied and the personality of the actor who is to do the embodying. Nowadays, the 'heavy' is, to a large degree, a reformed and more subtle creature, but in the eighteenth century the amount of his dramatic presence often equalled the amount of 'drama' involved in the character to be played:

> [James Quin's] utterance is a continual sing-song, like the chanting of Vespers; and his action resembles that of heaving ballast into the hold of a ship. In his outward deportment, he seems to have confounded the ideas of dignity and insolence of mien.[7]

But the 'dramatic' extends its tentacles into all aspects of the arts of drama and theatre, confusing any attempts to hold it steadily and designate its precise qualities. There is the drama of situations—sometimes called 'the dramatic moment'— which, indeed, the 'dramatic' actor will attempt to hold for as long as possible. It may happen as the result of a pause, or as the result of a sudden unexpected situation which arises because of some action or remark of a character. The result is to realign the situation which we are observing so that the play points in a different direction. An argument is going on between relatives and friends of a man who has recently died:

Stanton: Oh, drop it, man.
Gordon: You've got to answer.
Robert: I'll never forgive you for telling Martin what you did—by God, I won't!
Stanton: You've got it all wrong.
Gordon: They haven't, you rotten liar. *(Moves as if to strike him)*
Stanton: (Pushing him aside) Oh, get out.
Gordon: (Shouting and about to go for him again) You made Martin shoot himself.
Olwen: Wait a minute, Gordon. *(Everybody turns and looks at him)* Martin didn't shoot himself.

And thus at the end of Act II, J. B. Priestley's play, *Dangerous Corner*, dramatically swerves again.

These various types of the 'dramatic' encourage a number of generalizations when we think of them strictly in terms of theatre and drama, while tacitly allowing their appropriateness to the other public verbal arts. The first concerns the actual experience of the dramatic, whatever type we may have in mind, by the audience. The 'dramatic' has a far greater chance of making itself felt when it is exposed to a group. The audience, rather than the single individual, is the best catalyst to encourage it. The second is that the element of surprise seems to be a common denominator to all the types of 'dramatic'—what the audience does not know in contrast to what it finds out, and the way it finds it out, is the very stuff of dramatic experience. The third makes clear the extent to which language is responsible for what is dramatic and how both audience and (to a less extent) the solitary individual reader receive their experience through their responses to the effects of language. Even when a 'dramatic moment' occurs because of some twist in action or movement of character, it is more often the words that can be seen either to have initiated the movement or to clinch it. A young officer has died of his wounds in a dug-out in the trenches of World War I:

Still Raleigh is quiet. Stanhope gently takes his hand. There is a long silence. Stanhope lowers Raleigh's hand to the bed. rises,

13

and takes the candle back to the table. He sits on the bench behind the table with his back to the wall, and stares listlessly across at the boy on Osborne's bed. The solitary candle-flame throws up the lines on his pale, drawn face and the dark shadows under his tired eyes. The thudding of the shells rises and falls like an angry sea. A private soldier comes scrambling down the steps, his round, red face wet with perspiration, his chest heaving for breath.

Soldier: Message from Mr Trotter, sir—will you come at once. *(Stanhope gazes round at the soldier—and makes no other sign)* Mr Trotter, sir—says will you come at once! *(Stanhope rises stiffly and takes his helmet from the table)*
Stanhope: All right, Broughton, I'm coming.

The banality, almost the inconsequentiality of the words that are spoken, effectively highlight the poignancy of the boy's death. The visual is being enriched by the verbal—and the visual itself has been created by the dramatist.

Often, too, the 'dramatic' is associated with silence. Arthur Miller is a master of persuading silence to consort with language to produce a dramatic effect which is often complex in its significance. In *The Crucible,* Elizabeth asks to speak to her imprisoned husband, John Proctor:

Elizabeth: I promise nothing. Let me speak with him. *(A sound—the sibilance of dragging feet on stone. They turn. A pause. Herrick enters with John Proctor. His wrists are chained. He is another man, bearded, filthy, his eyes misty as though webs had overgrown them. He halts inside the doorway, his eye caught by the sight of Elizabeth. The emotion flowing between them prevents anyone from speaking for an instant. Now Hale, visibly affected, goes to Danforth and speaks quietly)*
Hale: Pray, leave them, Excellency.
Danforth: *(Pressing Hale impatiently aside)* Mr Proctor, you have been notified, have you not? *(Proctor is silent, staring at Elizabeth)* I see light in the sky, Mister; let you counsel with your wife, and may God help you turn your back on Hell. *(Proctor is silent, staring at Elizabeth)*
Hale: *(Quietly)* Excellency, let—*(Danforth brushes past Hale and walks out. Hale follows. Cheever stands and follows, Hathorne behind. Herrick goes. Parris, from a safe distance, offers)*
Parris: If you desire a cup of cider, Mr Proctor, I am sure I—*(Proctor*

turns an icy stare at him, and he breaks off. Parris raises his palms towards Proctor) God lead you now. *(Parris goes out)*

Such a use of the language of drama is characteristic of Miller. Several layers of characters' experiences and attitudes are revealed—and we learn something of the depth of relation-ships—in the silences bracketed by the words.

We should remind ourselves that dramatic elements akin to these can often be found in both the novel and (to a less extent) in poetry. The dramatist, therefore, must be sure that he is not writing his play in dramatic terms which are suitable only for novel or poem. The play, alone, when spoken aloud, has to be natural for speech, for embodied character and for action:

> Drama, by its nature, can come into being only when men are moved powerfully and suddenly to record the circumstances of life . . . The dramatist is for striking out his word and actions in the round, as it were; his people must stand by nature of their own concreteness— like chessmen ready to a player's hand, rather than figures worked in silk or an arras . . . The motive and the cue for the dramatist's real passion, then, is this quick desire to make real his imaginings—under the influence . . . of surprise.[9]

2 The Twentieth Century and the Language of Drama

In this century there has been, and there continues to be, a tremendous amount of discussion of drama. The discussion has been not only huge in volume but diverse in theme and motivation. Before this century, the bulk of discussion was largely confined to professional reviewing of plays in performance, literary criticism of themes and characters and language, and quasi-philosophical essays on the 'meaning' of plays. On the whole, prior to the twentieth century, the concern was more with plays strictly as literature to be regarded in much the same fashion as novels and poetry.

There is a multiplicity of reasons for the excited activity of this century. Increased literacy, new media for discussion and presentation, the discovery, certainly in the latter part of the century, of something called 'leisure': drama is conceived of by many people as part of the industry which caters for the unoccupied. The reasons abound, but they are hedged about with others no less palpable or pervasive. There has been a growth of sophisticated forms of theatrical presentation—themselves the inevitable result of technological discovery. The age of technology has, with the relentless inevitability we associate with battery-farming, brought the 'expert' into being. Experts in costume, set, paint, make-up, sound, lighting, synthetic materials, script-reading, publicity, and so on. Some of these experts who have worked for and received acclaim, have imposed their ideas, and their power has multiplied.

This restless century has progressively grown pernickety and dismissive about old forms of drama and traditional

16

methods of stage-presentation. The 'well-made' play has acquired the reputation among many theorists and practitioners usually reserved for some form of mental aberration. Admittedly, the innumerable examples of the type, both in the United States and Western Europe, sometimes tax the imagination, but there are occasions when one would trade in a dozen experimental pieces for dazzling custom-built products like *The Male Animal, Junior Miss* or *Night Must Fall*. Typed characters, stereotyped dialogue sometimes sounding as if a computer had made it, a dramatic pattern so predictable in its rhythm of climax and anti-climax, themes where the human predicament is generalized to the point of caricature, a decided sense of positive beginning, exciting middle and absolute end—all these characteristics have been brought forth as evidence against the well-made play. The worst of such plays certainly display them all in an extreme form, but the best of them make virtues out of what detractors consider to be inexcusable vices.

There are few prose dramatists of this century who have not, to one degree or another, embraced, or used as a starting-point, the concept of the well-made play. Theatregoing would, indeed, have been a poorer activity if the enemies of this genre had had their way and denied us some of Shaw, some of Coward, Somerset Maugham, J. B. Priestley. Lilian Hellman, Chodorov, Joseph Fields and Thurber—the list is longer even than this, though to increase it hardly adds to its distinction. The proscenium-stage, regarded by so many as the emblem of well-made restrictiveness and mechanical artificiality, is spoken of as if it were a Thespian's cemetery. The century has searched both diligently and sometimes frantically for new modes and sometimes ended up with a mere fad. As the practitioners have searched, so the theorists, agog with partisanship, have subjected the results to minute though not always rational scrutiny.

Among the new forms which drama and theatre have had thrust upon them rather than developed from their traditional soil are radio, film and television. The first impact, certainly of television, seemed to put the very existence of traditional dramatic forms and theatre into jeopardy. There has been close examination, the result of a reaction to the effects of television, of the traditional forms and the Johnny's-come-lately. This examination was bound eventually to become more than an argument about artistic matters, and to spread to include the sensitive matter of the place of drama in society. Never has there been more discussion than in the period since 1945 of the *use* of drama to its human environment. Putting aside its role as a leisure-filler, drama, in company with other arts, has come under the scrutiny of sociologists and quasi-sociologists. This scrutiny and the general discussion has two aspects.

First, there is the obvious possible use of drama to promote mental attitudes, philosophies, political ideologies relating to the way society is or should be organized. This involves both the study and the practice of drama and theatre as a means of social comment and as an implement for social change. At worst, it is propaganda, at best it is proselytization graced by entertainment. Overall, it is part of the twentieth century's growing assumption that everything, including art, must justify itself in terms quite different from those now called 'esoteric' or 'élitist'. Oscar Wilde might not have found himself in Reading Gaol for saying that 'Art itself is really a form of exaggeration; and selection, which is the very spirit of Art, is nothing more than an intensified mode of over-emphasis', but he would, today, have found it not an over-popular remark.

Second, the emphasis on drama's relationship to society's needs has created a climate of conviction about what kind of communication is best calculated to serve those needs. Directly, then, the whole matter of the language of drama is itself involved in all this cerebration. This aspect is very closely connected to yet another element which has taken drama very much to its domain. The 'educational' case for drama has and is being stated ad infinitum. Because of drama's inherent ability to 'release' the individual's imagination and, if the individual is a participant, to engage him fully by its demands on his physical and mental resources, other subjects in the school curriculum are drawn into its orbit. Those subjects taught by exposition and recourse to memory and judgment (a process, unless carefully handled, always inclined to bore or disengage) are now receiving the benefits of drama and can be shown to be revivified by its effects—particularly history (an

18

obvious case for treatment) and geography. Needless to say, the awesome features of the gymnastic repetitiveness of the old PT lesson have been softened by the cosmetic application of drama in dance form.

In both the sociological and educational justifications which are made for drama's more integrated role in society, there is frequent emphasis on the physical as an expression of the inner being, and a depreciation of the notion of the 'play' performed in the traditional way—the 'aesthetic' of the old school year. In other words, the tendency in late twentieth-century theories about the adaptability of drama seems to be away from the aesthetic and verbal, and towards the functional and physical.

The more extreme effects of the twentieth century's unique preoccupation with drama did not make themselves apparent until after World War II, but, throughout the century, the amount of external pressures affecting the language of the dramatist have been of a proportion much higher than in previous centuries. The growth of mass-communications has made every artist nearer to the front-line, so to speak, of his society. Shaw, Priestley, Coward, Miller, Albee, themselves 'early' twentieth-century dramatists reveal the effect of political, sociological and military events. Furthermore, we have to notice that the preoccupation with drama has been matched by an obsession with the forms of theatre. The language of theatre, as we have already seen, has become progressively more advanced, even strong and vociferous. Indeed, one of the marked characteristics of the preoccupation and obsession has been the frequent blurring of the language of drama and theatre. From Gordon Craig at the beginning of the century to Peter Brook today the pressing direction has been to lump theatre and drama together as one art. When a play is received into a theatre it is certainly entering into its correct environment, but it brings a great deal with it. That environment means nothing without the language which drama brings to it—the medium is not the message. But, to understand this it is essential not to confuse the two.

The old, well-used, customary divisions of prose and poetry are still viable and convenient enough to form the basis of understanding the language of drama. In the sixteenth and seventeenth centuries there was some blurring of definition

19

between the two forms of communication—manifest, for example, in some mediaeval and Elizabethan drama. The earliest novels, *Euphues* and *Arcadia,* seem to exist in a hazy no-man's land, neither completely occupied by the ordered ranks of prose, nor by brave cohorts of poetry. But in the eighteenth and nineteenth centuries, distinctions became very much clearer; in the earlier period because of the directing effects of neo-classical rules of form and expression, in the latter because poetry became regarded as the language of the sublime spirit, and prose the language of mental processes and human affections. The nineteenth-century prose-melodrama play was distinct in both form and tone from, say, Tennyson's *Queen Mary.* During the late nineteenth century there gradually arose a conscious application of what, eventually, seemed to be self-evident—that is that poetry concerned itself with the non-naturalistic and prose with the naturalistic. This distinction was intensified during the first two decades of the twentieth century, when the very phrases, 'prose naturalism' and 'poetic symbolism', had a vogue. This distinction, in practice, is almost graphically represented in the difference between Galsworthy's dramatic language and Yeats's. Equally graphic is the distinction (self-consciously perpetuated in her essay on the subject) between Virginia Woolf 's and Arnold Bennett's novels. To Virginia Woolf, Mr Bennett's prose naturalistic novels could only be described in one word—'materialistic'—'they write of unimportant things . . . they spend immense skill and immense industry making the trivial and the transitory appear the true and the enduring'.[1] Although she does not mention Galsworthy's plays, she says she has a 'quarrel' with his novels—for their 'materialism'. If prose-naturalism, then, was regarded as anathema by many, poetic non-naturalism was hailed as the antithesis. Yeats, writing about his play *Deirdre* said—'I discovered that my language must keep at all times a certain even richness . . . I had forgotten in a moment of melodrama that tragic drama must be carved out of speech as a statue is out of stone.' As if to emphasize the difference between what prose can do and what poetry can achieve, he wrote about *The Player Queen*—'I have finished the prose version of what is to be a new verse play.'[2]

Prose is commonly believed to be the 'language of the

everyday', although what we use everyday is more accurately to be thought of as speech, which, either tacitly or explicitly, is taken to be concerned with the expression of what is called the actual. Prose as one kind of literary language has become confused with ordinary speech, to such an extent that any dramatist who indulges in undecorated prose communication is ipso facto deemed to be dealing with the individual as he exists in his society, and as he has to face the day-to-day problems which his society hurls at him. Today, prose is regarded as not only the language of the individual in society, but that of conflict. Plain, unvarnished, even gnarled, possibly crude, language is habitually regarded as being the language of that class whose relationship with society in the twentieth century is largely a history of conflict—those who toil to create society's material wealth. On the other hand, poetry is commonly taken to be the language of some other-where. It is habitually taken to be the language of man not as a critic of the palpable world, but as a citizen of his own private world—if prose is what we speak in society, poetry is the only way to express the inner soul of man.

Twentieth-century drama is distinguished by the extent to which the language of man in his society—commonly prose —and the language of man in his private world—habitually poetry—have both been exploited.

Twentieth-century man has created and, hence, had to confront a very obvious choice in his consciousness and experience of existence. The growth of literacy and quasi-literacy, the effects of political dogma and creeds, the levelling out of class distinctions, have had the effect of turning man outwards, so to say, in an effort to understand his environment, control it, and above all, to ameliorate his status within it. Plain prose, demotic speech, unvarnished diction has come naturally to be considered as the language of this process—a language which leads to social action.

On the other hand—and partly as a reaction—man has been subjected to pressures which have forced him to look inward. The decay of public religious observance, the onslaughts of new media of communication, the often fearful discoveries and prognoses of psychology—these, among other effects, tend to make him into a scared introvert. Such a posture also

21

requires its language: poetry has maintained its traditional role as the language of the inward-looking man, the language of reflection.

So, an antithesis exists between two kinds of consciousness and two kinds of communication. It is not a new one, but in no other century has it been so distinct, sharp and disturbing in its implications.

The twentieth century—particularly since the end of World War I—has given us, then, schizoid man (to adopt a popular and characteristic twentieth-century usage). This is man in a state of constant oscillation between an awareness of himself as himself, and of himself as an inhabitant of his environment. The language of drama reflects this condition perfectly.

One of the most outspoken of American theatre-historians, Robert Brustein, makes the distinction, between a prose and a poetic medium, and the place of drama abundantly clear. In *Theatre of Revolt* Brustein presents a case that most of the major dramatists of this century, and in particular Ibsen, Shaw, Strindberg, Chekhov and Beckett, Pirandello and O'Neill, are 'rebellious' artists. Each, he says, is, in his own way, at fierce odds with something—with God, society, existence itself. His main thesis may be arguable, but what is remarkable and germane is the frequency with which Brustein either directly states or implies the dichotomy we have discussed—as it appears to the artist:

> . . . and herein lies the paradox of the rebel artist. He would exalt the ideal, yet he is imprisoned by the real. He would vindicate the self, yet he must also examine the claims of the others. He would sing of ecstasy, wildness and drunkenness, yet he must cope with the tedious, conditioned world.[3]

T. S. Eliot did not see twentieth-century dramatists in Brustein's terms, and he was, in any case, at least as much interested in expression as in content, but he, too, expresses a sense of dichotomy.

> It seems to me that beyond the namable classifiable emotions and motives of our conscious life when directed towards action—the part of life which prose drama is wholly adequate to express—there is a fringe of indefinite extent, of feeling which we can only detect, so to speak, out of the corner of the

eye and can never completely focus. There are great prose dramatists—such as Ibsen and Chekhov—who have at times done things of which I would not otherwise have supposed prose to be capable, but who seem to me, in spite of their success, to have been hampered in expression by writing in prose. This peculiar range of sensibility can be expressed by dramatic poetry, at its moments of greater intensity. [4]

Ignoring the merest whiff of grapeshot around the ghosts of Ibsen and Chekhov, and the severe schoolmastery in which prose is firmly put in its place, Eliot's remarks are both illuminating and useful. They clearly show that one of the century's greatest critics and most memorable playwrights was not, as some of his detractors have assumed, classically remote from the way the world wags but had shrewdly judged the direction of the wind. But what is to be particularly noticed is that although what Eliot writes does not go as far as Brustein in seeing the artist as torn between being a citizen of two opposed worlds or consorting with one while yearning for the other, there is still, in Eliot, a sense of two kinds of consciousness and experience with appropriate language for each. The useful and important difference between Eliot and Brustein is that the former does not find a Berlin Wall separating that part of life 'for which prose is wholly adequate' from that part of life for which poetry is the best communicator, but only a fringe of indefinite extent, through which the other world can be glimpsed. For Brustein, it would seem, the dramatist has to make a choice between living in and expressing one world or the other, for Eliot it appears that no severe choice is necessary.

For Eliot, ' . . . to go as far . . . as it is possible to go, without losing that contact with the everyday world with which drama must come to terms, seems to be the proper aim of dramatic poetry'. In fact, Eliot wanted a dramatic language (what he terms a 'dramatic poetry') flexible enough to meet both the requirements of workhorse prose *and* intensely sophisticated poetry. He struggled to find it and nobly failed. His plays, even the best—*Murder in the Cathedral, The Family Reunion* and *The Cocktail Party*—give the impression that, at times, his language is suffering from its impossible task of having to do too many incompatible jobs—notably, the sophisticated poetic structure has sometimes to pretend, not without embarrassment, that it is mere workaday stuff; conversely his sometimes self-consciously artisan verbal profile has to try to shuffle itself quickly back into the posture of a nobler function.

The differences between Brustein and Eliot are not merely of emphasis. They suggest a very important general distinction between two cultural genres. Eliot was a man of western Christendom in the sense that he believed in the integrated reality of God's created universe. For Eliot there was no sharp distinction between man's consciousness of what Brustein calls the 'tedious conditioned world' and 'a world elsewhere', any more than there would have been for a fourteenth-century poet, any more than there was for Gerard Manley Hopkins, for unity is the context for his attempts to achieve a 'oneness' in his dramatic language, which would slacken or tauten between the extremes of poetry and prose as it responded to Eliot's attempts to express life in all its complicated totality. Indeed the form of Eliot's expression of this is twentieth century, but notionally it is mediaeval. Its cultural matrix is western Christendom:

> For it is ultimately the function of art, in imposing a credible order upon ordinary reality, and thereby eliciting some perception of order *in* reality, to bring us to a condition of serenity, stillness, and reconciliation; and then leave us, as Virgil left Dante, to proceed toward a region where that guide can avail us no farther.[5]

But Brustein is not expressing the idea of an integrated universe. There is nothing mediaeval in his expression of a choice between two modes of consciousness, two worlds, two forms of expression for them. It is, rather, post-Renaissance in the absolute severity of its distinction between 'ideal' and 'real', 'tedious' and 'ecstasy'. It is characteristically mid-twentieth century. It reflects an age which, having abandoned many of its ineffable unseen gods, has found it necessary to replace them by expedient and palpable ones. Having, to a large extent, given up its faiths, it still finds it has its own imaginative world to contend with. Having become militant about its claims to the environment it actually inhabits, it seeks, often in bafflement, for a less physical, less painful, less divisive, less strident world in which, if only intermittently, to rest its perturbed spirit. The twentieth century has discovered the efficacy of prose in which to express its hold on the planet, but it often tacitly acknowledges without assertion that a simple and temporary grasp on day-to-day actuality is not enough. Almost winsomely it seeks for a less expedient, less precarious, less evanescent reality, and seems half to realize that only poetry can unlock the door to this.

It can be described in many different ways, and given different names—'the ecstatic world', 'the metaphysical world'—and it need not have religious affiliations or implications. For Eliot it did—God lay at the centre of it. For J. B. Priestley, it does not:

> What we must do now . . . is . . . to live . . . not throwing away our science and the mechanistic view of things it necessitates, but retaining them as an instrument of power, a tool against the stubborn earth, while at the same time we live at heart like poets and priests, aware that this is still a magical world moving with wonder and awe through a mystery.

'Magic', 'imagination'—each word, and others, can equally well serve to designate those regions to which man fugitively aspires—and to which poetry has been assigned for the task of satisfying the aspiration.

But neither was Eliot nor is Priestley, in his quite different way, alone in the attempt to create a dramatic language which could accommodate both the grosser and the grander vestures. In some Irish dramatists, notably O'Casey and Synge, we find a dramatic language which is flexible and verbally rich enough to encompass many themes, many visions, many attitudes. And, indeed, it encompasses the arc from earth to heaven and heaven to earth with beguiling ease and profound effect. O'Casey's language is as capable of communicating a fierce naturalism convincingly as it is able to take flight into the worlds of the imagination. Synge's, basing its rhythmic structure and vocabulary upon the actualities of heard peasant speech, can express the day-to-day existence of those from whom it derives as eloquently as it harbours their dreams and the illusions they court.

25

It is always tempting to account for some characteristic or other in Irish writers by some quirk in the Irish 'temperament'. Indeed, it is quite remarkable how much greater an involvement is argued for by critics, of the 'personality' of being Irish, in the act of writing, than that of any other nationality. Perhaps, fancifully, we may think of accounting for the presence in major Irish dramatists of a comprehensive dramatic language by declaring that schizoid man is not to be found in the Celtic races—for what is true of Irish dramatists is true also of Welsh drama. Can it be that for some reason beyond total comprehension the Celts have an ability to harmonize even the most rabid aspects of the material world and the most romantic facets of the imagination? Certainly, it is very apparent that an interaction of the unexceptional and the amazing is a marked characteristic of Celtic responses to any situation—'Isn't life terrible—thank God,' says Polly Garter, turning the banal into a paradoxical benediction! It is inescapable—the Irish and the Welsh, in their drama, display far less of the divisiveness which characterizes twentieth-century English dramatic history.

Yet there is a strange exception to this rule, to be found in English plays of the 1920s and 1930s. These plays form a significantly large enough body of dramatic writing to merit comment. They are not to be accounted as among the very best that the century has produced, but countless theatregoers over the age of fifty would regard them as the most poignantly affecting theatrical experiences of their lives: for many they are the be-all and the end-all of what they mean by the enchantment of theatre—and against what they provide all other theatrical experience is judged. It is not easy to give this body of drama a generic name because it encompasses a variety of both themes and forms. A sense of it may, however, be gained from an account of its sources.

World War I bequeathed the world many grim legacies, but none more poignant than the heirloom of human loss, sometimes on a multiple scale. Few families were immune from the telegrams that expressed official regret for the death of husband, brother, fiancé, sweetheart, cousin, uncle. The world of the 1970s lacks the heirs of virtually a whole generation. This loss has been bitterly and compassionately recorded by writers like Robert Graves, Siegfried Sassoon and J. B. Priestley in essays or poems, but it is also embodied in a large amount of drama. In the 1920s and 1930s we find plays which express something that to the more cynical 1970s might seem a kind of pathetic fallacy. It is a passionate faith that the loved ones who, in reality, had been blown to pieces in the trenches had passed on to a bourne from which they could not return but which was a place of happiness and content. Moreover, it had some accessibility for those left behind, in the sense that, eventually a joyful reunion would take place but that, in the meantime, contact was possible. It is with this possibility that many such plays were concerned. Astrology, seances, clairvoyance, mediums, all flourished in the 1920s and the 1930s as desperate and grief-stricken people strove to contact the loved ones. These purveyors of access to another world traded, to a large extent, on an extensive belief in it and, indeed, on its presumed difference from a grievous everyday existence in which mortal life is spent. Barrie, Sutton Vane, Priestley, Bridie, each in his own way and with his own emphasis, was concerned with this and with another world of experience. The dramatic landscape of the twenties and thirties is dotted with examples of their work and of that of others, and we find them in the most surprising places. Noël Coward, an unlikely necromancer, wrote *Blithe Spirit*; it is not merely a delightful take-off of the world of the medium, but a gently acerbic satire on the state of mind of those who believe in that world.

On a more apparently intellectually rigorous level there is a related body of drama, of which by far the most important writer is J. B. Priestley. In this, the belief in the existence of some other-where is derived not solely from the harrowing creativity of grief and nostalgia or romance but from an unlikely source. Priestley would claim that there is every possibility that there is a whole area of consciousness outside so-called normal experience which may, in time, be scientifically verifiable. Parallel with the phenomenon of reliance on the astrological and clairvoyant in the 1920s and 1930s, was a deep and passionate interest (often displayed by those to whom clairvoyance was a dangerous anathema) in the mysteries of time. Among the most read writers were time-theorists like Dunne, E. A. Abbott and Ouspensky,[6] and

many plays exploited and manipulated what they wrote in
many and various ways. But there was a common factor—time, it said, can provide an escape of one kind or another
from the restrictions of the everyday and, if we are prepared to
allow ourselves to fall under its spell we are likely to experience a quality of being which is less materialistic, less
restricted, than metaphysical and free. Priestley exploits this
frequently and in many cunning ways, but the basic meaning
never varies.

In the 1920s and 1930s society was fast relinquishing its grip
on conventional religious faith and observance, so that such
'secular', serious and apparently soundly-based intimations of
immortality had a vital fascination—whether expressed in
serious or romantic terms; whether the play be *I have been here
before* or *Berkeley Square,*[7] many members of the public were
beguiled and comforted.

Both related types of drama—the more necromantic and the
quasi-scientific—accept the existence of two contrasted
worlds and states of consciousness—speak a particular kind of
language. It is one that is designed either to reconcile the two
worlds or to effect the transfer between one and the other.

Mary Rose: Yes. *(She rises)* Bad man.
Harry: It's easy to call me names, but the thing fair beats me. There is
　　nothing I wouldn't do for you, but a mere man is so helpless.
　　How should the likes of me know what to do with a ghost that
　　has lost her way on earth? I wonder if what it means is that you
　　broke some law, just to come back for the sake of—of that
　　Harry? If it was that, it's surely time He overlooked it.
Mary Rose: Yes.
　　(He looks at the open window)
Harry: What a night of stars! Good old glitterers, I dare say they are
　　in the know, but I am thinking you are too small a thing to get a
　　helping hand from them.
Mary Rose: Yes.
　　*(The call is again heard, but there is in it now no unholy sound. It is a
　　celestial music that is calling for Mary Rose, Mary Rose, first in
　　whispers and soon so loudly that, for one who can hear, it is the only
　　sound in the world. Mary Rose, Mary Rose. As it wraps her round,
　　the weary little ghost knows that her long day is done. Her face is
　　shining. The smallest star shoots down as if it were her star sent for her,
　　and with her arms stretched forth to it trustingly she walks out through*

the window into the Empyrean. The music passes with her. Harry hears nothing, but he knows that somehow a prayer has been answered)[8]

The words 'she walks out through the window into the Empyrean' resonantly embody the play's attempt to link Earth and Heaven, Here and There. The language of the dialogue, while it has Barrie's characteristically soft burr, is made up of ingredients which are to be found, in certain measures, in all the dramatists who wrote in this genre. The apparently naturalistic, demotic, like 'but the thing fair beats me' is part of an attempt to give the credibility of actuality to what is done and said; but Barrie, not wishing the play to have too much earth on its feet so that its flights are clogged, intersperses the naturalistic (even in the same character's mouth) with highly-wrought phraseology—notice how the demotic ('glitterers') leads into the plangency of, 'I dare say they are in the know, but I am thinking you are too small a thing to get a helping hand from them.' It is surely highly symptomatic of an urge by Barrie to introduce a kind of lyrical tone that he should employ an Irish usage 'but I am thinking you are' (with all its associations with lilt and sentiment) despite the fact that the speaker is an Australian! Mary Rose's succession of single-word affirmatives (each succeeding 'yes', we may assume, intended to be breath-ier than its predecessor) introduces both a rhythmic pace and 'mysterious' atmosphere into the situation. The end-result of this mixture of ingredients is a language that is unnatural, is neither quite 'prose' nor 'poetry', is not, in a sense, even 'poetic prose'. It is, in fact, a kind of literary custom-built product. It has no strong affiliations with the accepted resources of language-communication; it is not intended either to perform the resolute and familiar tasks of prose nor the more subtle and emotive ones of poetry. It is neither this nor that, nor is it the language of Here or There. It is, in fact, the language of a third world of consciousness and feeling and tries to attain the status of credibility by taking only what it wants or can invent (not what is forced upon it) from this world and a world elsewhere. It is, essentially, the language of illusions—beautiful, poignant, evocative, wry, nostalgic, even comic, but essentially artificial.

The justification for separating out and designating this body of play-writing as a significant and familiar genre is surely confirmed by its recognition by perhaps the most sensitive barometer of public taste and mode—*Punch*. On 1 January 1930 its theatre critic wrote of Frank Harvey's *The Last Enemy* at the Fortune:

> One does not somehow connect Mr Tom Walls with stage-plays having a theological, mystical or metaphysical basis, and therefore one must suppose that some deep note of serious intention in Mr Frank Harvey's *The Last Enemy* urged him to finance and produce this interesting if rather unconvincing play—unconvincing perhaps only if you are disinclined to read your theology in the book of the theatre, and have a prejudice against the wailing of female voices in the Mary-Rosy manner, and Gordon Craigish staircases piled against a star-spangled sky as indications that you have passed beyond the borders of earthbound life and are on the First Landing on the way to Heaven.

It would be grossly unfair to dramatists of the calibre of J. B. Priestley, James Bridie and Emlyn Williams, but particularly the first-named, to seem to imply that the worlds they create in those of their plays which belong to the general category under discussion are no more than whimsies whose language is merely obtrusively artificial. In Priestley's *I Have Been Here Before*, *Eden End, Johnson over Jordan* and *Time and the Conways*, for example, character, plot and theme are of a different and higher order of creation than anything written by any other writer of the genre. Neither, indeed, should Bridie's moral strength in *Tobias and the Angel* or even Sutton Vane's devious psychology in *Outward Bound* ⁹ be judged as whimsical and without consequence. Yet, in all of them, including Priestley, a special language-pattern frequently emerges—neither completely 'prose', nor 'poetry' nor even 'poetic-prose' but a constructed amalgam which takes from Here and from There in order to try and communicate the existence of a world of consciousness which is neither completely of this earth nor completely of a world elsewhere. It is 'artificial' for this reason—but because Priestley's purpose is, unlike Barrie's, not whimsical but, in the long run, metaphysical to a degree, the artifice of his language becomes, to an extent, absorbed and only intermittently obtrusive.

Again, the extent to which Priestley's particular and fecund explorations of time-themes and other-worldliness—most important features of the genre—had passed into the jargon of the self-consciously literate is amply demonstrated:

> It seems sometimes, sir, as though the past isn't the past! I believe there's been a play on in London about something like that. There's something in it, sir—there really is. There's a feeling comes over you—as though you'd done everything before.

Thus speaks Tressillian, a butler, in Agatha Christie's *Hercule Poirot's Christmas.* No less than *Punch,* the novels of Agatha Christie were accurate measures. By the time a preoccupation had reached the pages of Agatha Christie one must presume, without being pejorative, that it had achieved the common touch!

But it must be remembered that this drama and its language stands between the two dominating extremes of prose-naturalism and poetry. It takes sustenance from both, but it is, in the eventual result, neither precisely the language of man in or out of his own society, his own time, his own normal existence. It is a hybrid, a charming and, at times, a poignant one in the world of dramatic communication which, as the century wears on, shows more and more dissonances rather than reconciliations in both theme and communication.

Part II
The Language of Prose-Drama

3 Bernard Shaw and the Language of Man in Society

Bernard Shaw is the great exception to the notion that the dramatist who deals with 'contemporary life' must, in order to be direct and successful, use, in its raw state, the language of the populace. But he affirms the proposition that the language of man in society is prose. Any examination of Shaw's dramatic communication must start with the proposition that his plays are, in a very special set of ways, 'literary', and that he is not a naturalistic dramatist in the sense that he attempts to produce an accurate photograph of life. That it is neither arrogant to assert the first point nor naive to urge the second, is strongly evidenced by his own words and by the strong associations that have been made between Shaw the dramatist and the working-class community of the first twenty years, at least, of the twentieth century. Such an association existed, but it had little to do with a stark employment of the dramatic language of the artisan. Again, he is commonly accused of completely lacking or avoiding 'poetry', the implication being that his language is so much of the earth, earthy, that it never aspires to flight.

To say that his is a 'literary' language does not mean that he abandons the idiomatic in favour of an invented sophistication. Indeed he prided himself on his phonetician's ear for spoken speech, but what he made of it in his plays renders it, in fact, into a different status of communication.

> My dear Hamon,
>   In Brassbound, Drinkwater does not talk much slang. In the Socialist movement I met a costermonger who was quite an

32

effective public speaker. He was very fluent, and had a copious vocabulary, as he was fond of reading. But he spoke with the strongest Whitechapel accent; and the contrast between his comparatively literary style and his appalling pronunciation was very quaint.[1]

Idiom never appeared in his dialogue before it had passed the test of clarity and had acquired style. The indefatigable Siegfried Trebitsch, Shaw's German translator, was bombarded with advice on matters concerning 'correct' idiom, but always, the correctness had to be measured by artistic propriety.

> . . . I do not believe a bit in your schoolmasters and professors and people. I notice that they do not know that when an Englishman names an hour with a 'the' before it, he always means a train. Thus, when Frank Warren says that his mother has gone up to town by the 11.15, he means that she has gone to catch the 11.15 train . . .[2]

He congratulates Trebitsch on his accuracy, and adds that his translation 'seemed to me to have a distinct style, and to be not only accurate in the schoolmaster's way, but artistically expressive'.

He defined style as 'a sort of melody that comes into my sentences by itself '. In fact, what this style amounts to is the result of a painstaking and conscious refinement (at times it amounts to purification) of ordinary speech and dialect. The result is to give his dialogue the miasma of public speaking—an art which habitually takes the ordinary and, without losing some touch with it, makes it extraordinary, with a ring of authority and a memorable shape. He gently castigated J. L. Shire who appeared in the first production of *John Bull's Other Island* in 1904 for his handling of some of the dialogue. It must have been unnerving for the man to realize that Shaw was, as he puts it in a letter, 'jotting' down the fluffs and flaws and cuts he was guilty of. It is noticeable that Shaw is particularly sensitive to anything that diminishes this style:

> Act IV, page 8, 'He'll tell it himself as if it were one of the most providential episodes in the history of England and Ireland.' You generally forget the word providential, and in your agitation extemporise the most amazing variations on the whole sentence.[3]

A dramatist whose attitude towards his language was so conscious and rigorously on guard, and who wrote with such deliberation and sense of purpose, would not find it easy to accept any interference with it either by actor or director. It is no exaggeration to say that, in a sense, Shaw's plays are written in such a way as to make interference either impossible or very difficult. Shaw, in any case, had an ambivalent relationship with the acting profession; he was capable of adoring actresses and greatly respecting actors, but he was equally given to regarding them as morons where sensitivity to language and meaning was concerned. He never harboured (except in the transports of a blind affection—which he was quite capable of allowing to overcome him) any illusions about his view of the mental capacities of the acting profession. Neither was he at all doubtful about what their rightful place was in the hierarchy—at the very top of which stood the dramatist.

> Born actors have a susceptibility to dramatic emotion which enables them to seize the moods of their parts intuitively. But to expect them to be intuitive as to intellectual meaning and circumstantial conditions as well, is to demand powers of divination from them; one might as well expect the Astronomer Royal to tell the time in a catacomb.[4]

Shaw trusted the emotional intuitions of the players much more certainly than their intellectual capabilities, but he was as much prepared to guide their intuitions as he was determined to direct their mentalities. He even offered some advice to Henry Arthur Jones, his fellow-playwright, on this:

> You have to know how to write down the sounds so that the musician, reaching his part (like the actor reaching his part), may, as far as he is capable, make the sounds as or when you want them.[5]

Clearly, to Shaw, his text was definitive. He was genuinely prepared to allow the actor to 'find' the part in his own way, but he took pains to see that that way was charted for him:

> . . . follow your own feeling and make the most of your own skill: turn the whole thing inside out if you like—in fact you won't be able to help yourself when the spirit takes possession

of you at full pressure—but don't hesitate on my account to make the part entirely your own: my idea of having my play acted is not to insist on everybody rattling my particular bag of tricks . . .[6]

But he had already prefaced this apparently genial liberality of advice to the actor with the words: 'I think I am probably nearly right as to the best changes and stopping places on the journey.' Throughout his life, Shaw never budged from the belief that the playwright's 'own view of his work can only be conveyed by himself'.

The apparent rigidity of his approach to the work of dramatist has encouraged a belief that Shaw not only constantly interfered in rehearsals of his own plays, but that his ideal performance of them was that in which he played all the roles himself. To read some of his letters and comments seems only to reinforce this belief, but, with the evidence of a typical example before us, we still have to remember first, that few actors and actresses either resented Shaw or found him to be wrong in his advice, second, that he was an uncommonly fine actor and, third, that he often expressed himself with more enthusiastic and mischievous diligence than he intended:

> My dear Trebitsch
> Good: we can do no more now as to the text.
> Now as to the general philosophy of the thing. I know that the transfer of any work to the professional stage means desecration, prostitution, sacrilege and damnation. It means this *at best*. At worst it means mere ignorant rascality, lies, cheating, evasion, and interpolation of obscenities and idiocies. But you must never admit this, or make any truce with it, or allow anybody to tell you that it is the custom . . . In a theatre you must always assume that the noblest aims, the highest artistic integrity, the most scrupulous respect for artistic considerations, the most strenuous fidelity to the poet's text, are the law in that particular house, and that it is only in third rate places and among the lowest class of actors that malpractices occur and liberties are taken. Never let them put you in the position of a novice who does not know what theatres are really like: .put *them* in the position of having to act up to your high estimate of their conscience and respectability.[7]

We have to temper any conclusion that Shaw was unique in

35

this assertion of the playwright's authority by looking at what he wrote, said and did in the context of its time. The proselytization of the status of the dramatist was, in fact, not a Shavian innovation. It is to be found in a number of late nineteenth- and early twentieth-century dramatists and Yeats is often taken to be a founding father. But, as so often in theatre history, we have to turn to a relatively unknown critic to find the fullest and deepest examination of this particular doctrine of infallibility. Arthur Symons (who was so sceptical about Shaw's plays), aesthete, follower of Walter Pater, poet, dramatist, critic, wrote very trenchantly on the subject but with a more theatrically apocalyptic sense than Shaw:

> I am inclined to ask myself why we require the intervention of any less perfect medium between the meaning of a piece, as the author conceived it, and that other meaning which it derives from our reception of it. The living actor, even when he condescends to subordinate himself to the requirements of pantomime, has always what he is proud to call his temperament; in other words so much personal caprice, which for the most part means wilful misunderstanding; and in seeing his acting you have to consider this intrusive little personality of his as well as the author's. The marionette may be relied upon. He will respond to an indication without reserve or revolt; an error on his part (we are all human) will certainly be the fault of the author; he can be trained to perfection . . .[8]

Shaw's assumption of the authority of the playwright obviously had compatible surroundings in which to parade itself. But even if he was not the 'onlie begetter' of the doctrine, his addiction to it was far from being a mere reaction to those surroundings. An amalgam of several elements was responsible: his self-willed temperament, his nationality perhaps, his experience (limited though it was) as a novelist, his career as a public speaker and, perhaps, even a realization of favourable monetary return, all combined to drive him towards an assertion of the status of the creative single man. In the preface to *Widowers' Houses* (called, both pertinently and pertly, *Mainly about Myself*) Shaw announced what he obviously wanted to be accepted as a new art-form—one in which the dramatist/creator's sanctity and authority was preserved, while the actor/manager's opportunity was (apparently) ensured. The form in which he published *Widowers' Houses* was intended to attract the general reader who was used to the amplitude of the novel as well as the professional man-of-the-theatre who expected an 'acting-text'. At a stroke, Shaw both proposed and effected a text which he believed fulfilled both the requirements of a novel and of a play. Throughout his career he never significantly modified either his purpose or his practice—and, as a result, his conception of the nature of dramatic language, and a good deal of his practice, remained the same as it did when he set out with such cheery, but sometimes solemn, confidence at the end of the nineteenth century. He writes to the Rev. Montagu Villiers: 'My own profession is the same as yours, my inspiration the same as that of the prophets you expound, my heritage every word they uttered, my responsibility great in proportion to the numbers of people I reach . . . A theatre is a place where 2 or 3 are gathered together; & an actor one whose function is fundamentally priestly.'

Shaw's words are too tempting to decline asking the question—if the actor is priest, the audience congregation, the theatre a place of worship, who then is the playwright? Somewhere, in his declaration to the revered gentleman, there is a flaw. Shaw's profession cannot be the same as his, if the actor is the priest. There are, in fact, only three occupations vacant—sidesman (not one Shaw could contemplate), saint, or God!

Shaw's edicts (for they are often expressed as such) about the new art-form he intended to formulate are to be found as part of the preface to *Widowers' Houses* and, scattered, in his letters. It is too much to expect that, in the matter of text, Shaw would be able to forgo a pejorative reference to Shakespeare, who, for his shortcomings in preparing his text, 'has left us no intellectually coherent drama, and could not afford to pursue a genuinely scientific method in his studies of character and society'. Shaw's ability both to invent and use history was phenomenal, but his actual knowledge of historical activity was often threadbare, or occasionally conveniently pushed aside. He regrets the fact (and seems to blame Shakespeare for it) that we do not have complete prompt copies of the plays, no 'descriptive directions which the author gave on the stage', no 'character sketches'. He concludes that 'we should have had all this and much more if Shakespear [sic], instead of merely writing out his lines, had prepared the plays for publication in competition with fiction as elaborate as that of Meredith'. Time and time again, Shakespeare is castigated because he did not have the advantages of living as a contemporary of Shaw; time and time again he judges Shakespeare, who lived in one clime, by the laws of another.

It is important to understand Shaw's unsteady and capricious hold on historical actuality, and his treatment of Shakespeare is a notable example of his occasional mixture of pigheadedness and incomplete knowledge. Shaw either did not know, or chose to forget, that Elizabethan stage and social conditions made it impossible for Shakespeare to be as Shaw wished, and he is reckless in his generalizations about Elizabethan acting. Nevertheless, it is from his reflections on sixteenth-century theatre and Shakespeare that the germ of his new art-form grew. He claims that the dialogue of an Elizabethan play, with the exception of 'half a dozen lines', can be understood without difficulty, but that many modern plays cannot be intelligible by mere reading—since so much depends on visible stage business. He believes that the reluctance of the British public to read plays is the result of a bafflement which the published texts induce—'nothing in them but bare words, with a few carpenter's and costumier's directions . . .' And so his proposal is made—and we may think of that motivation of favourable economy when we consider that royalties may well increase when plays are both seen and read.

> The case, then, is overwhelming not only for printing and publishing the dialogue of plays, but for a serious effort to convey their full content to the reader. This means the institution of a new art; and I daresay that before these two volumes are ten years old, the bald attempt they make at it will be left far behind, and that the customary brief and unreadable scene specification at the head of an act will have expanded into a chapter, or even a series of chapters. No doubt one result of this will be the production, under cover of the above arguments, of works of a mixture of kinds, part narrative, part homily, part description, part dialogue, and (possibly) part drama: works

that could be read, but not acted. I have no objection to such works; but my own aim has been that of the practical dramatist: if anything my eye has been too much on the stage. At all events, I have tried to put down nothing that is irrelevant to the actor's performance, and, through it, to the audience's comprehension of the play . . . But if my readers do their fair share of the work, I daresay they will understand nearly as much of the plays as I do myself.

The manifesto explains Shaw's published texts, it explains, to a degree, the nature of his dialogue, and it accounts for the existence of the Prefaces whose presence has so unaccountably puzzled both so many critics and general readers. The prefaces are logically necessary in order that the readers, if they 'do their fair share of the work, . . . will understand nearly as much of the play as I do myself '.

Shaw is the greatest prose dramatist of the twentieth century, because the prose he uses has a virility, clarity and colour unmatched by any other dramatist, save Shakespeare and, at his best, Congreve. Of the many critical reflexes Shaw's language has galvanized the most persistent are that he lacks a poetic sense, that his characters discuss but little happens, that he is a realist, not a romantic, that his major contribution to the history of English drama is 'social' plays which deal with the problems of men in contemporary society.

It is not Shaw's language but his political and sociological ideas and attitudes that gave his plays their astonishing currency. This was not confined to Shaftesbury Avenue, but spread throughout the land, often circulated more in educational circles than in the theatre. The phenomenon of Shaw and the Workers' Educational Association is absolutely unique in the annals of the effect of writers upon their society. The WEA grew into being to meet a certain and urgent need for the educationally dispossessed and socially underprivileged to attend series of evening lectures, when the day's task was done, on a whole variety of subjects. It goes without saying that the most popular subjects in the early days of this movement were economics and politics—miners, railwaymen, dustmen, postmen wanted to try and understand the theoretical bases for the economic and political maelstroms in which

their lives seemed to be spent. So far as literature was concerned the most popular was that which seemed to reflect, in
some way or other, the facts of life of society. Dickens,
Galsworthy, Gissing were names that appeared time after time
on the syllabuses of classes held in places as geographically
separated as Cradley Heath in the Black Country and Port
Talbot in South Wales. But the name of Shaw was predomin-
ant. He appeared in courses not only on literature but on
economics and politics. For the liberal-minded God-fearing
miner in Wales, Scotland or England, the Bible, Shaw and *The
Daily Mail* were constant reading. For the bolshie militant it
was *Das Kapital,* Shaw and *The Daily Worker.* Shaw became
not merely the darling of the so-called working class; he
became its temporal deity. No criticism of Shaw was brooked;
no other dramatist had ever seemed to get anywhere as near to
expressing what many felt but was ne'er so well expressed.
Yet, and this is a paradox of great proportions, Shaw did *not*
express what so many accepted in a language which was
theirs. There is little that is exclusively horny-handed and
demotic about Shaw's prose.

If it has an echo of 'real' speech about it at all, it is the speech
of the uncommonly articulate, not the inarticulate. Beatie, in
Wesker's *Roots* aspires to unforced fluency of thought and
speech, and discovers eventually that she has it:

Beatie: The writers don't write thinkin' we can understand, nor the
painters don't paint expecting us to be interested—that they
don't, nor don't the composers give out music thinking we can
appreciate it. 'Blust,' they say, 'the masses is too stupid for us to
come down to them. Blust,' they say, 'if they don't make no
effort why should we bother?' So you know who come along?
The slop singers and the pop writers and the film makers and
women's magazines and the Sunday papers and the picture
strip love stories—that's who come along, and you don't have
to make no effort for them, it come easy. 'We know where the
money lie,' they say, 'hell we do! The workers've got it so let's
give them what they want. If they want slop songs and film
idols we'll give 'em that then. If they want words of one
syllable, we'll give 'em that then. If they want the third-rate,
blust! We'll give 'em *that* then. Anything's good enough for
them 'cos they don't ask for no more!' The whole stinkin'
commercial world insults us and we don't care a damn. Well,

Ronnie's right—it's our own bloody fault. We want the third-rate—we got it! We got it! We . . .
(Suddenly Beatie stops as if listening to herself. She pauses, turns with an ecstatic smile on her face—)
D'you hear that? D'you hear it? Did you listen to me? I'm talking. Jenny, Frankie, Mother—I'm not quoting no more.[9]

But she is an amateur compared with the ratiocinative and splendidly rhythmical Alfred Doolittle:

Doolittle: I don't need less than a deserving man. I need more. I don't eat less hearty than him; and drink a lot more. I want a bit of amusement, cause I'm a thinking man. I want cheerfulness and a song and a band when I feel low. Well, they charge me just the same for everything as they charge the deserving. What is middle class morality? Just an excuse for never giving me anything. Therefore, I ask you, as two gentlemen, not to play that game on me. I'm playing straight with you. I aint pretending to be deserving. I'm undeserving; and I mean to go on being undeserving; I like it; and thats the truth. Will you take advantage of a man's nature to do him out of the price of his own daughter what he's brought up and fed and clothed by the sweat of his brow until she's growed big enough to be interesting to you two gentlemen? Is five pounds unreasonable? I put it to you: and I leave it to you.
Higgins: (Rising, and going over to Pickering) Pickering: if we were to take this man in hand for three months, he could choose between a seat in the Cabinet and a popular pulpit in Wales.[10]

In fact, Shakespeare's Shallow and Silence utter in a way far closer to the dust than Doolittle. The nearest Shaw gets to the truly demotic is a kind of linguistic artful dodgery which he expresses in what he has obviously taken pains to render into Cockney. Unless the actor or actress bravely forgets Shaw and trusts his or her own ear, the result can be very contrived:

Drinkwater: (Bursting into tears) Clawss feelin! thets wot it is; clawss feelin! Wot are yer, arter all, bat a bloomin gang o wust cowst cazhls [*casual ward paupers*]? . . . Better ev naow fembly, an rawse aht of it, lawk me, than ev a specble one and disgrice it, lawk you.[11]

The miracle of Shaw's hold upon the educationally and economically dispossessed, in the 1920s and 1930s, is that the very elegance of his basic prose style and the very artificiality of his excursions into dialect did not daunt his admirers —indeed, it might almost be said that an aspiration to speak like Shaw and to seem to be able to argue from point to point, as he seemed to do, towards an inexorable QED, prevented any disaffection. And, in any case, the sheer weight of Shaw's plays was enough to push aside any worries about dialect that Shaw's rank and file acolytes might have. It cannot be too strongly emphasized that the effects of Shaw's style on those now middle aged and elderly, and who still publicly fight what is called the 'class struggle', are still working. The sweet reasonableness, which is often more apparent than real, the absence of verbal decoration which, nevertheless, does not preclude the use of the occasional portentous phrase, the repetition, the subtle use of the rhetorical question—these characteristics of platform prose have their roots deep in the Shavian soil. Shaw's characters do not speak the language specifically of the possessed or the dispossessed, but one which the former feels is suitable to their station and which the latter feels might enable them to raise their station. It is, in fact, an elevated language.

It would be natural to expect that a man who had begun his career as a novelist could not easily throw off the influence of that more discursive art when he came to write plays. It is a remarkable and abiding achievement of Shaw's to have so successfully fended off, so far as his dialogue is concerned, the most baleful effects of novel-writing. J. B. Priestley alone, in the twentieth century, surpasses Shaw in his ability to step cleanly from one art-form into another. But, to varying degrees, others have been less successful—Maugham, Charles Morgan, Graham Greene. Shaw's own temperament and skilled knowledge of the arts of theatre ensured that his language would be dramatic enough; his experiences of the novel's opportunities for descriptive writing admirably fitted his intention to write readable plays.

The nature, manner and effect of his descriptive material in his first play—*Widowers' Houses*—is to be found, mutated, but with the basic intentions unaltered and recognizable, in all his plays. This material is, naturally, mainly concerned with location and with the appearance and identification of the main attitudes of characters. In the former, detailed information is clearly given to the director, but Shaw is never averse to embodying the factual necessities in atmospheric description.

It is in initial descriptive directions for acts that Shaw's intention to make his text readable as well as actable can be most clearly seen. In *Widowers' Houses* this is, curiously, less apparent than in later plays, but the novelist's eye is unmistakable:

> In the garden restaurant of a hotel at Remagen on the Rhine, on a fine afternoon in August in the eighteen-eighties. Looking down the Rhine towards Bonn, the gate leading from the garden to the riverside is seen on the right. The hotel is on the left. It has a wooden annexe with an entrance marked Table d'Hôte. A waiter is in attendance.
>
> A couple of English tourists come out of the hotel. The younger, Dr. Harry Trench, is about 24, stoutly built, thick in the neck, close-cropped and black in the hair, with undignified medical-student manners, frank, hasty, rather boyish. The other, Mr. William de Burgh Cokane, is probably over 40, possibly 50: an ill-nourished, scanty-haired gentleman, with affected manners; fidgety, touchy, and constitutionally ridiculous in uncompassionate eyes.

In *Too True to be Good*, the visual beginning of Act II is designated in a form which takes it out of the terms in which a play can viably be presented. It is a sharp reminder not only of Shaw's novelist-style but of the extent to which he accepted what to us is a quite old-fashioned attempt at illusion provided by the box-set and the back-drop:

> A sea beach in a mountainous country. Sand dunes rise to a brow which cuts off the view of the plain beyond, only the summits of the distant mountain range which bounds it being visible. An army hut on the hither side, with a klaxon electric horn projecting from a board on the wall, shews that we are in a military cantoonment. Opposite the hut is a particolored canvas bathing pavilion with a folding stool beside the entrance. As seen from the sand dunes the hut is on the right and the pavilion on the left. From the neighbourhood of the hut a date palm throws a long shadow; for it is early morning.
>
> In this shadow sits a British colonel in a deck chair, peacefully reading the weekly edition of The Times, but with a revolver in

his equipment. A light cane chair for use by his visitors is at hand by the hut. Though well over fifty, he is still slender, handsome, well set up and every inch a commanding officer. His full style and title is Colonel Tallboys, v.c., d.s.o. He won his cross as a company-officer, and has never looked back since then.

He is disturbed by a shattering series of explosions announcing the approach of a powerful and very imperfectly silenced motor bicycle from the side opposite to the huts.

The visual illusion and atmosphere that Shaw wants certainly strained the audience's willing suspension of disbelief and, perhaps, the capacity of the technical resources of the theatre of his time. The discrepancy, for example, between what Shaw is able to people our mind's eye with, and what even a director in the more sophisticated 1970s can achieve, is implicit in his visual directions for Act I of *Caesar and Cleopatra*. Some of the photographs of early production-sets of this play—and making allowances for the possible deceptions of the camera—can surely leave little doubt that they were inadequate. Shaw had a strong visual imagination, which was of a romantic kind, in the sense that it was constantly inclined to rove from the practical to the picturesque, from the clear to the indefinite. This gives many of his descriptive directions a lyrical and acceptable quality, but it dooms the reader of his plays to a startling bump to earth when he becomes a member of an audience:

> An October night on the Syrian border of Egypt towards the end of the XXXIII Dynasty, in the year 706 by Roman computation, afterwards reckoned by Christian computation as 48 B.C. A great radiance of silver fire, the dawn of a moonlit night, is rising in the east. The stars and the cloudless sky are our own contemporaries, nineteen and a half centuries younger than we know them: but you would not guess that from their appearance. Below them are two notable drawbacks of civilisation: a palace and soldiers.

The truth is that, quite apart from this disposition to be romantic, Shaw's visual notions of his plays, certainly the early ones, were frequently bigger than what the plays in terms of theatre require. There is a sense in which one experiences a Shaw play (when the director has assiduously tried to

make Shaw's winged prose take practical flight) where what is
being seen and what is heard are incompatible. Sometimes
Shaw tries to put quarts into pint pots. His descriptions frequently give the reader (and, by an act of faith, the playgoer) a
geographical context, a glimpse of a larger world which, in
strictly theatrical terms, is dangerously close to affluent irrelevance.

> The same darkness into which the temple of Ra and the Syrian
> palace vanished. The same silence. Suspense. Then the black-
> ness and stillness break softly into silver mist and strange airs as
> the windswept harp of Memnon plays at the dawning of the
> moon. It rises full over the desert; and a vast horizon comes into
> relief, broken by a huge shape which soon reveals itself in the
> spreading radiance as a sphinx pedestalled on the sands. The
> light still clears, until the upraised eyes of the image are distin-
> guished looking straight forward and upward in infinite fear-
> less vigil . . .

But the confrontation between Caesar and Cleopatra which
takes place creates too sensational a contrast:

The Girl: Old Gentleman.
Caesar: Immortal Gods!
The Girl: Old Gentleman: dont run away.
Caesar: Old Gentleman: dont run away!!! This: to Julius Caesar!

Would that Shaw's descriptive directions were always as
theatrically appropriate as they are in the opening scenes of
Widowers' Houses and *Mrs. Warren's Profession.* More often,
however, they impose a strain both on the reader's credulity
and on the technical resources of the theatre. Paradoxically,
though, they can still be an aid to the actor in the preparation of
his role. The actor is enabled to satisfy the universal need of his
profession to feel the 'reality' of his role growing inside a
context, an atmosphere. With most dramatists the actor has to
invent the context—'out of the blue', so to say; sometimes he
has to 'transplant' his role in a recalled or surrogate background. It is not often that he is helped by the playwright. But
Shaw treats his players well and, time and time again, the
mode of the descriptive direction helps to satisfy their need to
know how to fit the fictional character into a background:

> Higgins . . . appears in the morning light as a robust, vital, appetising sort of man of forty or thereabouts, dressed in a professional-looking black frock-coat with a white linen collar and black silk tie. He is of the energetic, scientific type heartily, even violently interested in everything that can be studied as a scientific subject, and careless about himself and other people, including their feelings. He is, in fact, but for his years and size, rather like a very impetuous baby 'taking notice' eagerly and loudly . . .

Shaw's directions per se are more helpful than the frequent discrepancies which arise between affluent description and scenic possibility on stage. The actor is, unusually, put into the same position as a member of the audience who has read the play. The possibility of discrepancies seems not to have crossed Shaw's mind. As late as 1949 he was castigating those playwrights who wrote 'as poets and novelists indulging their imaginations beyond the physical limits of "four boards and a passion".' The phrase occurs in an essay entitled 'Rules for Directors'.[12] In this Shaw discusses in detail the methods of the director in rehearsal on the a priori assumption that 'the most desirable director of a play is the author'; but remarkably, treatment of the play in visual terms is categorically left until the very end where it is dealt with peremptorily—not without some naiveté. Having expressed approval of Restoration stage-architecture he goes on:

> Old toy theatres preserve this type of stage. Every director should preserve one; for effects are possible on it that are not possible in modern built-in sets. For instance, when there are three wide entrances between the wings on both sides of the stage a crowd can be cleared off it almost instantaneously. The very few who are old enough to have seen Queen Elizabeth and her court apparently sink into the earth and disappear when Ristori, as Marie Stewart, called her 'the Bastard of England', will appreciate how a modern director is hampered by having to clear the stage through one door.[13]

This is, of course, not to say that Shaw was insensitive to or ignorant of the work of the visual artist in the theatre—his letters to Gordon Craig are ample evidence of his knowledgeable interest in the art of the set-designer. Moreover, he gave generous praise to designers who had provided the sets for his own plays.

Yet, in the long run one cannot escape the impression that, for him, the visual was implicit in the verbal; that what he wanted his audience to see was already satisfactorily contained—waiting only to be released and embodied—in his stage directions:

> Do you realise that my plays are being kept alive by desperate little bands of enthusiasts, mostly very poor, who perform them in all sorts of out-of-the-way valleys and villages, and pay me author's fees which sometimes do not exceed ninepence? These people have to buy my plays in the printed book, and get up their shows from the directions in them.

It is when the actor reaches the stage that his problems arise with a Shaw play. Time and time again in revivals which have remained faithful to Shaw's text—since there is precious little else that they can do—a sense is created that the set and what it embraces are at odds. Even if a modern director abandons what seems to Shaw to have been the ideal stage-setting and relics, let us say in *Caesar and Cleopatra*, on lighting and impressionistic background, the extraordinary force of Shaw's language seems to make the visual effort inappropriate, sometimes even ludicrous. In any case, however much of an embarrassment objects like the Sphinx are to set-designers, it is astonishing how often such embarrassments are called for by Shaw. He requires the Sphinx here, and a mill to be used in *John Bull's Other Island*, in which a car is also required, 'a monster jaunty car, black and dilapidated'; a cannon in *Major Barbara*, a jungle in *Androcles and the Lion*, followed by an Emperor's box at the Coliseum, not forgetting a lion's cage with a heavy portcullis grating. By comparison, the specific requirements of the Garden of Eden in *Back to Methuselah* seem small beer!

In that play where he might have been expected to indulge himself in a largesse of description in his directions he is, relatively, parsimonious—indeed, in the first act—'The Garden of Eden'—positively niggardly. Shaw significantly tempered his descriptive directions, with one or two lapses, after and including *Heartbreak House*—though the 'after-part' of a

47

'high-pooped ship' is a daunting challenge for any set-designer.

He seems, after this play (and particularly excepting *Too True to be Good*) to have had some access of mercy towards his set-designers. He gave them much more allowance of freedom to solve visual problems by not overloading his descriptive rifts with often charming but embarrassing ore. He does not, however, stint himself on an incredible amount of small set details—particularly of furniture. But gone, largely, is what seems to have been an early obsession to ensure that the large outside, the great globe itself, yea and the heavens, should be glimpsed from his specific stage-locations. Perhaps, after *Heartbreak House,* there was less he wished to see out of his windows and from his balustrades.

Even *St. Joan,* his historical magnum opus, has to be content to open on 'a fine spring morning on the river Meuse' and Scene vi is designated merely as 'a great stone hall in the castle, arranged for a trial-at-law'. He disciplines himself, too, even for the marine vistas of *The Simpleton of the Unexpected Isles.*

There is, however, for many of Shaw's plays no way in which they can satisfactorily be represented without, at one extreme (impressionism) seeming irrelevantly unreal or, at the other (naturalism) seeming awkwardly artificial. In either case the play is put at odds with itself, and the actor seems to be wandering in a misplaced limbo or an oversize Pollock's cut-out theatre. Perhaps, indeed, the great Shaw revival which his admirers long for will only come when people stop reading his plays, and, thus, stuffing their imaginations with visual expectations the stage cannot handle. They might, then, just be prepared to accept Pollock's cut-outs as a quaint curiosity and give their attention to the play.

The bulk of the responsibility for ministering both to the actor and to the reader in Shaw's plays falls on what are habitually called Stage Directions, although, in view of their dual function, the title is misleading, the more so when they are examined closely. Indeed their function often merges with that of the descriptive directions so that their specifically theatrical indications are often more apparent than real. In pursuance of his new 'art-form' Shaw thus produced a different kind of direction which would be more than a simple indication to an actor of what was required at any given point in the text. Shaw also had his readers much in mind who had to be told the 'why', 'how' and 'with what result' of the direction. We will find, for convenience sake, and perhaps with an added degree of accuracy, that the phrase 'active-direction' may be used of these sign-posts for both the actors' skills and for the readers' imaginations.

Shaw's 'active-directions' are of several kinds. These are sometimes deceptive in the sense that they can seem innocently simple and yet, on examination, can be found to be not for the actor alone—they are absolutely necessary to the reader as well. In *Widowers' Houses* there is a stark example of this. The dialogue printed without directions reads:

Blanche: (   ) Has papa made any difficulty?
Trench: (   ) No. None at all. (   )
Blanche: Harry: are you too proud to take money from my father?
Trench: Yes, Blanche: I am too proud.
Blanche: (   ) That is not nice to me, Harry.
Trench: You must bear with me, Blanche. I—I cant explain. After all, it's very natural.
Blanche: Has it occurred to you that I may be proud, too?
Trench: Oh, thats nonsense. No one will accuse you of marrying for money.
Blanche: No one would think the worse of me if I did, or of you either. (   ) We really cannot live on seven hundred a year, Harry; and I dont think it quite fair of you to ask me merely because you are afraid of people talking.
Trench: It's not that alone, Blanche.
Blanche: What else is it, then?
Trench: Nothing. I—
Blanche: (   ) Of course it's nothing. Now dont be absurd, Harry: be good; and listen to me: I know how to settle it. You are too proud to owe anything to me; and I am too proud to owe anything to you. You have seven hundred a year. Well, I will take just seven hundred a year from papa at first; and then we shall be quits. Now, now, Harry, you know youve not a word to say against that.

There is very little in the language alone to indicate the degree of tension that is intended by Shaw to exist between Trench and Blanche. The most that the language of itself

49

provides is that Blanche does not think she can live with him on seven hundred pounds a year and that there is some unexplained reason for his refusing to take money from her father. There is no suggestion of anger, no suggestion of explosively suppressed emotions, of a deep-seated aversion to taking money, very little indication of Blanche's changes of mood. There is a flatness, a one-dimensional quality, so to speak, in the dialogue. Without the active-directions the reader might be justified in concurring with Arthur Symons that Shaw's prose is cold stuff. But, with the active-directions, the temperature rises and meaning and mood begin to flourish:

Blanche: (He shakes his head) Has papa made any difficulty?
Trench: (Rising with a sigh and taking his chair back to its former place) No. None at all. *(He sits down dejectedly. When Blanche speaks again her face and voice betray the beginning of a struggle with her temper)*
Blanche: Harry: are you too proud to take money from my father?
Trench: Yes, Blanche: I am too proud.
Blanche: (After a pause) That is not nice to me, Harry.
Trench: You must bear with me, Blanche. I—I cant explain. After all, it's very natural.
Blanche: Has it occurred to you that I may be proud, too?
Trench: Oh, thats nonsense. No one will accuse you of marrying for money.
Blanche: No one would think the worse of me if I did, or of you either. *(She rises and begins to walk restlessly about)* We really cannot live on seven hundred a year, Harry; and I dont think it quite fair of you to ask me merely because you are afraid of people talking.
Trench: It's not that alone, Blanche.
Blanche: What else is it, then?
Trench: Nothing. I—
Blanche: (Getting behind him, and speaking with forced playfulness as she bends over him, her hands on his shoulders) Of course it's nothing. Now dont be absurd, Harry: be good; and listen to me: I know how to settle it. You are too proud to owe anything to me; and I am too proud to owe anything to you. You have seven hundred a year. Well, I will take just seven hundred a year from papa at first; and then we shall be quits. Now, now, Harry, you know youve not a word to say against that.

Almost all (in depth of perspective, relating to motive, mood and action) that is missing in the emasculated version we first printed, is here as Shaw intended it to be.

In other examples, however, which, again, can be found throughout his dramatic career, the language itself, in dialogue form, embodies the direction; it is, in fact, fulfilling the requirements of being dramatic language—by embodying the drama within itself. There is no doubt about the mood, tone and disposition of the characters here:

Trench: (   ) I will not. It's a damnable business from beginning to end; and you deserve no better luck for helping in it. Ive seen it all among the out-patients at the hospital; and it used to make my blood boil to think that such things couldnt be prevented.

Lickcheese: (   ) Oh indeed, sir. But I suppose youll take your share when you marry Miss Blanche, all the same. (   ) Which of us is the worse, I should like to know? me that wrings the money out to keep a home over my children, or you that spend it and try to shove the blame on to me?

The missing directions are—'rising angrily', 'his suppressed spleen breaking out', 'furiously'—but, significantly, the dialogue itself carries these emotions within itself. The directions are hardly required.

Caesar and Cleopatra is particularly replete with such apparent directive superfluity. At times it gives the play an unfortunate melodramatic posture. In this short example the direction 'interrupting her' has already been made superfluous by the way the preceding line of dialogue is constructed and printed:

Cleopatra: (In a stifled whisper) Ftatateeta, Ftatateeta.
Ftatateeta: (Hurrying to her from the table and petting her) Peace, child: be comforted—
Cleopatra: (Interrupting her) Can they hear us?
Ftatateeta: No, dear heart, no.
Cleopatra: Listen to me. If he leaves the Palace alive, never see my face again.
Ftatateeta: He? Poth—
Cleopatra: (Striking her on the mouth) Strike his life out as I strike his name from your lips. Dash him down from the wall. Break him on the stones. Kill, kill, kill him.

And, indeed, the direction—'striking her on the mouth' is equally unnecessary.

51

The occasions when we find unnecessary stage-directions like this can be balanced by those when they are, although lengthy, of precise theatrical point and help. Such a one, very typical, is to be found in Act II of *Caesar and Cleopatra*:

> Caesar, seeing that Rufio's temper threatens to get the worse of him, puts his hand on his shoulder and brings him down the hall out of harm's way, Britannus accompanying them and posting himself on Caesar's right hand. This movement brings the three in a little group to the place occupied by Achillas, who moves haughtily away and joins Theodotus on the other side. Lucius Septimius goes out through the soldiers in the loggia. Pothinus, Theodotus and Achillas follow him with the courtiers, very mistrustful of the soldiers, who close up in their rear and go out after them, keeping them moving without much ceremony. The King is left in his chair, piteous, obstinate, with twitching face and fingers. During these movements Rufio maintains an energetic grumbling, as follows:

This is 'blocking' to an extent rarely found outside the director's production text. Apart from the reference to the state of mistrust it is strictly a stage not a descriptive direction. It is fascinating to ponder on which kind of direction a producer of Shaw's plays would prefer—one like this which, almost literally, gives neither him nor his actors room to manoeuvre, or the elaborate descriptive directions which seem to give a visual freedom but, in fact, can be a hindrance and a trap.

Or, one wonders, would he be happier with a direction which is a mixture of both stage and descriptive. There is, again in *Caesar and Cleopatra,* a typical example of Shaw's hunting with the hounds and running with the hare; he has one eye on his readers and another on his audience. This scene is worth some exploration since it so clearly indicates the problems Shaw can create by, so to speak, mixing up the language of theatre, the language of drama and, indeed, the language of narrative prose:

> Meanwhile Rufio, the morning's fighting done, sits munching dates on a faggot of brushwood outside the door of the lighthouse, which towers gigantic to the clouds on his left. His helmet, full of dates, is between his knees; and a leathern bottle of wine is by his side. Behind him the great stone pedestal of the lighthouse is shut in from the open sea by a low stone parapet,

with a couple of steps in the middle to the broad coping. A huge chain with a hook hangs down from the lighthouse crane above his head. Faggots like the one he sits on lie beneath it ready to be drawn up to feed the beacon.

Caesar is standing on the step at the parapet looking out anxiously, evidently ill at ease. Britannus comes out of the lighthouse door.

The scenic implications of the one word 'meanwhile' are packed with snags. In a novel its use would allow the reader to click on that mental switch which allows him to experience apparent simultaneity of actions which, in fact, have to be presented, for obvious reasons, serially in the text. But how do you translate 'meanwhile' in active theatrical terms? Is it feasible that an important character (Rufio) would be allowed to remain 'munching dates on a faggot of brushwood' while, 'meanwhile', a very contentious episode is taking place between Ftatateeta, a porter and a sentinel? If, however, we grant that he does 'meanwhile' munch his dates, is it not likely that his presence will distract us from the Ftatateeta scene that is being played 'meanwhile'?

But if 'meanwhile' is intended to indicate that as Ftatateeta's scene is ending we become aware of Rufio date-munching, how is this achieved? Does he walk on? Is he 'discovered'—but how?

Another kind of stage-direction which, upon examination, proves not to be theatrically 'pure', although apparently quite straightforward, is exemplified in *Widowers' Houses*. It occurs in Act I following a conversation between Trench and Sartorius:

Sartorius: I will leave you to yourself then. *(He hesitates, the conversation having made him self-conscious and embarrassed; then recovers himself with an effort, and adds with dignity, as he turns to go)* I am pleased to have come to an understanding with you. *(He goes into the hotel; and Cokane, who has been hanging about inquisitively, emerges from the shrubbery)*

Three words in this apparently bland stage-direction must give us pause. They are—'has been' and 'inquisitively'. 'Has been' suggests Cokane's presence throughout the scene. 'Inquisitively' suggests that the audience is aware of this presence in the bushes and the nature of his demeanour. But when did Cokane go into the bushes? If we search back we will find that the previous stage-direction involving Cokane occurs before the Trench/Sartorius scene and states—'He walks away'. No direction for hiding is given, nor, indeed, for inquisitiveness.

If we *read* the play we experience the surprise suddenly of discovering that Cokane 'has been' lurking inquisitively in the shrubbery. If we *see* the play we presumably observe him as 'he walks away' into the shrubbery earlier (though Shaw does not tell us that it is to the shrubbery) and, apparently, we watch his reactions. Truly, as reader we get one kind of experience, as audience we get quite another.

If Shaw's prefaces are, in a way, a sort of sub-text to his plays, his directions provide us with a good deal of evidence about the nature of that part of his imagination in which form has its genesis, and where the conflicting demands of one kind of embodiment or another are either resolved, unresolved or, as seems the case here, partly resolved.

Much has been made by both sympathetic and unsympathetic critics of the assumption that Shaw's characters so often merely sit down and talk. Sometimes this is taken to be a proof of his addiction to argument and discussion and, less kindly, as an earnest of a failing in theatrical versatility. Another explanation seems to have escaped both his admirers and his detractors, and evidence for putting it forward may well be to hand in the nature of Shaw's stage and descriptive directions.

It is clear that it is misleading to take all Shaw's directions at face value. They are often not the simple things they seem to be, for Shaw consciously (and perhaps sometimes unconsciously) tried to cater for both reader and audience. This, in itself, would tend to introduce some clumps of stasis—some implication, we might say, of the total reliance of the reader on the verbal when he reads a novel.

But there is something else, and we can introduce it by reference to directions from four plays written in different periods. The first is from *Widowers' Houses* (1895):

> Lickcheese comes in with Trench and Cokane. Both are in evening dress. Cokane shakes hands effusively with Sartorius.

Trench, who is coarsened and sullen, and has evidently not been making the best of his disappointment, bows shortly and resentfully. Lickcheese covers the general embarrassment by talking cheerfully until they are all seated round the large table: Trench nearest the fireplace; Cokane nearest the piano; and the other two between them, with Lickcheese next Cokane.

The second from *Androcles and the Lion* (1912):

Behind the Emperor's box at the Coliseum, where the performers assemble before entering the arena. In the middle a wide passage leading to the arena descends from the floor level under the imperial box. On both sides of this passage steps ascend to a landing at the back entrance to the box. The landing forms a bridge across the passage. At the entrance to the passage are two bronze mirrors, one on each side.

On the west side of this passage, on the right hand of anyone coming from the box and standing on the bridge, the martyrs are sitting on the steps. Lavinia is seated half-way up, thoughtful, trying to look death in the face. On her left Androcles consoles himself by nursing a cat. Ferrovius stands behind them, his eyes blazing, his figure stiff with intense resolution. At the foot of the steps crouches Spintho, with his head clutched in his hands, full of horror at the approach of martyrdom.

On the east side of the passage the gladiators are standing and sitting at ease, waiting, like the Christians, for their turn in the arena. One (Retiarius) is a nearly naked man with a net and a trident. Another (Secutor) is in armor with a sword. He carries a helmet with a barred visor. The editor of the gladiators sits on a chair a little apart from them.

The third from *Heartbreak House* (1917):

Lady Utterword: . . . (*She goes to the window seat and sits down, turning away from them ill humoredly and looking into the garden, where Hector and Ellie are now seen strolling together*)

Mrs. Hushabye: I think you have not met Mr. Mangan, Addy.

Lady Utterword: (*Turning her head and nodding coldly to Mangan*) I beg your pardon. Randall: you have flustered me so: I made a perfect fool of myself.

Mrs. Hushabye: . . . (*She goes to the window to look*)

Randall: . . . (*joining them at the window*) . . . (*he sits by Lady Utterword on her right*)

. . .

(Ellie and Hector come in from the garden by the starboard door. Randall rises. Ellie retires into the corner near the pantry. Hector comes forward; and Lady Utterword rises looking her very best)

And the fourth from *The Millionairess* (1936):

> Sagamore places the chair for Patricia next the table. Alastair shoves the broken chair back out of the way with his foot; fetches another from the wall, and is about to sit on it next Patricia when Epifania sits on it and motions him to her own chair, so that she is seated between the two, Patricia on her left, Alastair on her right. Sagamore goes back to his official place at the table.

These passages span four decades, but they demonstrate a persistent and obvious characteristic which can be compared to the constant preoccupation in Shakespeare's writing with notions of order and disorder. The persistence of an obsession with a dominant element in an artist's creative span may well be taken as an indication not only of a basic motivating power but maybe as one proof of an overriding and absolute dedication to the efficacy of art. The obsession, when it exists, has to be resolved by the artist, and his unchanging decision is that only artistic expression can resolve it. In Shakespeare's case the constant preoccupation with the virtue of order and the vice of disorder is no technical matter; it seems to reside and force itself out of his very heart and soul. To describe it as a 'theme' in his plays is a poor designation of its overmastering presence in his imagination. In Shaw's case, however, we seem to be dealing with something that is not only equally pervasive but which straddles both what we habitually refer to as 'technique' and that which we call 'imagination'.

In the four examples (and, it must be emphasized, such examples abound) we can observe how Shaw creates either static friezes with his characters, or moments in which movement seems to be directing itself towards that condition. It is as if they are being arranged in a deliberate design, aspiring towards a ritual stillness. The drive towards this is very apparent in the direction from *Widowers' Houses*. Like the frustrated individuals on Keats's Grecian Urn—we have the strong impression in the reading—that Cokane will be forever shaking Sartorius's hand, that Trench is condemned to an eternally resentful bow, that Lickcheese will ever chatter.

In *Androcles and the Lion,* stasis, in an almost ceremonial form, is completely achieved. Nothing of movement disturbs this frozen ritual. In *Heartbreak House* the process by which the moment of stasis or semi-stasis is achieved can, fascinatingly, be followed by the reader—and, it must be recognized, should be conveyed to an audience. Lady Utterword goes to the window-seat and sits down; she looks into the garden where Hector and Ellie are seen strolling together; Mrs Hushabye goes to the window to look; Randall joins them at the window; he sits by Lady Utterword; Ellie and Hector come in from the garden. Suddenly all is gathered together. To see it happening is almost hypnotic in its effect.

In *The Millionairess,* the frieze effect is virtually announced to us. The chair, we are told, is to be its focal point, the group gathers about it, the picture is made—the conversation can begin.

The technical implications of this persistent element in Shaw's plays cannot, indeed should not, be completely dissociated from the imaginative. Still, it is worth suggesting that one explanation as to why Shaw's plays so often seem to be more talk than action is simply because he so frequently employs this method of halting or virtually halting action. But this need not be because of a deficiency in his theatrical skill, as is sometimes claimed. We have to ask, why he so frequently does it, and why is it so often of a ritualistic or quasi-ritualistic nature?

Deep down, but not all that far down, in Shaw's make-up lay the orator. His record as a public speaker makes it clear that this was not a frustrated part of him. The orator requires stasis, certainly physical, if not mental, stasis, in order to fulfil his verbal mission. There is a ritual about the orator's situation; the survival of his status depends on his audience taking up positions of rest which are to be maintained while he takes up and retains his ritual stances before them. The art of the camera can reveal that at any given moment, there is a significant and concentrated and ritual physical relationship within the oratorical situation. Time and time again we experience this significant moment in Shaw's plays. In *Widowers' Houses* when, after the postures are made, Lickcheese says, 'Here we are', and begins. In *Androcles and the Lion* when, after the stances are fixed, the call boy shouts, 'Number six. Retiarius versus Secutor.' In *Heartbreak House* when Mrs. Hushabye announces—'Hector, this is Addy.' In *The Millionairess* when Patricia sounds as if she's to start upon a long story—'You see, Mr. Sagamore, it's like this. Alastair—.' In Shaw's plays characters are always brought together with tremendous purpose. It is an important moment and an important event when this happens—and it happens with great regularity and frequency.

But is there more to the ritual? The realm of supposition is a happy and indulgent haven and it is one which Shaw himself often visited. We may perhaps try to emulate him and indulge a fancy that there was in him (possibly in a rather less comprehensive sense than with Shakespeare's obsession about order) an aspiration for pattern, for order, for gathered orderliness which had less to do with an overwhelming desire to see it fulfilled in all mankind's works and activities than with his deep, wise, balanced and loving care for and knowledge of music. Perhaps, if fancy may be allowed to curl about a supposition once more, Shaw's true language was a musical one, his true artistic métier a musical one. Can it be that the formalism of his verbal communication, the concern for 'style', the immaculate quest for the right verbal note, the pernickety notation of his 'slang' language, the creation of pattern we have noted, the neatness and orderliness of the progression of his plays, the sense of beginning and of finish, are all musical surrogates? Oratorio and orator are, after all, consanguineous.

Shaw's language almost invariably gives off an air of confidence and an assurance about itself, so that the reader seems constantly to be breathing in a spirit of optimism. Since, as is axiomatic, language *is* character, this spirit pervades the creatures who inhabit the plays, often even when what they have to say seems to contradict it. What gives the language this spirit is a constant enthusiasm—the characters are glad to be able to speak—even the least educated of them are never at a loss to express or imply their enthusiasm about communicating.

Only in *Heartbreak House* do we find any lengthy departure

from this spirit of optimism and it may well be that the writing of the play came out of a rare depression of the soul suffered by Shaw, or it may be, in this 'most allusive and poetic of his plays' he penetrated deeper into himself than he ever had or would again. Certainly, the play stands curiously isolated. For the rest, they seem to have been written, both before and after *Heartbreak House,* not, perhaps, without fits of disillusion, dissatisfaction, but out of a consistent faith in the power and necessity of words.

The inevitable consequence of such a pervading faith in the efficacy of verbal communication is the creation of a recognizable 'style'. You can no more mistake a Shavian speech for any other dramatist's work than you can believe that any other dramatist could have created a Shavian character. This style, in tone and pace, is confident, assured; its form inevitably brings about clarity of meaning; in nature it is Socratic to a very large extent.

The actor has to recognize this strongly individual style as surely as he must recognize that of Restoration comedy. In fact, so individualistic and pronounced is it that his communication of it must include both a recognition of its characteristics and a surrender to its 'stylishness'. In order to speak the language of Restoration comedy a certain studiedness is essential; the same is true of Shaw. The terse offhandedness which Pinter sometimes seems to demand, the emotional charge that Miller expects his actors to generate, the fervent cynicism of address which Osborne requires, the calm intellectuality which Eliot seems to ask for, will not work for Shaw. Moreover, it goes without saying that modern naturalistic acting, where clarity of verbal expression often has to take second place to brash physical presence, is quite anathematic to Shaw's language. A recent critic comments that 'although it would be inaccurate to describe his drama as a comedy of manners, his best drama is never very far away from that social sphere, and the comedy of manners which he was able to create from it'.[14]

Shaw's language makes three demands. First, the actor must have an unsullied directness of address. This is particularly noticeable in the dialogue of Shaw's women. The danger is that speeches will become fervent monologues, but Shaw gives every opportunity to avoid this by his wit and irony. But there is rarely any faltering in address:

> You remind me of Liz a little: she was a first-rate business woman—saved money from the beginning—never let herself look too like what she was—never lost her head or threw away a chance. When she saw I'd grown up good-looking she said to me across the bar 'What are you doing there, you little fool? wearing out your health and your appearance for other people's profit!' Liz was saving money then to take a house for herself in Brussels; and she thought we two could save faster than one. So she lent me some money and gave me a start; and I saved steadily and first paid her back, and then went into business with her as her partner. Why shouldnt I have done it?[15]

It should be noticed that this habitual requirement goes in parallel with the need for the actors to face one another squarely. Physical candour, one may call it—when eyes meet eyes square on—is a marked corollary of the directness required by the language. Even hesitation is expressed with a certain candour.

Second, the actor has to convey the habitual confidence, the enthusiasm, of the language—its celebration, so to speak, of its own potency. So often, in Shaw, there is a sparkling, liquid utterance which, at times, it must be admitted, is slightly embarrassing—as if a bright young thing was showing off. Yet this is a mere stain in a pellucid flow which is a joy to listen to:

Eve: Your hood is most lovely. *(She strokes at and pets the serpent)* Pretty thing! Do you love your godmother Eve?
The Serpent: I adore her. *(She licks Eve's neck with her double tongue)*
Eve: (Petting her) Eve's wonderful darling snake. Eve will never be lonely now that her snake can talk to her.
The Snake: I can talk of many things. I am very wise. It was I who whispered the word to you that you did not know. Dead. Death. Die.
Eve: (Shuddering) Why do you remind me of it? I forgot it when I saw your beautiful hood. You must not remind me of unhappy things.
The Serpent: Death is not an unhappy thing when you have learnt how to conquer it.
Eve: How can I conquer it?

The Serpent: By another thing, called birth.
Eve: What? *(Trying to pronounce it)* B–birth?
The Serpent: Yes, birth.
Eve: What is birth?
The Serpent: The serpent never dies. Some day you shall see me come out of this beautiful skin, a new skin with a new and lovelier skin. That is birth.
Eve: I have seen that. It is wonderful. [16]

Third, the actor must be constantly aware that his position in the play's dialogue is essentially part of a designed pattern. This is saying more than that any actor in any play must be aware that others are on the stage. In a Shaw play if you forget your colleagues you are doomed and damned not simply because a play is fully achieved only when its constituents are unified, but for another reason. There are few Shaw plays which do not have a sense of logical progression. It is not of that kind which makes the 'well-made' play so mechanical, but of a much subtler nature. The movement of the main ideas and attitudes of a Shaw play always seems to be a matter of logical progression; every constituent is a part of this aspiration towards a QED—not necessarily of plot, but of ideas. We may well wonder who Eliza married at the end of *Pygmalion*, but there is no doubt that the 'ideas' are resolved—Galatea is separate from Pygmalion, will has broken loose from its constraints. In order that this resolution, and indeed the resolutions of all Shaw's plays, can be achieved, the actor, at any given point in the play, has to be aware, more assuredly than with any other dramatist save Shakespeare, of where his dialogue now stands, as it were, in its relation to this oncoming resolution. This awareness of the 'intellectual' signposts puts a particular strain on the attempt to delineate the emotional life of the character. It is not that Shaw's characters are deficient in emotion; it is that emotion has to take its rightful and allotted place in the inexorable journey towards QED. In Shaw, emotion is neither frozen nor scanty, nor is it at the mercy of a ruthless intellectuality. It is, as in a piece of chamber music, an inseparable part of the movement towards complete fulfilment of meaning.

These three requirements—of directness of address, of conveying the confidence and enthusiasm of the language, of awareness of his position in the overall design of the play—ask the actor to take on a style, as we have seen. It is a truism to say that the proof of this lies in our experience of seeing a Shaw play well done. Most dramatists do not require the kind of transubstantiation Shaw demands: you cannot miss the changes that have occurred in an actor when he steps correctly into a Shaw play.

But there is a further consideration. Restoration comedy is untranslatable into a modern idiom either of dress or language, partly because of the conspicuous stylishness of its form and manner. The same is true of Shaw's plays. They could not survive the move, not always because their themes are dated, but because, their style being broken or bent, their essential design is destroyed. Shakespeare can survive such treatment (though not always unharmed) because his plays do not expect such an adamant fixation to an intrinsic style.

Within the general pattern of the stylish language there are, of course, variations, though they are only variations; at no point in his career did Shaw fundamentally depart from the kind of verbal architecture we have noted. But if we seek for a source for the clear directness of the language, and, to a degree, for its basic confidence, it is hardly necessary to seek further than Bunyan, whom Shaw seems to have revered hardly this side idolatry. A good deal of his attitude towards Shakespeare and, at the same time, his vulnerability to Bunyan's influence was explained in a review entitled *Better than Shakespeare* in 1897. In a group of plays which fall under Shaw's judging gaze, there is 'a mystery play, with music, in four acts' which is founded on *The Pilgrim's Progress*. Shaw take it as an opportunity to berate Shakespeare, and gives us an opportunity to understand why his language is as it is. He writes:

> All that you miss in Shakespeare you find in Bunyan, to whom the true heroic came quite obviously and naturally. The world was to him a more terrible place than it was to Shakespeare; but he saw through it a path at the end of which a man might look not only forward to the celestial city, but back on his life and say: 'Tho' with great difficulty I am got hither, yet now I do not repent me of all the trouble I have been at to arrive where I am. My sword I give to him that shall succeed me in my pilgrimage,

and my courage and skill to him that can get them.' The heart vibrates like a bell to such an utterance as this: to turn from it to 'Out, out, brief candle', and 'The rest is silence', and 'We are such stuff as dreams are made of; and our little life is rounded by a sleep' [*sic*] is to turn from life, strength, resolution, morning air and eternal youth, to the terrors of a drunken nightmare.

The truly heroic is that which conquers evil and comes to a City. The unheroic is that which is evil and seeks nothing but destruction. Bunyan writes what is truly heroic, Shakespeare does not. It is quite surprisingly thrilling to find Shaw allowing his emotional slip to show when he declares, 'The heart vibrates like a bell to such an utterance as this . . .'

Shaw's excitement about Bunyan which seems to have persisted throughout his life is symptomatic of a great deal. Bunyan, the self-made man, could not fail to strike a chord in Shaw—who prided himself on the success of his own, a similar, creative exercise:

> Bunyan learnt his lesson, not only from his own rough pilgrimage through life, but from the tradition of many an actual journey from real Cities of Destruction (under Alva), with Interpreters' houses and convoy of Great-hearts all complete.

In Bunyan's forthright heroics and faith Shaw seems to have found an echo of his own mental, emotional and dramatic optimism: this is why his heart beats like a bell when he reads him. In Bunyan's grand, clear and candid prose is to be found the source of Shaw's open-hearted, spirited and rational language. Shakespeare, because he 'never thought a noble life worth living or a great work worth doing, because the commercial profit-and-loss sheet shewed that the one did not bring happiness, nor the other money' never 'struck the great vein'. This vein he finds constantly in Bunyan who told:

> . . . of that 'man of a very strong countenance' who went up to the keeper of the book of life and said, not 'out, out, brief candle', but 'set down my name, sir', and immediately fell on the armed men and cut his way into heaven after receiving and giving many wounds.

Shaw's dramatic language is written in a heroic spirit, and its tendency is always to elevate, to a degree, what it communicates into the grandiloquent or the celebrative or the potent or the brightly witty, or the momentous. It is the language of an imagination which never forgot that what is heroically conceived must always be expressed by a kind of oratory.

4 John Galsworthy and the Language of Man and Society

A remark by Bernard Shaw is a useful starting-point for assessing the work of a dramatist who is regarded by many as a follower of Shaw and by some as an unfulfilled dramatist. He is commenting on Granville-Barker's plays and how he feels he has to read them several times before he can grasp them, and he concludes:

> . . . I tell my story and fling my meaning at the audience with an old-fashioned violence which seems downright barn-storming in contrast with the subtler ways of Mr. Barker and Mr. Galsworthy . . .[1]

Shaw, at least, does not wish his ways to be confused with Galsworthy's. Yet, an influential American critic includes the latter in a section entitled *Shaw's Fellow-Travellers* in a book on twentieth-century drama. In it, he writes:

> Galsworthy's talent was, in short, too temperate and circum-spect to rank him with the giants of the drama. He was deficient in the heat of passion on the one hand, and in the cold fire of intellectual display on the other.[2]

If this is intended to distinguish what is taken to be Galsworthy's modest talent from Shaw's towering genius, it is curiously worded. Shaw's passion is not hot, but neither is his intellectual display that of a 'cold fire'. This critic seems to have followed the lead of many others in consigning Galsworthy to a satellite posture to Shaw without fully understanding how different he was. In fact, Shaw has it in one word—'subtle'. There is about Galsworthy's best plays a kind of stealth of technique, a quiet deviousness in characterization and, above all, a quality of associativeness in the language which is completely lost on anyone who only reads its surface and concludes that here we are face to face with a 'poor man's Shaw'.

The most remarkable testimony to Galsworthy's durability and to his deeply ingrained dramatic sense is to be found in the success of his adapted novel—*The Forsyte Saga*—and of his plays on a medium unknown to society at the time of his death—television. Television ruthlessly shows up any play which relies on a mere bull-at-a-gate naturalism of language and character. The concentration of the viewer on to the small area of the screen has an in-built expectation of something more than meets the eye or the ear; any sensitive imagination is incited, by television, to search for nuance, for what is subtle. When it is found the medium itself seems justified, when it is not, both the product and the medium seem mechanistic and unprofitable. A BBC production of *Strife* in 1972, perhaps encouraged out of curiosity, after *The Forsyte Saga,* about how a Galsworthy play would 'translate' to television, revealed his astonishing dramatic power and subtlety. Moreover (and this is of singular importance in view of the allegation of the 'quaintness', 'old-fashionedness' of his language) the play (without having been updated) forcefully spoke to the emotions, the sensibilities and the conscience of the 1970s.

The subtlety which Shaw refers to in Galsworthy is a quality of the language, the characterization and the construction of the plays, and it is highly individual. But Galsworthy learned from Shaw that the thesis play was a very viable commodity for the English theatre. It is in Galsworthy's conception of the role of the thesis play in its society and in his use of prose that he differs most from Shaw.

In a series of fascinating comments under the general title of *Some Platitudes Concerning Drama,*[3] Galsworthy distinguished three types of dramatist. The first gives the public that view of life in which it either already believed or wished to; the second gives the public a view of life in which the dramatist believes; the third presents the phenomenon of life, selected but not distorted by the vision of the dramatist, and the public is left to draw its own conclusions. He himself belongs to this third category, Shaw clearly belongs to the second. We have, then, one dramatist (Shaw) who presents a thesis according to a view he himself holds—this is the proselytizing dramatist; the other (Galsworthy) tries to present life as it is, selected, fined down to fit the three-hour traffic of the stage, but dedicated to attempting to retain the truth of life. This is the neutral dramatist, arbitrating neither for one thing nor another; he 'shows our eyes' and if it 'grieves our hearts' it is we, having been given the evidence, who draw our own conclusions and make our responses.

We may reflect here that, despite their differences, they shared at the time (and perhaps Shaw deserves the credit for teaching this to Galsworthy) an abhorrence of Victorian sentimentality in the depiction of human problems. But both may have learned from T. W. Robertson that a truly 'modern' drama was possible, in the sense that people were prepared to listen to plays about contemporary problems.

What makes the American critic misjudge Galsworthy's potency is precisely that whereas Robertson was prepared to satirize his society and Shaw was vehemently prepared to show its vices and suggest remedies, Galsworthy neither did nor seemed to want to do either. He is more like the inspector in a public inquiry who does not make the law but tries to be impartial about the relevance of evidence. Indeed, perhaps Galsworthy's legal training had much to do with his quite unusual impartiality and with his subtlety. This emerges time and time again—sometimes as the matrix for the overriding theme of the play, sometimes as the shaping element in an incident. Its effect is always to set one's emotions in motion against the immovable object of one's reason.[4]

Even his most socially abrasive plays do not offer, as Shaw's do, any kind of solution to the human problems that they have displayed to us. But this is not a symptom of uncertainty or tentativeness, rather is it a kind of courage—Galsworthy did not know what the solution was because he does not pretend to understand humankind—he is a committed observer:

Tench: (Approaching Harness) It's a great weight off my mind, Mr Harness! But what a painful scene, sir! *(He wipes his brow. Harness, pale and resolute, regards with a grim half-smile the quavering Tench)* It's all been so violent! What did he mean by: 'Done

us both down?' If he has lost his wife, poor fellow, he oughtn't
to have spoken to the Chairman like that!
Harness: A woman dead; and the two best men both broken!
(Underwood enters suddenly)
Tench: (Staring at Harness—suddenly excited) D'you know, sir—these
terms, they're the *very same* we drew up together, you and I,
and put to both sides before the fight began? All this—all
this—and—and what for?
Harness: (In a slow grim voice) That's where the fun comes in! *(Underwood without turning from the door makes a gesture of assent)*[5]
The curtain falls

The nature of his commitment brings us close to the qualities of his subtlety. Lurking within the often sparse, apparently bare plots and situations are irony, pity and indignation.
These are exerted not in order to make a judgment upon any
specific character's position relative to the plot, or on the
moral stance the theme requires from him. They are used in a
way more akin to Thomas Hardy than to Shaw or Arnold
Wesker. They comment on the folly of mankind rather than
on the iniquities of any particular member of the human race.
Galsworthy's commitment is to the 'pity of it', and we are
lured to believe that, like Hardy, the context against which he
sees the tragi-comedy of man being played out is not that of
the specific life-span of any particular play, but of eternity.
It is of the utmost importance to realize his awareness of the
context—brooding, half-apprehended, fugitive, but always
there. Its presence is, itself, enough to reprieve Galsworthy of
the charge that he is a naturalistic dramatist concerned only
with certain restricted issues of some moment to his own
contemporary society. The theme of *Strife* alerts us to Galsworthy's spacious imagination; its theme, like a wound, is as
open and painful now as it was in his time.
Galsworthy rejected 'naturalism', except in a very specific
sense. He did not wish to be regarded as a 'naturalist' in the
sense commonly used at the time to indicate a dramatist who
dealt with contemporary issues in a prosaic way. He wished to
reserve the word for a much narrower definition. Galsworthy
strongly affirmed[6] that 'realism' and 'realistic' should not be
applied to a writer's technique—for that, 'naturalism' and
'naturalistic' were more apt. He also claimed that a 'realist'

68

writer (contrary to accepted belief) exercised as much imaginative power as a romantic writer and, indeed, did not have to be tied down to a naturalistic technique. The realist could be idealistic, poetic, fantastic, impressionistic—almost anything except romantic. For Galsworthy, the true realist occupied himself with showing the way in which what he called 'the spirit of life', thought and personality were inter-mixed. His categorical distinction between naturalism and realism is of importance to an understanding of what he asks of his language in his plays. His definition of realist, and the implication that he regards himself as one, gives him plenty of elbow-room in theme, characterization and language. This realist did not think of himself as a dramatist who, to adopt Arthur Symons's notion of the 'realist' was one who merely 'dealt with the accidents of life and the vulgarities of nature'.

Galsworthy's work exemplifies his definition. There are no vulgarities of nature in *Joy* where, in Act III for example, 'It is evening; a full yellow moon is shining through the branches of the willow tree. The Chinese lanterns are alight. There is dancing in the house; the music sounds now loud, now soft.' There are no accidents of life in *The Little Dream;* and where, indeed, is the Galsworthy who, according to tradition, trafficked only in terse clipped prose? *The Little Dream* is replete with clouds with silver wings, dewdrops that vie with pearls, and the distant piping of a shepherd. Indeed, in this play, we are nearer to the symbolic world of Maeterlinck than to Shaw's kind of realism.

Certainly, the example is taken from a minor play and, certainly, the Galsworthy most familiar to us is the one who, in the best-known plays, does concern himself with matters nearer to the common usages of the everyday. Yet, how familiar are we, really, with this 'familiar' Galsworthy? In *Justice,* beneath the 'everyday speech' of the characters there can, very frequently, be discerned another language. Part of the subtlety of Galsworthy is in his double focus on what is happening. There are many examples of it. A notable one is the scene in *Justice* where the witness, Ruth, is being cross-examined about her relationship with Falder. Her monosyl-labic replies of 'yes', interspersed with glances at Falder in the dock and with longer but still metallically dull responses to questions, gradually create a contrapuntal effect of meaning and feeling far beyond what is actually said.

In the Prologue to *Escape* there is a convincing example of verbal subtlety of a different kind. Here the terseness of the questions and answers produces, in a manner akin to Harold Pinter, a growing tension between the characters and, as a consequence, between the characters and the audience. Moreover, the relationship between dialogue and stage-directions (always more economically practical than Shaw's) creates a situation which is theatrically potent:

> *The Girl shifts forward on her seat as he approaches. He is going by when she looks suddenly up and says in a low voice:* 'Good evening!' *He halts, looks at her, gives a little shrug, carries his hand to his hat, and answering,* 'Good evening!' *is moving on when she speaks again.*
> Girl: Have you a match? *(She is holding out a cigarette; he stops and hands her his cigarette lighter)*
> Girl: *(Fingering the lighter)* Gold?
> Matt: Brass.
> Girl: Have one? *(Offering her cigarette case)*
> Matt: Thanks, I'm smoking. *(He shows her his cigar; resting his foot on the seat and dangling his race glasses)*
> Girl: Been racing?
> Matt: Goodwood.
> Girl: I went to see the Jubilee this year.
> Matt: And what did you back?
> Girl: Everything that didn't win. It's rotten when you don't back winners.
> Matt: Don't you like the horses?
> Girl: They look pretty.
> Matt: Prettiest things in the world.
> Girl: Pretty as women?
> Matt: Saving your presence.
> Girl: Do you mean that?
> Matt: Well, you get a woman once in a way that can arch her neck.
> Girl: You don't like women—that's clear.
> Matt: Not too much.

But Galsworthy's rich and subtle realism is not confined only to the language which we hear. Galsworthy vies with Pinter for recognition as the greatest master of pause, but he has no rival in creating *tableaux vivants*, in the twentieth century. Ironically (since they were poles apart in belief and temperament), the 'language' of physical movement, of significant gesture, beloved of Symons, had its best and most lasting expression in the plays of Galsworthy.

It has a number of facets. One of them presents us with an interesting difference from Shaw's use of stage-directions, or 'descriptive' directions, which we have noticed. Shaw's fascinating evocations of the appearance and disposition of characters often have a novel-ish air to them. Galsworthy, the much more considerable novelist, also provides descriptive directions but they are almost always both evocative *and* of extremely practical help to the actor. The stage directions in *The Silver Box*[7] are a masterpiece of the art of observation—not only of human beings, but of the actor's art. Truth to nature and fidelity to the requirements of illusion, are in perfect harmony:

Jack: (Jones gives him the whisky he desires, together with a squirt of syphon) Wha' I was goin' tell you was—I've had a row with her. *(He waves the reticule)* Have a drink, Jones—sh'd never have got in without you—tha's why I'm giving you a drink. Don' care who knows I've scored her off. Th' cat! *(He throws his feet up on the sofa)* Don' you make a noise, whatever you do. You pour out a drink—you make yourself good long, long drink—you take cigarette—you take anything you like. Sh'd never have got in without you. *(Closing his eyes)* You're a Tory—you're a Tory Socialist. I'm Liberal myself—have a drink—I'm an excel'nt chap. *(His head drops back. He, smiling, falls asleep, and Jones stands looking at him; then, snatching up Jack's glass, he drinks it off. He picks the reticule from off Jack's shirt-front, holds it to the light, and smells at it)*

Jones: Been on the tiles and brought 'ome some of yer cat's fur. *(He stuffs it into Jack's breast pocket)*

Jack: (Murmuring) I've scored you off! You cat! *(Jones looks around him furtively; he pours out whisky and drinks it. From the silver box he takes a cigarette, puffs at it, and drinks more whisky. There is no sobriety left in him)*

This harmony is to be found in the slightest of directions. Marlow enters in *The Silver Box*—'Incidentally a butler, he is first a man.'

The above extract is more than an example of stage directions and dialogue in consort, it exemplifies how a Galsworthy text flows, carrying its literary and theatrical content, completely harmonized, with it. The visual and the physical are neither an adornment to the words nor a hermetically sealed activity in themselves. They proceed directly from the words—they have inevitability about them.

The most remarkable example of Galsworthy's use of the language of theatre, wordless but imparted with meaning, is in *Justice*. Act III, Scene iii is entirely without dialogue. This scene, with its lack of words, counterpoints a long verbal section of Act II, Scene ii where the defence counsel makes his final plea on behalf of the prisoner whom, in this later scene, we are to observe in his prison cell. The defence counsel's speech is long, superbly architectural, and entirely uninterrupted until the judge addresses the jury, and judgment is at hand. The prisoner's wordless actions in the later scene in the cell are eloquent of his despair and anguish, finely and economically ordered by Galsworthy, completely uninterrupted until the cell light clicks on and 'a sound from far away, as of distant, dull beating on thick metal, is suddenly audible'. This, we may believe, is what judgment really means.

Galsworthy's expertise as a novelist has stood him in excellent stead in creating this scene, though it has never obtruded. This long descriptive direction (because this is what the whole scene amounts to) is over 650 words in length, but not a word is devoted to 'literary' realization, except perhaps in the mention of the novel which the prisoner is reading and which lies on the table. It is of no theatrical consequence that the novel is *Lorna Doone*. The novelist's imagination is at the beck and call of the playwright's sense of drama and theatre and this reveals itself in the careful attention to detail here.

One of the most telling features of this quite literally astonishing scene is its clear justification of Galsworthy's dicta about naturalism and realism and its tacit rebuttal of the Symons view of realism. There is an orchestration of effects here which amounts to a perfect demonstration that the realist 'may be poetic, idealistic, fantastic, impressionistic . . .', and is 'by no means tied to naturalistic technique'. After the initial bare, accurate and prosaic details of the set, there follows the restless ritual of the prisoner's movements, where the body tells of the mind's agony. How long this lasts we do not know—it must be the actor's judgment but, whatever it is, Galsworthy relentlessly takes us out of clock time; this man is in a terrible timeless moment. The naturalistic details which have given place to ritual, now virtually disappear, after the cell-light is clicked on, and we and the prisoner are thrown into a symbolism of light and noise. 'Yet there are some who think,' wrote his first sympathetic critic, R. H. Coats, 'that Galsworthy is not a poet!'[8]

One indication of a dramatist of the highest class is the extent to which his dialogue 'contains' more than is said, so that the actor, the designer, the director find in it a theatrical language as well as the dramatic language of the playwright. We have noticed how Shaw, certainly in his earlier plays, is deficient in this. This is not to say that he does not have compensating virtues. The truth is, however, that he some-times seems less a natural dramatist than Galsworthy though he has, by far, the wider imaginative and intellectual breadth. Time and time again we find that Galsworthy's language 'contains' what the actor needs to know.[9]

But the proof absolute of Galsworthy's claim to be regarded as 'subtle'—not perhaps quite in the sense which Shaw meant, but in a deeper sense—must lie in the deeps of his language. It is here that we must look for the conclusive proof that Gals-worthy is much more than a prosaic naturalist, a dedicated photographer of passing actuality. That his imagination is not, by any means, a stranger to poetic impulses is shown in such examples as that of the prisoner in his cell. That his language aspired to poetic flight is exemplified in plays like *Joy* and *The Little Dream*. It is not a flight that seems at all sure of itself—it sometimes is guilty of self-display, on occasions of a kind of sentimentally motivated swooping upon the affections of the reader or auditor, and often its beating progress seems unnatural, related neither to the element it is trying to conquer nor to the observer.

If Galsworthy had attempted to write his best plays—*Strife, Justice, The Silver Box, The Skin Game, Escape*[10]—in an explicitly poetic medium we could, on the evidence, be confident that they would not have possessed the powerful impact which, well directed and acted, they had and still have. But we have to call upon another concept of poetry—one which, increasingly, in the twentieth century, and specifically with Harold Pinter, seems apposite—to test the nature of Galsworthy's plays. Simply expressed, it amounts to an artistic vision which sees beneath the surface of things—a surface which changes as time and mutability ruffle it—to the unchanging depths beneath. One critic expresses it, in terms of Galsworthy, in this way:

> It is in its appeal for imaginative sympathy, therefore, more than in any naturalism of manner or accompanying spirit of irony with which that appeal is expressed, that we must find, at last, the quintessential flavour of a Galsworthy play.[11]

But it is Galsworthy himself (a remarkable but comparatively unremarked theorist of art in general and drama in particular) who expresses it most pertinaciously and eloquently:

> It can be seen how a dramatist, strongly and pitifully impressed by the encircling pressure of modern environments, predisposed to the naturalistic method, and with something in him of the satirist, will neither create characters seven or even six feet high, nor write plays detached from the movements and problems of his times. He is not conscious, however, of any desire to solve those problems in his plays, or to effect direct reforms. His only ambition in drama, as in his other work, is to present truth as he sees it, and, gripping with it his readers or his audience, to produce in them a sort of mental and moral fermenting whereby vision may be enlarged, imagination livened, and understanding promoted.[12]

It is *Strife* more than any other of his plays which shows the extent to which Galsworthy sought and achieved that 'only ambition'.

A superficial reading of it might well lead to the conclusion that it gains a great deal of dramatic force for the quite fortuitous reason that it deals with matters very germane to our society today—capital versus labour. Despite this, the extent to which the play, in circumstances and detail, is of its own time, might lead to the conclusion that its relevance to us is mainly antiquarian; its interest being analogous, so to say, to the realization of the connection between Leonardo's flying machine and a modern jet airliner.

The issues that are fought over in the play can be justifiably regarded as having been, certainly in their most stark form, settled. No member of a Board who wished his company to avoid bankruptcy would now dare to speak in the terms used by Wilder in the opening of *Strife*, where his attitude and that of most of his colleagues is one of barely concealed contempt towards workers and their trade unions, although you cannot, even now, be sure that you will not stumble across such antediluvian responses as are represented in one particular imbecility of Wilder's. His anxiety to get the business done—a business which will involve men's livelihoods and has already brought them, their wives and their children, to the edge of starvation—is not based on humanitarian grounds but is simply because he has to take his wife to Spain the following day.

We must not overlook Galsworthy's grim, sardonic irony, and we have to remember that these events and attitudes were true to that time. Indeed, television trades upon the curiosity of our age to learn about the day before yesterday in innumerable evocations of upstairs, below-stairs, and so on. Our contemporary urge for equality appeals for its evidences of inequality, of the class struggle, time and time again to the society which Galsworthy depicts with such clear zeal and truth to fact.

But, if the play's actuality has been overtaken, just as our day before yesterday has been superseded by ourselves, and as we will be by our children's time, its fidelity to unchanging human truths has not. Its power does not rest alone in its accidental contemporaneity of theme, but in its ability 'to present truth . . . and, gripping with it his readers or his audience, to produce in them a sort of mental and moral fermenting, whereby vision may be enlarged, imagination livened, and understanding promoted'.

In few other dramatists of the twentieth century can one find better justification for an assertion of the peculiar uniqueness of the language of the playwright. It is a severe task to express the quality of Galsworthy's subtlety in this respect, because of the immediacy of his communication. We are lured into assuming that immediacy is all. It is not.

We must begin with structure, for Galsworthy's imagination not only seems to begin with a sense of pattern, but to take flight from it—perhaps even to harbour a grave joy in it. His

sense of structure is both judicial and judicious in that it strives
for an impartial balance of forces and, to do it, selects, with an
impeccable feeling for what is credible and viable. Two
worlds are depicted and with equal clarity of vision and fair-
ness of view. In one sense the one world is a mirror image of
the other—every character in the world of capital has its
counterpart in the world of labour. Climaxes which occur in
the one are reduplicated in the other, human values which
come up for inspection repeat themselves. One world has a
protagonist, so has the other; they are utterly opposed in class,
yet in belief, principle, motivation and ambition they are
curiously interchangeable. If they exchanged positions each
would act as the other does.

The architectonics, alone, of this play remove it from the
customary superficialities we associate with plain naturalistic
writing. Everything seems fixed, immutable, in its place—it
is as apparently ordained as it was so fervently believed the
universal order was in the fourteenth and fifteenth centuries.
More than this the clash of two men of implacable will and
power has, in its pride, arrogance and dedication that brash
assumption which, in Greek tragedy, called down the wrath
of the gods. Almost every other character in the play moves
like a satellite around one or other of these two men—the
capitalist Anthony, the labour man Roberts—and is dragged
into their huge gravitative force, but becomes an instrument
of their destruction.

The sense of a destiny working itself out transcends absolutely the play's very occasional lapses into what now seems a
kind of emotional mawkishness. Yet we must not allow this to
devalue Galsworthy's achievement in creating a tragedy out of
a clash of worlds, one of which (the world of labour, of the
'lower orders', of the dispossessed) would not have been
considered as capable of supporting the tragic experience;
axiomatically, tragedy, both of the Aristotelian and English
renascence variety happened only where the great were; the
rest of mankind looked on or were sucked into the deadly
maelstrom of the mighty.

Within this pattern an inevitability works itself out, but
what is to be emphasized is that however fixed the pattern may
seem to be the communication is variable in both style and

effect. It is essential to say this in view of the commonly-held belief that Galsworthy wrote a flat advocate's prose which became dramatic only because of his range of characters and employment of devices like irony, bathos and climax. Again, we have to remember that it is language, and language alone that creates both character and the devices which give the play's communication its variety of dramatic effects. A sharp example of the way in which character and language are, so to speak, one flesh is to be found in the depiction of Scantlebury. His 'H'ms' and 'Dear, dear's' dotted about his speech give warning of insecurity—it amounts to a nervous cough, a tic of the conscience; his repetitions emphasize this—they bespeak a man desperately trying to convince himself that he is right. But sometimes they have the slight frenzy of a man whistling in the dark.

What Galsworthy allows this man to show us of himself through his own mouth is confirmed by the comments of others. Scantlebury is trapped in a totality of exposure, he is rounded off and up by Galsworthy's relentless pursuit of him. But Scantlebury's interest for us does not end here. His relationship to the crux of the play's theme is expressed in one scene for which only the word 'symbolic' seems right. It is the first scene, in which Scantlebury complains with some inordinateness about the heat in the room in which the managing director is holding a meeting. The screen which he calls for is as much a defence-mechanism as a physical protection. He cowers from the fire as he cowers from the heat of controversy. As Roberts says—'I looked into his eyes and I saw he was afraid'—the ritualistic biblical rhythm of the phrase in itself curiously heightens the symbolic effect.

There is one scene in which a non-representative intention comes completely into the foreground of communcation. It is, by any standards of theatrical risk-taking (something Galsworthy seemed to revel in) a quite remarkable scene. In Act II, Scene i Mrs Roberts, wife of the militant steel-plate worker is obviously dying; her husband is torn between wanting to stay with her and his implacable sense of duty as a striker. As he leaves, a small boy, Jan Thomas, enters 'in clothes too big for him, carrying a penny whistle'. He is followed by Thomas, an old man, his daughter Madge, and her fiancé, Rous. There is a desperate row between the young couple, with Madge tauntingly attempting to persuade Rous to blackleg the strike.

Throughout the entire scene the young boy plays his penny whistle, imitating the call of the cuckoo. It is a wry, strange obbligato to the ferocity of the emotions that have been released. It amounts to a wordless comment on man's stupidity; it is as if Feste or Lear's Fool, in the guise of a child, had entered and in their sad objective way, punctuated the harsh reality of this world with the timeless irony of 'but that's all one'.

Galsworthy seizes every opportunity to bring the poetic imagination to the service of the practicalities of dramatic communication. The language has moments when it seems to move into a near-lyrical utterance before ebbing back into hard naturalism—but not before a sense of depth has been achieved:

> *Roberts.* . . . *I* tell you if a man cannot say to Nature: 'Budge me from this if ye can!'—*(with a sort of exaltation)*—his principles are but his belly. 'Oh, but,' Thomas says, 'a man can be pure and honest, just and merciful, and take off his hat to Nature!' *I* tell you Nature's neither pure nor honest, just nor merciful. You chaps that live over the hill, an' go home dead beat in the dark on a snowy night—don't ye fight your way every inch of it? Do ye go lyin' down an' trustin' to the tender mercies of this merciful Nature? Try it and you'll soon know with what ye've got to deal. 'Tes only by that—*(he strikes a blow with his clenched fist)*—in Nature's face that a man can be man. 'Give in,' says Thomas, 'go down on your knees; throw up your foolish fight, an' perhaps,' he said, 'perhaps your enemy will chuck you down a crust.'

Occasionally, indeed, the cadences of Synge seem to have entered Galsworthy's head, and we are made aware that it is more than a clash between labour and capital that we are witnessing—but another demonstration of the eternal struggle of man in his occupancy of this planet:

> *Roberts:* 'Tis not for this little moment of time we're fighting *(the murmuring dies)*, not for ourselves, our own little bodies, and their wants, 'tis for all those that come after throughout all time. *(With intense sadness)* Oh! men—for the love o' them,

don't roll up another stone upon their heads, don't help to blacken the sky, an' let the bitter sea in over them.

These verbal rises and falls have their counterpart visually. Galsworthy's keen eye for the language of theatrical effect was never better demonstrated than in his 'placing' of visual effects, so that what seems naturalistic, ordinary, suddenly acquires another dimension. In the introductory stage-direction to Act II, Scene ii we are told that the location is an open muddy space crowded with workmen. This is where the crucial strike meeting is to take place. It is a bitter, cold, joyless landscape with a canal towpath in the background. On this towpath two bargemen 'lounge and smoke indifferently'. They are not of the strike, they are observers. But, from time to time Galsworthy uses them as comments on the action—comments which are as trenchant as they are silent. At one point they are *seen* laughing; at another, one of the barge-men looks after Harness who has made a speech and jerks his pipe with a derisive gesture. But perhaps the most telling moment is when Roberts, the fiery eloquent leader pushes forward to speak to the crowd. He faces them, holding them with his eyes and silencing them. As he begins to speak one of the distant bargemen rises to his feet and is still. It is as if everything has frozen for a moment. All is still and silent, and in this stillness and silence, in the background, this one figure rises and stands. The importance of the moment is, so to speak, etched for us visually, but, more than this, we seem to be taken out of time by this one single movement—as if eternity were being represented in this one figure who has, before, shown derision and laughter in turn; now he listens.

Only to a degree is Galsworthy's estimate of his own characters and, by implication, the way he has created them, correct. He contrasted himself with Shaw and wrote: 'It might be said of Shaw's plays that he creates characters who express feelings which they have not got. It might be said of mine, that I create characters who have feelings which they cannot express.'[13] Roberts, in *Strife*, expresses his feelings in no uncertain terms, about his attitude to capital, about his principles; yet, it is true that in his personal confrontations both with his wife and the leader of capital, something seems to be withheld. In point of fact, this is true of all the major characters in Galsworthy's major plays. They express themselves most cogently on matters which are germane to the play's main line of thematic development, but they all have a secret area whose nature we can only guess at. The existence of this ambivalence is reflected in a technical sense. Those feelings or attitudes which are directly aroused by the play's theme are expressed directly, in the robust language we have noted. Those that are held from us are hinted at obliquely—either by the use of silence, or tableaux in which a minimum is said (as in the final scene of *Strife* and *Justice*) or by statements which are so tantalizingly incomplete in what they tell us of the character's true feelings *behind* what is being said, as to amount to a kind of irony.

Galsworthy is a superb ironist, but it is important to realize that his deployment of it has a double effect. The first is to convey, more certainly as the play progresses and the stock of irony mounts up, a sense of deus ex machina (with much the same effect as in Thomas Hardy's *Dynasts*): the impression, therefore, of some other kind of view, some other focus, only half-perceived, is very strong. That, as Harness mordantly says in *Strife,* is 'where the fun comes in'. But the joke is enjoyed, sardonically, on a detached level; there is a hint of cosmic laughter. There is no greater hint of this than the ambiguity of the end of *Justice*—'No one'll touch him now! Never again! He's safe with gentle Jesus.'

Shaw and Galsworthy together, form the basis upon which the prose language of the drama which shows society to itself has been built. There is no dramatist in this century who has not, in some way, in his attempts to grapple with man in his environment, been influenced by them. But their reputations are not in a state of balance. True, Galsworthy was by no means as prolific as Shaw, neither was he able or willing to embrace huge contemporary issues like a prophet new inspired. But the speech of men in society as it has been depicted in so many naturalistic plays of the century owes as much to him as to Shaw. Indeed, if Shaw gave clear expression a dignity, excitement, passion, rhythm and wit, Galsworthy gave it economy, irony, pathos and a sense of depth. He is, in a sense, nearer to being the poet than Shaw because his prose is less tied to the specific issues it has to express; it also traffics with what used to be called eternal truths or values or conditions. Consequently, at its best, it has dated less than Shaw's.

Ironically Galsworthy, who is often designated as the arch prose-naturalist, created a dramatic language which, at its most mature and subtle, testifies against the widespread assumption that to write of man in his environment it is necessary to forget the deeps of poetry and concentrate entirely on the broken surfaces of prose.

Whatever later naturalistic dramatists learned from Galsworthy's language, many of them failed to recognize that he, like Shaw, did not subscribe in either theory or practice to the assumed divisions between the public and the private world. Most of them have benefited from his sparseness, his directness, his idiomatic expertise, without realizing his allusiveness. Sadly, his sense of intellectual and emotional depth, his fugitive rhythm, the trace-elements of symbolism, the subtleties of irony have not commonly been realized. He was, perhaps, the last prose dramatist of undoubted importance who realized that prose itself need not be the servant alone of the world of public man but can minister to matters more deeply interfused and less palpable.

5 Naturalism, Wesker and Osborne

Many English dramatists are associated with what came to be known and enshrined as the 'new wave' of dramatists in the 1960s. Each commentator and critic has a personal view of the scope and nature of this dramatically-named phenomenon, but there is a consensus set of generally agreed characteristics. A number of young dramatists, Arnold Wesker, Shelagh Delaney, John Osborne, achieved widely publicized productions of their work; this was acclaimed by many as symptomatic of a 'breakthrough', a 'change', a 'revolution' in dramatic history; this event was variously interpreted but it seemed generally accepted that it had something to do with youth, irreverence, social significance and language.

Young men (typified by Jimmy Porter in *Look Back in Anger* who for many people became hopelessly confused with his own creator, John Osborne) angry with the blind ostrich deference to a social, economic and political status quo began, so it was said, irreverently to cry out against what they took to be the tyranny of convention, tradition and authoritarianism in every conceivable activity of life. In a post-war world which fell very far short of being a land fit for returned heroes to live in, the shouts of the angry young men went out and, in drama, their accents were far from being those of the 'establishment' drama of Eliot, Christopher Fry or, in a different vein, Terence Rattigan. It was said that these young people spoke the raw prose of a frustrated generation, impatient of poetry; so urgent and anxious were they that they spoke from the shoulder not from frilled cuffs—they spoke the language, that is, of 'real' people.

At least, that is how it all seemed to some commentators at the time. Their conclusions had an apparent confirmation in certain phenomena of the sixties in England—the permissive Teddy boys, the licentious and dangerous gangs, the crudities of fashion that blatantly defied convention. Youth was about to grasp the helm, it seemed. Unfortunately, such is the way of mass communication media, only that segment of youth which didn't care a damn if the ship foundered was given publicity.

Young dramatists, novelists and, to a far less extent, poets, became identified with this phenomenon. Osborne, Wesker, Delaney became automatically associated with permissiveness of communication and anti-establishment themes. It was only a short step from this to their designation as 'new naturalistic' dramatists. It is the term 'naturalism' that has stuck to and with them ever since.

'Naturalism' is almost automatically associated by the majority with place and with language. What is most common and, indeed, commonplace, is deemed to be most 'natural' and 'real'—and prudence is placed at hazard by yoking these words together. The evidence upon which most people base their justification for describing something (whether it be in art, or elsewhere), as 'natural' or 'naturalistic' is derived from what is called actual experience—that is, experience emanating not from mental or imaginative activity, but from the palpable activity of everyday life. The greater the common denominator of that experience the more 'natural' and 'real' it is deemed to be. Both in life and in art, but particularly in drama, the greatest effects of place and language are to be found operating on individuals—on characters. The final test of whether any situation is to be passed as 'natural' or 'naturalistic' is the extent to which the characters involved in it seem to be actual—to be, that is, what the observer regards as actual. This final judgment will depend to a very large extent on the place and the language which are the observer's —humankind's notion of what is real is inevitably based on the premise that what is most real is that which is most familiar. Miss Gwendolen in *The Importance of Being Earnest* was glad to say she had never seen a spade; it formed no part of her conception of the actual or the real and certainly not of the natural because it was unfamiliar to her. Our environments prejudge our conception of the natural—'t'ain't natural' simply means—'I've never before experienced it—it probably isn't real.'

The 'naturalism' which was observed in the plays of the young dramatists of the early 1960s was, as some of them have testified, not just a response to specific phenomena. In some cases there was no expressly conscious response to outside stimuli at all—the playwright was concerned to write a play as ably as possible. Yet, to do that in itself implies that the artist must allow himself to be open, at the very least, to the effect of osmosis; he may not seek out his themes and characters in his surrounding environment, they may find him.

What (whether by design or by osmosis), many of the young dramatists found had become their material was not so much specific and unique symptoms of a restless society, as incessant, deep movements of change. Religion, politics, education, the law, social habits and *mores*, culture—all these were beginning to lose what seemed to a young generation to be the monolithic unchanging face of centuries. The drive towards a classless society, towards equality of opportunity, a relentless growth of opposition to élitism, formed the material out of which the 'new naturalistic' drama was created. The conditioned reflexes of centuries by which significant drama had, certainly since the seventeenth century, been associated with the upper and middle classes, were stunned. Some critics found *Look Back in Anger* anathema to them not so much because they believed it to be an inefficient play, but because they could not really recognize the place, the language, the characters—it was not 'natural' to them. One, however, reckless in his praise of its dramatic value, recognized it only too clearly and shouted Hallelujah:

> . . . Osborne struck a representative note, he summed up the sense of inverted rage, the bitter raging against the cramped, *pusillanimous* forms of life which stifled Jimmy Porter. If Porter was unbearable, as the stiffer critics said, it was because many of us were on the edge of finding all our relationships unbearable. And what we found in *Look Back* was the language which, at least at that moment, contained something of our sense for life. Constantly critical, it yet called out something more than a reaction in us: it gave us lessons in feeling.[1]

Another, echoing praise, assumed that what was naturalistic in the kitchen-sink plays, was natural for all:

> To talk as we do about popular theatre, about new working-class audiences, about plays that will interpret the common experiences of today—all this is one thing, and a good thing too. But how much better even, how much more exciting, to find such theatre suddenly here, suddenly sprung up under our feet! This was the first joyful thing about Theatre Workshop's performance of *A Taste of Honey*.[2]

And still another triumphantly found his finger (a little incontinently perhaps) on the spot and declared:

> . . . 'The whole stinking commercial world insults us,' says Beatie, now speaking for herself, 'and we don't care a damn . . . . We want the third rate, we get it.'
> The quality of *Roots* lies in the evolution of this accusation from a naturalistic drama; it emerges without the chilly, antitheatrical flavour of something tagged on or schematic. Middle-class playwrights would be incapable of finding the objective correlatives for such a statement in a community dominated by 'guts ache', trivial family quarrels, threats of dismissal to casual labour and culture diffused by television. Most of those who did know the community would be incapable of dramatizing the statement. Wesker succeeds on both counts.[3]

The new naturalism was 'new' in place, in language and in character. Those who had found their naturalism heretofore in iambic pentameter, in the custom-built obsolescences of 'well-made' language, in the orotundities of measured prose, were now faced with a 'new' species of dramatic actuality—drawn, as the so-frequent phrase had it, 'from life itself'. For it is essential to understand that the claims of the proselytizers of the 'new naturalism' were largely based on the proposition that, in language and character, this new drama was nearer to what most people experience (though, of course, patterned, selected and designed) than most drama that had ever before been written in theatrical history: 'I write,' said Shelagh Delaney, 'as people speak.' It was, at the least, naive to ask 'which people?'.

Kings, princes and, to a less extent, nobility—all those who,

by ceremony, status and power hold sway over other mor-
tals—or people of singular and notable individuality, are not
commonplace. They were, in the 1960s, and they certainly are
now, correspondingly less easy to assimilate as 'natural' or
'naturalistic'. They do not, so we think, believe, behave, feel,
think, even look or speak 'as people speak'. A charitable view
of them, in so far as they are experienced as creatures in
fictional work like drama, is that they belong to a now-defunct
'heroic' stage in the history of drama.

Perhaps more people than is imagined realize with a start
that heroic drama is now no more. The 'new naturalism'
became the brazen antithesis of the old conventional 'heroical',
though, for some, the newly elevated commonplace has a kind
of sentimental heroic patina to it—the halo of almost total
perfection of the ordinary.

The retreat from conventional heroic drama did not begin in
the mid-twentieth century, though it began to gallop then.
The 1960s and 1970s completed, by particularizing and celebrating the antithesis of the heroic, a process which had begun
much earlier. It is to Galsworthy, and unsung writers like
Knoblock and Greenwood, that we must turn to find the
beginning of the apotheosis of the commonplace—though in
Galsworthy the commonplace is only apparent. Shaw is a
throwback. He certainly denudes his Caesars—of whatever
kind they are—of pomp, circumstance and glamour. But he
does not, by any means, abandon the heroic. Many of his
characters act and speak on a grand scale. They are marked off
from other men by the size of their personalities. Indeed, Mr
Doolittle reminds us that you can abandon much of your
class-label without losing your dignity, your principles, your
prejudices or indeed, your language—so long as you are an
extraordinary not a commonplace man.

The 'new wave' of dramatists in the 1960s created an environment for the flourishing of the non-heroic character. With
few exceptions the best-known dramatists of the 1960s and 1970s
have created characters whose social status, personality, intellectual capacity have been in most respects unexceptionable; whose
power over their environment and their contemporaries has
been, at best, fugitive, temporary and unremarkable. Their
strength (using the word in the sense of a pronounced and

consistent dominant capacity) has lain in their emotional 'presence'—the demonstration of all kinds of passion—love, hate, envy, compassion *et al.*—has been the most remarkable feature of both protagonists and secondary characters in the drama of the sixties and seventies. It is quite extraordinary, but with very few exceptions it is difficult to remember even their names, though one can remember their emotional dispositions. But one remembers the tone of their language. It is 'naturalistic' in the sense that it has its roots deep in actual speech—in the commonplace speech of the 'non-heroic' in society. Such characters and such speech are not to be found in 'heroic' places. The people and the language we experience in the most characteristic drama of the sixties and seventies is that of the bed-sit, the attic room, the digs, even the loo. Glamis and High Dunsinane, the middle-class respectability of *Candida*, and even the unaffluent but tidy pride of Galsworthy's lower orders are gone. A naturalism which equates immediacy, significance, drama with what Lindsay Anderson has called 'the common experiences' of today must, presumably, use the 'common' language of today. It is described variously as 'direct', 'salty', 'earthy', 'contemporary'. By any other name the kind of language meant is non-literate, unsophisticated, idiomatic, slangy—in all quite unrelated to any form of verbal communication which has about it the taint of formalized convention or authoritarianism. It is sometimes called 'working-class' language. This description is useful but only if it is employed to mean the language of people who, after the sixteenth and before the twentieth centuries had short shrift in the dramatic history of England. It is not one language—for it can be derived from dialect or occupation—but it has one powerful motivation behind its use in drama since the 1960s. That motivation is the desire to say—'Look, it's us who are speaking, who've never had the chance to speak before.' This desire is seen in its most passionate form in the work of Arnold Wesker.

All Wesker's plays seem to be written out of a huge inner compulsion, but especially the earlier ones when Wesker's youthful committal to the underprivileged in an 'unfair' society was both passionate in its expression and deep in its compassion. It would be tempting to explain this in biographical terms—his own experience and observation of deprivation, the rich emotive Jewish background—except that there is little that seems overtly self-indulgent about it, and that the care and compassion are very outward-looking. What is more important than a source that cannot be traced is the effect of the compulsion to write as he does on the language of his plays.

Accompanying this strong sense of a compulsion is a less intense but equally persistent feeling that the drama is not Wesker's natural form of expression. His Trilogy[4] has a panoramic width of reference and an episodic rhythm which is characteristic of the novel—as if *The Forsyte Saga* were the story of entirely below-stairs. It may be that what is taken to be Wesker's compulsion (more apparent in the early part of his career than now) to broadcast his thoughts and feelings about the underprivileged had the effect of pushing him towards that form of communication which had the widest and most dramatic effect—theatre. His work, valiant, and flawed partly because of an embarrassing mode of enthusiasm which, some may have thought, was condescension, to bring culture to the masses, suggests a man prepared to exploit the most public of the arts to proselytize his beliefs. But, as an individual artist, his bent seems less for the play than for the pamphlet, or for a kind of sociological treatise which allows as much scope to the heart as to the head.

There are many points in both the more successful earlier plays and the less successful later ones when one feels doubtful about Wesker's own comfort in using the language of drama. This is no condescension to him, for, unlike many writers about contemporary society, there is an immense warm attractiveness about the aura of his plays. Shaw seems pert by comparison, sociologists seem uncaringly cold, left-wing poets seem tartly nagging. There is no other dramatist writing about society in whom one can feel this warmth—it seems, indeed, to be a kind of vulnerability.

The decline of Wesker as a dramatist was one of the sad phenomena of the 1960s and it is difficult, in hindsight, not to attribute it to his apparent increasing inability to keep his language on a straight dramatic course. In what seem like hard-fought attempts to identify his own language, correct for what he wants to say, he has moved from the speech of man in society, which characterized the style of his early works, to a more private one—that of man living within himself. The irony is that thematically Wesker has never lost his passion for keeping a watching brief on man's status in society, but the language of the later plays embroiders rather than embodies that passion.

The record of durable dramatists inevitably shows that one element in their durability is a very particular quality in their language—an unchanging quality. The prism, so to speak, remains the same shape and size and of the same material, throughout the dramatist's career, but, at different times, is seen from different angles, so that different colours emerge, depths of penetrations of light increase as the dramatist becomes more adept at discovering new dimensions and in relating his vision to the prism. This is essentially true of the great dramatists, notably Shakespeare and Congreve and Shaw. The language, for example, of *Love's Labour's Lost* and of *King Lear* may not seem to have much in common at a mere ear's glance but, in fact, there is much that makes it absolutely plain that they were written by the same man—the unique imaginative opulence, the astonishing counterpointing between informal and formal statement, the risky but almost always successful punning, the inventiveness in imagery, the constant implied awareness of the needs of the actors in communicating the language, the ease with which prose sits with verse, the acceptance that dramatic effect is often obtainable when metrical pattern is broken rather than slavishly maintained. All this makes the 'immature' play irrevocably the child of the same imagination which created the 'mature' play—the difference is in quality and direction of vision, experience and expertise, not in kind.

Dramatists who radically 'experiment' or seek too zealously for new styles or mistake one kind of language for another in mid-life are usually those who have lost something of a grip, or perhaps never absolutely possessed one, on their basic, green style. Examples, it is true, may be urged from all arts of the opposite being true. Picasso, it seemed at the time, drastically changed direction several times in his life. But the operative phrase is 'at the time'. The sense of development is, now, more obvious than any sense of staccato advance and revolutionary change.

But Wesker seems, during his lifetime, to be not so much in a state of continuous development, as in uncertain and uneasy movement. If this is true then it is to be regretted not only because of the nature of Wesker's themes, the intensity of his committal to them, but because, to a point, his dramatic language in the early plays has a quality which, if not unique (as was claimed by some) in English drama, is uncommon enough to be regarded as important.

This is his use of the demotic, which in some ways is comparable to Galsworthy's, particularly in the deployment of verbal surprises, in the emotional overtones that he can give to ideas, in the use of irony (though it is not so fierce as Galsworthy's). But, especially, few dramatists in the history of drama in this country have used dialect as convincingly as does Wesker in his Trilogy. It is easy to underrate what he has achieved in this respect because it is so very convincingly and naturally exploited. In fact, Wesker contrives to make dialect sound authentic while at the same time firmly embodying it in the reality of the play; in other words there is artistic cohesiveness between the dialect and the play's world. This point is worth elaborating if only to a small extent.

On the whole British dramatists have failed lamentably with dialects. Shakespeare very wisely did not allow himself too much indulgence in using them and it is not without some significance that he is far more successful in his depiction of his (virtually) native Cotswold speech (in *Henry IV*) than in his erratic forages into Anglo-Welsh in *Henry V*. With Shallow and Silence he realized that you best convey a dialect not by larding your prose with it, but by a light brush stroke. Wesker's Norfolk is as keenly heard and communicated as is Shakespeare's Cotswold, and it is as economically applied as is Shakespeare's. This in itself is a signal achievement, but the integration of the dialect with the play's meaning is, in the final analysis, a greater one. If we merely glance at some of the attempts at dialect writing which, with the growing obsession with prose-naturalism, became popular with dramatists during the first half of the twentieth century, we will find ourselves notably embarrassed. First by its painful ineffici-

90

ency, and second by the lack of integration. Dialect, to most of
the dramatists, simply meant that the speaker was a member
of a lesser social order, no doubt great-hearted, strong-willed,
sincere, honest—but inferior. Indeed the very possession of a
dialect was itself a mark of inferiority. So that dialect speech
merely tried to fulfil the relatively simple job of conveying to
the audience, first where the person came from, and second,
what his class was. The inefficiency of any attempt to create
dialect in collusion, so to speak, with simple mechanistic
function, inevitably separates it off from even an approxima-
tion to harmony with the play's heart and theme. The dialect is
phoney and its function is limited and stilted. In Wesker, it
plays a significant part in the development of the theme and
delineation of character.

In *Roots*, Beatie does not have to break out of, or abandon,
her dialect in order to prove her sudden consciousness of being
really articulate for the first time in her life. She feels she can
stand up and be counted among the literate and, therefore, the
privileged, but not at the expense of forfeiting what is natural
to her tongue.

Those critics who lauded Wesker for being the first
dramatist to give the artisan class a voice in English drama
missed the truth about what he achieved. What he did in his
Trilogy was to dissociate dialect from inferiority, and to give
it a valid currency for expression. He gave loamy voices a true
tone and articulacy which, other than in Shakespeare and
intermittently in other dramatists, it had never possessed.

But Wesker does not confine himself to the Norfolk dialect
in his early plays. In his Trilogy, particularly and, to a degree,
in both *The Kitchen* and *Chips With Everything* Wesker's
passionate urge to make public the extent of the dispossession
of the working-class beats with energy and urgency. But the
dispossession is not only the political and economic one which
Chicken Soup with Barley is largely concerned with. Wesker,
probably uniquely in the history of English drama, realized
and movingly communicated, particularly in *Roots*, the deprivation or devaluation of the individual's means of expression:
it is as if he were saying that if you are deprived of the
birthright to a fair share of the world's wealth and power to
govern a society you are automatically liable to fall short of a

full expression and fulfilment of yourself and your class in both a cultural and linguistic sense. Wesker, so eloquent himself, is extremely sensitive to any individual or group or class which has not had the opportunity to learn how to speak or the recognition of the validity of what it speaks. In this he is, of course, at the opposite end of the spectrum from Shaw who never seems to have equated any kind of disinheritance with this particular deprivation.

Wesker's early drama then, can be said to be 'democratic' in the sense that it attempts to give a language to the dispossessed, the underprivileged. It is for this reason rather than for any overt or explicit political stance that Wesker adopts in his plays that he is important. It seems that most critics have forgotten or not realized that his work is the culminating success of a thin red line of effort in the twentieth century to wrench the working class out of a position which it had occupied in drama for centuries. In the Middle Ages the artisan had a naturally easy equality with his social superior—so far as drama was concerned. Mediaeval morality drama is, perhaps unexpectedly, 'democratic' in this respect—citizenry and nobility, shepherd and king, labourer and lord had equal opportunity for expression which is often eloquent. Shakespeare dignified the 'lower orders' by a constant adherence to the principle that all men are equal in the sight of God, though the social divisions that man created seemed to ordain otherwise. In the long run his kings, as many of them testify, not only have to face, eventually, the great leveller, Death, but without the trappings of authority and ceremony are no better, no different in shape, in needs, indeed in any respect, from the meanest beggar.

But after Shakespeare (with some exceptions) the ordinances of society rather than of God dominated the way in which the working class was depicted in literary forms—particularly the drama and the novel. Wesker did not alone restore the working class to the human status it occupied in Shakespeare's plays. Galsworthy and Hardy have far more right to claim a larger part in the process than he has. But, more than them and more than Shaw—with his tortuous attempts to convey dialect by notation—Wesker gave underprivilege a language and a voice which sounded authentic.

The truth of the judgment that Wesker's ear is so extraordinarily acute that the speech of his people in *Roots* has immense conviction has been countered by an opinion that questions whether his notation of Norfolk speech is indeed accurate. It is claimed that while it is not standard mummerset it nevertheless bears only a superficial resemblance to real Norfolk. But Wesker has neither attempted to give his actors the task of confronting Norfolk dialect 'straight' (and, incidentally, labouring the audience with the problems of understanding it), nor has he, like Shaw, attempted a phonetic representation of it. Wesker has in this respect remembered that the art of theatre is the art of illusion. You can, in the theatre, no more be strictly 'authentic' with dialect than you can with, let us say, trees, bushes, railway engines, waterfalls—and still preserve theatrical credibility. The 'authenticity' of Wesker's Norfolk speech lies not so much in a studied facsimile of reality, as in a version of it. Whistler's impressionistic painting, *Westminster Bridge*, ridiculed by Ruskin for its lack of actuality, is no less truthful to its subject than a photograph. Wesker's Norfolk language has maintained a characteristic rhythm, it has exploited, or enabled the actor to exploit, some typical and unique vowel sounds—particularly 'o' of Norfolk speech; it has superbly captured the somewhat anarchic way with some consonants—particularly 'h' and 'd'—which, occasionally, looking for a home, find themselves in quite the wrong company; it has judiciously used the tendency to phrase-repetition, and to the ubiquitous, urgent and endearing emphatic 'I say' or ''e say'.

Indeed, it is much further away from mummerset and much nearer the truth of Norfolk than Wesker's detractors realize. We have only to listen in our mind's ear for this to be apparent. Here is an example of 'authentic' mummerset, which happens to be of the Irish variety:

Michael: It's not enough fur a man an' a wumman til join han's. A want til see the whole wurl' at peace.

Mrs Rainey: Ye'll on'y git that be men an' weemen bein' at peace. Him an' her, Mickie, are bigger than the wurl', if ye on'y knew it. That man o' mine can't see fardher nor churches an' Or'nge Lodges, an' all the time there's men an' wimmen stan'in' about, waitin' fur somethin' til bring them thegither.

Michael: Aw, but selfishness is the curse o' the wurl. An' it's the curse
o' Irèlan' more nor anny other country. They wur alwis thinkin' o' their selves, the men an' weemen that might ha' saved
Irelan'.[5]

And this is from *Roots:*

Stan: Daf ' clothes? Blust woman! I got on half a cow's hide, what
you sayin'! Where's the gal?
Mrs Bryant: Beatie? She 'ent come yit. Didn't *you* see her?
Stan: Hell, I was up too early for her. She always stay the week-end
wi' Jenny 'fore comin' home?
Mrs Bryant: Most times;
(Stan sneezes)
What you doin' up this way wi' a cold like that then? Get you
home to bed.
Stan: Just come this way to look at the vicarage. Stuff's comin' up for
sale soon.
Mrs Bryant: You still visit them things then?
Stan: Yearp. Pass the ole time away. Pass the ole time.

But Wesker does not confine himself to Norfolk either in his
Trilogy or elsewhere. When his ear is unsullied by sounds and
rhythms 'far more deeply interfused'—which remain to be
discussed—he is just as at ease with Cockney, East London
Jewish of European origin and other dialects. As with Norfolk
the 'authenticity' lies not in an attempt at facsimile but in
precise 'impression' using the basic characteristics of a certain
dialect or speech pattern. In this short episode the marriage of
East End London and indigenous Jewish is complete and
totally convincing:

Sarah: Here, lay these out, the boys will be coming soon.
Harry: Good woman! I could just do with a cup of tea.
Sarah: What's the matter, you didn't have any tea by Lottie's?
Harry: No.
Sarah: Liar.
Harry: I didn't have any tea by Lottie's, I tell you. *(Injured tone)* Good
God, woman, why don't you believe me when I tell you
things?
Sarah: *You* tell *me* why. Why don't I believe him when he tells me
things! As if he's such an angel and never tells lies. What's the
matter, you never told lies before I don't think?
Harry: All right, so I had tea at Lottie's. There, you satisfied now?[6]

But, significantly, when Wesker moves out of the area of the dispossessed, the struggling, the frustrated but aspiring, his ear lets him down badly, sometimes sensationally. The Colonel in *I'm Talking About Jerusalem* requires little comment. Wesker has totally failed to come to terms with the speech of a character from the other side, the swanky side, of the tracks. He has fallen back on a blithering caricature:

Colonel: Yes, well, thought I'd pop over and see you were arriving safely. Come at a good time—we've had some rain but it's gone. Doesn't do to have too much rain.
Ada: (Not really knowing the reply) No it doesn't does it?
Colonel: Talking of rain, Simmonds, I'd advise you to buy yourself a tank to catch the soft water. Good stuff, that. Save you work, too. Not so much to pull up from the well. Buy one with a tap—easier. Don't drink it, though. Use it for washing and things.

Even more significantly, the characterization of Ronnie, whose real presence is experienced in *Chicken Soup with Barley,* whose influence is felt in *Roots* and who returns in the flesh in *I'm Talking About Jerusalem,* lacks credibility. The reason is clear. Ronnie, the son of Harry and Sarah Kahn, East End Jews, salt of the earth, credible, underprivileged, has acquired the confidence of self-awareness and articulate expression but his language has lost touch with any sense of actuality. It is an invented thing, an illegitimate offspring of the falsely demotic and the fulsomely literate. The awful worry arises that Beatie, who has been so real for us, will eventually begin to talk like this after she has found the wings of speech. Even more, the suspicion begins to grow that Wesker does not know what language his characters will speak once they find themselves completely shrived of their dispossession. To this extent he does not keep faith with 'natural' speech:

Ronnie: Christ! It's bloody cold in that room: I—now, then Harry— *(as though playfully scolding a child)* you know you must not read the letter, remember what Mummykins said. *(He moves to take it)*
Harry: (Retaining it) I want to see it; it's about me, isn't what's in it?
Ronnie: (Making another bid for it) Use some will-power, Dad; you know the letter is not for you. Now leave it be, there's a good boy.

This is artificial enough, but its effect is compounded a little later on in the scene:

Harry: You shouldn't do these things. I'm a sick man. If I want to open the envelope you shouldn't stop me. You've got no right to stop me. Now you've upset me and yourself—you silly boy.

Ronnie: Can't you see that I can't bear what you are. I don't want to hear your lies all my life. Your weakness frightens me, Harry —did you ever think about that? I watch you and I see myself and I'm terrified.

The gradual loosening of Wesker's dramatic grasp after the Trilogy is to be measured by the extent to which he abandoned his hold on a naturalistic expression of the truth of characterization. More and more he began to slip out of naturalism into allegory and symbolism and, as he did so, presented a classic example of the dichotomy which Brustein and Eliot, in their different ways, expressed. Wesker, even in the early Trilogy, showed a tendency to abandon the directness of straight prose-speech whenever he wished to express an 'inner' mood, compulsion, attitude, enthusiasm, emotion. Almost as if a lever has been pushed, Wesker's language shifts gear from 'speech' into 'prose' and, eventually ever more often into 'poetic prose'. Wesker, in a characteristically warm-blooded fashion, has vehemently declared that his critics have found symbols where they do not exist in his later plays.

But there is a relentlessly comprehensive body of evidence to suggest that it is not them but Wesker who, in his energetic and deeply-thoughtful quest for the right communication for what he has to say, has deluded himself. The process by which Wesker's dramatic naturalism began to decline into a hazy and 'literary' symbolism began to show itself with certainty in *The Kitchen*.[7] John Russell Taylor was the first to comment on this:

> The point is made clearly on a number of occasions that the kitchen is meant to stand in our minds for the whole dirty business of modern life: most explicitly in Dimitri's speech in the first act:
> 'This stinking kitchen is like the world—you know what I mean? It's too fast to know what happens. People come and go, big excitement, big noise. What for? In the end who do you know? You make a friend, but when you go from here—pshtt! you forget! Why you grumble about this one kitchen?'

Now, to establish the validity of a parallel like this, it is necessary that the realistic level should be self-evidently true and believable; there should be no suspicion that the truth is being doctored to fit the argument. But if one looks at the set-up in *The Kitchen* there is far too much evidence, even to the casual uninformed eye, that this is just what is happening here.[8]

What has begun to happen is that Wesker's own relationship to his material has changed, or begun to change. He has ceased to submerge himself and allow his characters to speak a language natural to them. He, Wesker, the creator, has become apparent, as a speaking observer, speaking a different language. This kind of 'interference' begins before the play starts and the 'all-too-visible puppet-master' shows his hand. We expect and accept an author's production notes, but Wesker in *The Kitchen* spends capital in his preliminary introduction to the play which should be invested in the play itself, as an entity:

> The lengthy explanations I am forced to make may be annoying; I am sorry, but they are necessary.
> This is a play about a large kitchen in a restaurant called the Tivoli. All kitchens, especially during service, go insane. There is the rush, there are the petty quarrels, grumbles, false prides, and snobbery. Kitchen staff instinctively hate dining-room staff, and all of them hate the customer. He is the personal enemy. The world might have been a stage for Shakespeare, but to me it is a kitchen: where people come and go and cannot stay long enough to understand each other, and friendships, loves, and enmities are forgotten as quickly as they are made.

Having gone to great pains to talk about who serves what—tarts, cheese, pastry—he suddenly departs from naturalism:

> Now to the cooks. At this point it must be understood that at no time is food ever used. To cook and serve food is of course just not practical. Therefore the waitresses will carry empty dishes and the cooks will mime their cooking. Cooks being the main characters in this play, I shall sketch them and their activity here, so that while the main action of the play is continuing they shall always have something to do.

Within the body of the play we find reminders of Shavian

'internal' directions, but they lack his clarity and disturbingly at times puzzle the understanding:

Max: (His soul not yet returned) Good morning.

The interference of the author becomes more obvious the longer the play lasts. There is a fatal assumption of familiarity and agreement between author and audience for example. This, in itself, weakens the play's credibility—it is as if our elbow is being jogged and we are being told—'That's what it means, doesn't it—d'you see?' Even more, there is a curiously naive impression that the author believes that the audience already accepts entirely his point of view; a sort of cosy conspiracy:

> *(And so he moves right off stage. Marango is left among his staff who stand around, almost accusingly, looking at him. And he asks again—)* What is there more? What *is* there more? *(We have seen that there must be something more and so the lights must slowly fade)*

Taylor comments on this:

> . . . Wesker is not yet finished with the problem which has plagued him throughout his career: the debilitating effect that his inability to see that things may in fact be other than he thinks they ought to be has on his ability to express his ideas in properly dramatic terms.[9]

The more the relationship between Wesker and his creation seems to change the more the language of his plays acquires clumps of dramatically incredible material that is theatrically inhibiting and sometimes embarrassing:

Peter: . . . When you go, when I go, when Dimitri go—this kitchen stays. It'll go on when we die, think about that. We work here—eight hours a day, sweat our guts, and yet—it's nothing. We take nothing. Here—the kitchen, here—you. You and the kitchen. And the kitchen don't mean nothing to you and you don't mean to the kitchen nothing. Dimitri is right, you know—why do you grumble about this kitchen? The world is filled with kitchens—only some they call offices and some they call factories. There, Irishman—what do you say to that?
Kevin: You want to come in one morning and find it gone?
Peter: Just one morning. Imagine it, eh? Gone. All this gone.

Kevin: So you'd be out of work!
Peter: So I'd die?
Kevin: It doesn't worry you, I suppose.
Hans: Du träumst schon wieder, mein Lieber.

The most corrosive effect of the declension from truly dramatic language is to be found in what appeared more and more in Wesker's plays as he went on his escape route out of naturalism. It has two aspects: the first is obvious, and is present to a degree in the Trilogy—particularly *Chicken Soup with Barley*. It is certainly the most obtrusive feature of the author's interference—it may be called 'manifesto language':

Monty: The boys! Listen. Hear them? You know, Sarah, that's the same cry the people of Madrid were shouting.
Prince: And they didn't get past either. Imagine it! All those women and children coming out into the streets and making barricades with their beds and their chairs.
Dave: (Sadly) It was a slaughter.
Prince: And then came the first International Brigade . . .

This is not only out of tune with the specific character speaking it but incompatible with any kind of characterization. It is not the language of drama, but of the pamphlet and the ranting soap-box. In the later plays, particularly *The Friends* and *Their Very Own and Golden City,* its form and tone are changed, but the effect is the same. What, earlier, sounded like the faceless language of a party manifesto is now transmuted into the highly-wrought verbology of the half-romantic, and quasi-philosophical. It is a kind of rhetoric. You feel it is full of meaning but it tends to obscure it; moreover, such language is a trap that the seasoned actor is well aware of. A partial diary of the progress of rehearsals for Wesker's own production of *The Friends* not only confirms this but highlights the nature of the corrosion of such language on the play—and its source:

By now the actors are beginning to vent their frustrations on the play itself.

Henry: (Of part of his text) You've not done bad, Arnold—it's all scraps: I'm not saying it's voluble plagiarism, it's more a sort of eclectic fluency.

Even the Stage Manager starts coming forward with points like 'Why are they all in the last scene?' When Wesker read the script yesterday Ian Holm came forward and said: 'That's it—there are no characters in this play.' It is part of the trouble: the director should be working with the actors to build up the parts away from the author. All the people in the play are too much the dismembered voices of Arnold Wesker, which he is trying to 'conduct' into a great ensemble of statement. The approach, however, is not going to work out, and Wesker has increasing doubts about himself as a director: at one point he says to me, 'I don't think I'm a director.' But in spite of this and the times when the actors say:

Holm: We're all helpless. We feel we should have this out.
Cropper: It's like floundering around in an oil-rink.

and other similar remarks, work ploughs on.[10]

The interference of Wesker is the intrusion of the private into what is a public art. The comments of seasoned actors only serve to emphasize that the main victim of the interference is character:

John Bluthal, towards the end of a scene, is distracted out of character by a noise, and triggers a reaction among the others:

Bluthal: Stop it—I've only got six more lines and I'm finished.
Holm: That's it—we've hit the nail on the head. I don't believe in any of the characters. It sounds like a thesis.
Henry: Seven parrots don't make a play.

A Canadian girl, Norma Levine, has written an interesting piece on Wesker and Victor Henry, giving a Manichean interpretation to rehearsals. Victor says to Wesker during this rehearsal:

Henry: It's only a Jew who would discover evil with sadness instead of despair. You wrote that.

Norma uses this line in her Bradleyan approach:

'Wesker's universe is one of the most carefully created order, from the shaping of the end picture of the play, to the tradition-ally structured plays he writes, to the creation of Centre 42, to his reasonability and assumption of a causal pattern of predic-tability in human relationships. His universe, both inner and outer is structured. "New knowledge disrupts me," says Man-fred in the play with the voice of Wesker. For both of them, evil is a piece of knowledge but knowledge unbacked by experience.'

I find curious the fact that many of the Jews I have known discover evil with sadness and despair. But what of someone who discovers evil with anger or a sense of betrayal? So many of the lines are like that relating, like romantic poetry, to a private situation.[11]

Time and time again, especially from *Chips With Everything* onwards we find that we are being forced (or we get the impression that we are being forced) to make a radical shift of focus on a character. If we are successful in doing this we find, uncomfortably, that the rest of the play has become re- or unaligned.

Taylor has indicated how *Chips With Everything* builds up an allegorical framework in which the characters 'assume the boldly conventionalized characteristics of figures in a political cartoon, and this, indeed, is very much what they are . . . we are not, presumably, meant to accept them primarily as human beings existing in their own right, but rather as quasi-allegorical type-figures of their respective classes'.[12]

Yet Pip, one of the chief characters, steps, as Taylor says, 'right out of the allegorical framework' as conclusively as Peter steps right out of a naturalistic one in *The Kitchen*. The effect on the auditor or reader is to cause him to doubt both the allegorical and the naturalistic experience that Wesker so energetically provides.

He has written about naturalism, and the apparent confusion between 'naturalism' and 'realism' is perhaps a mirror of a confusion within him:

I have discovered that realistic art is a contradiction in terms. Art is the re-creation of experience, not the copying of it. Some writers use naturalistic means to re-create experience, others non-naturalistic. I happen to use naturalistic means; but all the statements I make are made theatrically. Reality is as misleading as truth; realistic art makes nonsense. If I develop, it might be away from naturalism. I have discovered that this too can be constricting—but I will still be trying to re-create the reality of my experience. I would no more be non-naturalistic for its own sake than I was naturalistic for its own sake; I am concerned with both only in order to communicate what experience has meant to me.[13]

Ironically, the lack of precise definition here can best be encapsulated in Wesker's own words to describe the style of *The Friends*—he referred to it as 'stylized naturalism'. The rehearsals of the play and the text itself only confirmed the suspicion of contradiction in his description.

The relentless accretion of unfavourable critical comment about Wesker's later plays has spurred him to detailed responses. These have done little to expunge the strong impression that there is an impulse in him which is inclined to ignore that necessary safety barrier which every dramatist should heed. This prevents the dramatist from joining the citizenry of his own imaginative world. But, Wesker seems to leap the barrier and to want to be both creator and what-is-created:

> 'The characters are all me,' Wesker had said when casting the play, ' . . . at one time or another.'[14]

In the light of his unique contribution to the dignified installation of naturalistic dialect language in late twentieth-century drama, his honesty, passionate intensity and artistic sensibility, it cannot, surely, be an exaggeration to designate the shortcomings of his dramatic talent as tragic. But he seems sometimes to be a victim of an inability to create and to maintain the illusion that character in drama must have a life of its own. Unfortunately the quest for 'truth'—with which Wesker is honourably and deeply acquainted—is no guarantee of artistic quality.

Both Arnold Wesker and John Osborne have been hailed as exciting innovators in modern drama. Hindsight, which always has an opportunity to display a wisdom denied to contemporaries of an event, raises some doubts about both the extent and the nature of their innovations. Wesker, for example, now seems important less as the man who gave the working class the freedom of the stage, than for his use of the vernacular and for his contribution to the onset of anti-heroic drama.

Much larger claims were made for John Osborne after the admittedly sensational success of the first production of *Look Back in Anger* in 1956. The chief chronicler of the fifties and sixties, John Russell Taylor, is empyrean in his enthusiasm —for him Osborne 'started everything off '. Only slightly less ecstatic is his view that the play was the first 'type-image of the new drama'.

But Osborne has been worshipped—the word hardly seems inappropriate—for other reasons. His protagonist, Jimmy Porter, has been regarded as the first non-hero—an opinion which ignores Stanley Kowalski who, by the time *Look Back in Anger* was written was well known and had spawned, in films, a number 'of progeny of his own type. Again—and Taylor echoes this opinion—Osborne's Jimmy was said, and still is by some, to represent a post-war generation in his anger, petulance, dissatisfaction, infirmity of purpose, railing, complaining. All these descriptive words have been used by commentators to describe Jimmy Porter. Yet, which genera- tion is this supposed to represent? Many of Jimmy's age at the time would not have recognized themselves in him. What, more and more, seems to be nearer the truth is that Jimmy is a mouthpiece for one man's disillusion about the society he lived in. John Osborne has been no slouch since 1956 in reiterating his views about society as he sees it—more and more in many of his public pronouncements he echoes, in an older way, a younger Porter.

And, of course, the play was hailed for the raw naturalism of its language. While allowing for the strong possibility that, at a time when censorship existed and, apparently, was exerted on the play, the language seemed permissive, there now seems room to doubt whether the word naturalism is apt, and even 'raw' seems a relative word in the context of much of today's dramatic language.

The claims for Osborne's play have weakened, but the greatest blow was delivered by the author himself. He described it as a formal old-fashioned play. Osborne's candour is often mashed with what seems a mischievous compulsion to thicken the issue or stir contention, so that his own description must not be taken at face-value. In this case, however, a summary examination of the play reveals some interesting facts. It is a three-acter; it has a thoroughly conventional set; that is, in the old-fashioned sense, a box-set; the play has a very precise conventional pattern—statement, development, crisis and resolution—in dramatic and theatrical terms, even if, thematically, it is opaque and lacks direction; no special effects are required; the 'situation' is naturalistic in that it could well be equated with real-life events. Indeed, a cursory examination alone amply confirms that Osborne's view of his play, is, indeed, forthright.

The two most persistent claims to innovation have been the vehemence and comprehensiveness of the protest and the nature of the language. They are closely connected and may therefore be examined as one. The first and perhaps the strongest impression of all that we receive in either reading or seeing the play is the rhythm that is set up between monologue and dialogue. Indeed, merely to hold the pages before your eyes and to turn them slowly reveals a visual pattern consisting of solid clumps of print (Jimmy's monologues) strung upon the thin wire of isolated lines (the dialogue). The dialogue, as such, which, of course, often involves Jimmy, too, is, on the whole, a neutral speech. Little attempt is made by Osborne to characterize through it, or to indicate class or accent. We have an occasional 'girlie' and a 'not 'arf ' from Cliff the Welshman (to whom, unaccountably, 'not 'arf ' is confined), but otherwise, there is no identification, no individualization in this dialogue. For example, we may think here that this is yet another of Jimmy's self-indulgences—

> I was wrong, I was wrong! I don't want to be neutral, I don't want to be a saint. I want to be a lost cause, I want to be corrupt and futile!

—but we should be warned that it is, in truth, one of Alison's speeches! That is an example of an outburst, but the more moderate areas of dialogue reveal that we are very much in the domain of the 'well-made play', a genre which so many of Osborne's admirers thought he was, by his scything newness, demolishing for ever. The 'well-made' elements in the language have several aspects, and some of them are to be found in Jimmy's famous monologues, but the more obvious are in the dialogue.

The language of the 'well-made' play always raises a question—'did people ever talk like this?' We do not ask the question of, say, Hamlet, or Mrs Malaprop or Doolittle, not because their language is more 'real', but because it convinces us in a way the 'well-made' play is incapable of doing—it contains an illusion of actuality within the pattern of its design. The language of Shakespeare, Sheridan or Shaw creates, in relation to theme and plot, a truth of character: we are forced to believe, whereas with the well-made play part of the pleasure lies in the exercise of our disbelief.

There is a good deal of 'well-made' dialogue in *Look Back in Anger*. Not only did no one ever talk like this—it creates with artificiality—but no characters firmly emerge out of it. The words remain as words, they often create nothing; they merely pass information:

Colonel: Well, I'd better put this in the car then. We may as well get along. Your mother will be worried, I know. I promised her I'd ring her when I got here. She's not very well.
Helena: I hope my telegram didn't upset her too much. Perhaps I shouldn't have—
Colonel: Not at all. We were very grateful that you did. It was very kind of you, indeed . . .

We must remind ourselves that the proof is in the hearing, however. The proof here is the extraordinary effect of a lack of dimension these two characters have on stage, even when performed by the most accomplished of players. It is not fulfilling the first requirement of dramatic language—the embodiment of individual character.

Yet another 'well-made' feature of the language is evidenced by what may well be called by the actress playing the part the 'sacrificial' dialogue given to Helena. It is sacrificial because it puts the actress in a posture where she has little chance of initiating any kind of action herself. She becomes a mere victim for the other person on stage who holds all the verbal weapons. In the final act, in the long scene between Alison and Helena, many of Helena's 'speeches' consist of single sentences or phrases which either confirm something Alison has said or ask a question to enable Alison to proceed: 'And it was true'; 'I could hardly believe it myself'; 'Maybe not. But I feel it just the same.' The longer speeches, which these and other phrases interrupt, in which Helena tells of her feelings about Jimmy, are insufficient to quell the sense of a

105

kind of dramatic futility in the part. Helena is only half-alive, and the Colonel is barely alive because like so many of their ilk in the well-made play their language is merely functional —and often barely that. Alison and Cliff give the illusion of being more rounded characters only because they have more to say and are involved much more in give-and-take with Jimmy. But their language, per se, is lacking in personality.

It is to Jimmy's language that we must look for evidence of the raw naturalism which Osborne is said to have brought to the stage. It is naturalistic—that is, it has a degree of truth to actual spoken speech—but not in the sense in which the term is often applied today. That is, it is not naturalistic as so much contemporary dramatic speech is, using the lowest common denominator of the vernacular like Bond[15] for example, in *Saved,* or as so many television plays do. Jimmy's 'naturalism' is special (to this extent he would probably be considered an élitist by a proponent of the most typical drama of the 1970s).

In the first place it is eloquent. It is not so much raw as vehement in a very lucid way. It sounds like the language of an educated man (and Jimmy, of course, is a university graduate) which has been carefully honed for stage purposes. It is, therefore, several stages higher in articulacy than the language employed by Wesker in the greater part of his Trilogy or by Shelagh Delaney in her celebrated *A Taste of Honey*—both dramatists associated by the commentators, for reasons that now seem illogical, with Osborne. The language of Jimmy is very similar to that of Dixon in Kingsley Amis's novel *Lucky Jim.* Indeed, Dixon's language is more 'natural' to the group from which it derives than is Porter's. Osborne has amalgamated with the group-language a number of devices.

The group-language from which Jimmy's speech comes is undergraduate—not exclusively, but to a large extent, arts. It is a language which was and is acquired in the heady atmosphere of the favoured student pub, the common-room, the debating-society, the endless impromptu coffee-sessions in hall, house or digs. It is the language of educated youth feeling its feet and determined to put things right. It is the language of a certain conceit—often not a vicious or deep one, but a cosy one born of a self-awareness of intelligence, a sense of words, and a desire to chalk up a victory in the intellectual stakes.

It is, too, a language which many undergraduates never abandon. It is to be found, sometimes polished, sometimes sharpened, sometimes down-at-heel, sometimes sly, sometimes exactly the same, in parliament, in the law, in senior common-rooms, in reunion dinners, in the occasional door-to-door salesmen, in school staff rooms. Jimmy has it still in a pristine form, but its content has been soured by time and circumstance. It is a language that is catching—from time to time Cliff gives evidences of having been infected by Jimmy, but there is no doubt that his is a secondary version. He, as Jimmy reminds us, is uneducated.

The characteristics of the language are eloquence, as we have seen, frequent lucidity, a tendency to exaggeration through repetition. It is, in a general analysis, always seeming to be on the point of breaking into a public rhetorical speech:

> Reason and Progress, the old firm, is selling out! Everyone get out while the going's good. Those forgotten shares you had in the old traditions, the old beliefs are going up—up and up and up.

Because it is so aware of itself anything of depth which it conveys seems to be created by accident. It cannot be trusted to a consistency of logic or argument, though it can often suddenly illuminate an idea or a feeling or an intuition:

> If you've no world of your own, it's rather pleasant to regret the passing of someone else's. I must be getting sentimental. But I must say it's pretty dreary living in the American Age—unless you're American of course.

Its most consistent quality is its drawing of attention to itself, and it does this by a persistent attempt to be witty. It often is, but the wit is always aggressive. It cannot be quiet because quietness is an enemy to exhibition:

> All I know is that somebody's been sticking pins into *my* wax image for years. *(Suddenly)* Of course: Alison's mother! Every Friday, the wax arrives from Harrods, and all through the week-end she's stabbing away at it with a hatpin! Ruined her bridge game, I dare say.

But it can often be banal largely because it is always in danger of losing a sense of fitness and proportion. When it is banal it is then that a kind of youthful pathos can just be glimpsed behind the cataract of words:

> The heaviest, strongest creatures in this world seem to be the loneliest. Like the old bear, following his own breath in the dark forest. There's no warm pack, no herd to comfort him. The voice that cries out doesn't *have* to be a weakling's, does it?

To write of the language as if it were a dramatis persona may be objected to. The truth is, however, that in *Look Back in Anger* almost all that Jimmy is as character is derived from the personality of the language. The surface characteristics of this group-language added up give us the total of Jimmy Porter's temperament. To this extent, the language is protagonist. Except, that is, for two ingredients which Osborne has added.

The first is melodrama—that is, the use of language to appeal to the emotions in ways that are at best, obvious, at worst, crude. The 'anger' of Jimmy Porter consists largely of a set of melodramatic forages into certain territories, an anger which seems less an emanation of some faith, principle or belief than a function of language. Jimmy is angry at so many things, but it is impossible to find any real source for the generation of the anger. He shouts in different sharps and flats, but we don't know why. All we can be sure of is his ability to appeal to emotions.

In this context an interesting observation was provided by a young company of players of very high professional capability, which was far too young to have recalled the sensational effect of the play in 1956, when recently having a first reading prior to production. None had read it before. The reaction was, for an older auditor, quite unexpected. The actors did not find naturalism, rawness, social significance, anger; instead they found old-fashioned melodrama. The actor playing Jimmy inquired what accent he was to use for (as he put it) 'the different characters this chap pretends to be—most of them unconsciously funny'.

The other ingredient is sentimentality. Again this emerges less as an inevitable facet of character than as a function of language. Rhetoric is often the mother of sentimental expression, with its recourse to repetition, its self-regarding rhythms, its tendency to seem impersonal while pushing

unerringly towards the emotionally subjective. Jimmy Porter's character has a huge sentimental element within it—and,
inevitably, we find that we can attribute it clearly to no specific
experience he has had, or principle, or prejudice. It emerges
through the rhetoric of his speech and we can only come to the
conclusion that he does not so much feel it as luxuriate in the
indulgence of listening to himself expressing it. No part of
Jimmy's anger, hate, love, sentimentality is explicable except
in terms of self-indulgence. And even that is a shallow fickle
thing that is dependent upon the waywardness and versatility
of his ability to talk himself into one posture or another. There
is no surer evidence of this than in the famous speech about his
dying father, hailed by many as an example of an underlying
sensitivity and vulnerability in the angry, deprived, perturbed
spirit of Jimmy Porter. In truth, what is remarkable about the
speech is not any revelation of the deeper soul of Porter, but of
the utter shallowness of his responses. The language as it
grows more rhetorical, 'turns on' the sentimentality, and as
this proceeds, the object of the speech turns away from the
dying father to Jimmy himself. He has talked himself into
being a victim. His father was the stalking-horse for Jimmy's
self-indulgent eloquence.

It would not by any means be generally agreed that *The
Entertainer*[16] is a better and likely to be a more memorable play
than *Look Back in Anger*. Perhaps a consensus of opinion
would reveal the belief that its success was due to Laurence
Olivier's performance as Archie Rice.
  If a greater flexibility and variety in the use of language is a
criterion of quality then the general view has to be questioned.
The Entertainer seems to employ language in a richer dramatic
way than its more illustrious forerunner—though it may well
have pre-dated it, at least in a preliminary form of conception.
Certainly there are strong echoes of Jimmy in it particularly in
some of Archie's more rhetorical monologues; and over the
whole there is Osborne's characteristic eloquence and sheer
cleverness of phrasing. But the group-speech which is so
strong an informing element in *Look Back in Anger* is firmly
kept in place. It has to give room to very much more dramatically and theatrically rich speech; it does not have the chance to

109

persuade us, as it does in the other play, that we are listening less to a dramatic embodiment of ideas and characters than a subjective cri-du-coeur, half in love with listening to its own expressions of itself.

The measure of its superiority as a true dramatic piece is the comparative richness of characterization. Two of the secondary characters—Archie's wife and his father—have a far more credible presence than any secondary character in *Look Back in Anger*. Phoebe (the wife) takes life through her accent which is implicit in her language:

> Blimey, you should know better than to ask me that! You know what a rotten memory I've got. Well, cheerio! *(She drinks)* Oooh, that's a nice drop of gin—some of the muck they give you nowadays—tastes like cheap scent . . .

Phoebe's language is clipped, always on the edge of being formless, inconsequential. It has none of the listless functionalism of Helen, or the artiness of Cliff. Through what she says and the form in which she says it we know her.

The same is true of Billy (Archie's father). His innate kindness, his frayed but brave dignity, comes out of a kind of hesitancy of speech. He moves from phrase to phrase, not with the possibility of lurching into incomprehensibility like Phoebe, but with a bemused care for saying the right thing. Therefore, he turns from one theme to another, carefully, nervously, watchfully, and with a touch of grace:

> Billy: Oh, this is nice of you. Thank you. Still, if she stays in she only gets irritable. And I can't stand rows. Not any more. *(He stares in front of him)* No use arguing with Phoebe anyway. Would you like some beer? *(She shakes her head)* She just won't listen to you. Are you sure you won't?

Olivier or not, Archie Rice is a more explicable, credibly dynamic, affecting character than Jimmy Porter. His failure as a human being is an inability not so much to distinguish (as some critics have suggested) between illusion and reality, as to keep them apart. It has a piercing human relevance. The way in which the little world he dominates partakes of his own weakness is both poignant and bitter. And the particular nature of his failure is superbly embodied in his very employment—as a professional Fool.

110

The language of Archie Rice is formed in a mould similar to that used for the creation of Shakespeare's Fools. There is no evidence that Osborne was or is conscious of this, nor that he would accept the connection. Yet he, like Shakespeare, realized that a special language is needed to express a character whose very function—as professional entertainer—forces him to live constantly on the boundary that separates illusion and reality, fiction and truth.

Like Touchstone, Feste and Lear's Fool, Archie expresses himself in a language which is really in a state of flux between commenting upon reality and creating a fiction. All four characters have a good deal of motley on their tongues, but there are moments when they 'wear not motley in their brain'.

Sometimes, like the Fools, Archie bursts into a song and prefaces or follows it with tart comment; sometimes he wraps up meaning in an anecdote which does not always easily make its point; often, like the Fools, he is berated for flippancy or coarseness, and often, like them, he appears to talk in the wild hope of getting applause. But, always, the flux between his function as entertainer and his status as human being and the irony between the language of illusion and reality is at work.

In Act I, Scene iv of *King Lear,* the Fool, operating within the same flux, tries to convince Lear of the stupidity of his division of the kingdom. He does it with an anecdote which, typically, is a play upon words:

Fool: Nuncle, give me an egg, and I'll give thee two crowns.
Lear: What two crowns shall they be?
Fool: Why, after I have cut the egg i the middle and eat up the meat, the two crowns of the egg. When thou clovest they crown i the middle, and gav'st away both parts, thou bor'st thine ass on thy back.

In Scene viii of *The Entertainer,* Archie Rice mocks the pretensions of politics. It is no less self-consciously contrived than that of Lear's Fool; it is no less efficient in its punning; it is no less received with intimidation. Above all, it is of the same order of expression, coming from the same kind of dramatic agent. Archie and the Fools would understand each other perfectly:

Archie: There was a chap at my school who managed to get himself

into the Labour Government, and they always said he was left of centre. Then he went into the House of Lords, and they made him an honourable fishmonger. Well, that just about wraps up the left of centre, doesn't it?
Frank: You know, you don't know what you're talking about.
. . .
Archie: If you can dodge all the clichés dropping like bats from the ceiling, you might pick up something from me.

In more measured terms, this is what Lear's Fool is saying to Lear.

The close association of the language and character of Archie with the Fools is most poignantly realized in the relationship of songs to dialogue and to situation and, especially, in the end. The essential loneliness of the figure who always patrols the thin line between illusion and reality, truth and fiction, is as true of Rice as it is of Feste with his wind and the rain or Lear's Fool who goes to bed at noon. And, to complete their consanguinity, inside the loneliness of all of them, is the wry paradox—who is performer and who is audience? What is real and what is not? Who is Fool and who is wise man?

Why should I care,
Why should I let it touch me,
Why shouldn't I?—
(He stops, the music goes on, as he walks over to Phoebe, who helps him on with his coat, and gives him his hat. He hesitates, comes back down to the floats) You've been a good audience. Very good. A very *good* audience. Let me know where you're working tomorrow night—and I'll come and see you.

In *The Entertainer* Osborne handled language with a creative sensitivity he never again equalled except intermittently in *Inadmissible Evidence*. The nature of this creativity is an ability to endow character with language appropriate to it. The enemy to this is to allow language to be the slave of theme or attitude and, hence, to be the mouthpiece of the author. Osborne's strength as a dramatist lies first in the unremitting passion of his language enabling him to provide actors capable of taking it with the opportunity to produce memorable oratorical performances. He has, too, an immense virtuosity of theme and plot and a vigorously aggressive relationship to the follies of his times which, at best, is refreshing, at worst, excusable.

In *The Hotel in Amsterdam,* the character Laurie cries, 'I work my drawers off and get written off twice a year as not fulfilling my early promise by some Philistine squirt drumming up copy.' Twelve years elapsed between *Look Back in Anger* and that remark, but it sounds like Jimmy Porter—or Osborne. The early promise is constantly being fulfilled—but never overtaken.

Part III
The Language of Poetic Drama

6 W. B. Yeats—the Poet in the Theatre

> A verse play is not a play done into verse, but a different kind of play . . . the poet with ambitions of the theatre, must discover the laws, both of another kind of verse and of another kind of drama. (T. S. Eliot)

When we look back to the end of the nineteenth century we see the long presence of Bernard Shaw and his prose-drama, and grouped around him, the less well-formed, less richly deep shadows of Galsworthy, Granville-Barker and the small host of other prose-dramatists. They, to a degree, owed their artistic existence to the presence of Shaw, and with him they seem to represent the final triumph of prose as an acceptable and natural communication of drama.

The truth is less precise. At the beginning of the twentieth century there was a great amount of confidence in a possible resurgence of poetic drama. The powerful evidences of the efficacy of prose-drama did not in any way dampen the enthusiasm of a significant and cultivated number of writers, many of whom were not only dedicated to drama in poetic form, but strongly deprecated the incursion of prose and social realism. Symons, Yeats, Stephen Philips (the last, a virtually forgotten poet/dramatist) were powerful advocates of the non-naturalistic and, therefore, to them, the non-prosaic drama. The extent of Yeats's commitment to the compatibility of poetry and drama is succinctly if a little wryly indicated in Louis MacNeice's implied stricture of Yeats's plays —'Browning made the lyric approximate to the drama; Yeats, working on Pater's principle that art is the removal of surplusage, makes the drama approximate to the lyric.'[1]

114

The period from the 1890s to the beginning of World War I was replete with poetic plays—not one of which has survived the relentless effects of time and change. The explanation for this depends very much on the answers to the question—why the confidence in poetic drama, and why the amount?

Although it is now popular to devalue or discount the Aesthetic movement of the 1880s and 1890s (largely because it seems to give off an aroma of cultural élitism) of which Pater was the English prophet and Wilde the most permissive acolyte, it was important. It is usually regarded as an eccentric, shallow backwater, but its effects were not only deep but long-lasting. T. S. Eliot, as his early poetry amply shows, had strong affinities with Aestheticism, and in *The Sacred Wood*, pays tribute to the work of Arthur Symons—the movement's most typical poet and, by far, its finest critic. The early Eliot may not have had the 'scent of patchouli' (the name of a rare Indian plant used by a reviewer to emblematize Symons's Aestheticism) about him, but, in a way, his early poems are not surprising when one has seen photographs of the young man—the uncarbuncular, somewhat sartorially over-sophisticated, slightly tired late teenage Eliot. The curiously blasé impressionism, the sense of the transient, the air of unexplained mystery were as common to Eliot as they were to Symons:

> Under the archway sheer,
> Sudden and black as a hole in the placarded wall,
> Faces flicker and veer,
> Wavering out of the darkness into the light,
> Wavering back into the night . . .[2]

> The brown waves of fog toss up to me
> Twisted faces from the bottom of the street,
> And tear from a passer-by with muddy skirts
> An aimless smile that hovers in the air
> And vanishes along the level of the roofs.[3]

The nature of the Aesthetic poet is well described by Symons:

> The moods of men! There I find my subject, there the region over which art rules: and whatever has been a mood of mine, though it has been no more than a ripple on the sea, and had no

115

> longer than the ripple's duration, I claim the right to render, if I
> can, in verse . . .[4]

The early Eliot would have found little there to cavil at.

So, Aestheticism made its mark on one of the century's
greatest poets and indeed, for a time, another great one fell
even more certainly and enthusiastically under its spell.
Symons regarded Yeats for some time as the chief poet of
Aestheticism, and his praise of Yeats amounts to a definition
of the Aesthetic search and mode.

> . . . it expresses, with a passionate quietude, the elemental
> desires of humanity, the desire of love, the desire of wisdom,
> the desire of beauty . . .[5]

The Aesthetic writers, with their concentration on the
pleasures of seeking concentrated sensuous and sensual
experiences, their emphasis on the Aesthetic potentiality of
any experience, their abrogation of moral content, their detes-
tation of factualism, their insistence on delicate but definite
form, and their assertion of the self-sufficiency of art, constituted a movement whose whole tendency was towards elevated and rare communication. To them this meant poetry,
'but even their prose enshrined their esoteric theory and practice, and often had the flavour, colour and rhythm of poetry'.

Pater's and Symons's criticism, Wilde's stories and plays all
either haunt the frontiers of poetic communication or penetrate into an interior where mysterious introspection, delicacy
of phrase, rhythmic associations of words—all the 'reverber-
ate gossip' of poetry—have their currency.

The Aesthetic movement was regarded as a literary backwater by those (a majority) to whom it seemed distinctly
un-English in its rejection of moral content, its embracing of
any experience. It had a dangerous foreignness about it; it
seemed to have its cultural sources not in established and
recognizable watersheds, but on the left bank, haunted by the
dwarfish shadow of Toulouse-Lautrec. It was, in fact, an
'alternative' culture. Kipling, Gissing, Shaw flourished while
Oscar Wilde was demonstrating the attractions of inspired
flippancy; Aubrey Beardsley, with consummate finesse, trod
the bounds between art and pornography, Frank Harris
o'erstepped them.

The Aesthetes were conditioned to accept poetic cadence as the norm of verbal communication and, with the example of the Elizabethan age, in particular, before them, the relationship of drama and poetry seemed to them unbreakable.

The theorists and practitioners of poetic drama gained allies from what, in a sense, might seem an unlikely place. Few poetic dramatists at any period would be expected to react with enthusiasm to any prominence given to the visual in the theatre. The set-designer seems, on face value, to be the natural adversary of the poet. Indeed, this has sometimes been proven to be true. But from the 1890s to the beginning of the 1920s developments in the theory and practice of stage-design paradoxically helped to prevent the course of poetic drama from being lost or submerged by the onset of prose-naturalism. The process was fired from the same tinder which gave poetic drama its renewed currency in the same period—the Aesthetic movement.

Adolphe Appia and Edward Gordon Craig reacted against the monolithic naturalism of contemporary stage setting and against the obsession with historical accuracy—exemplified most exhaustively in the revivals of Shakespeare in the latter quarter of the nineteenth century, and described by Symons as 'this costly and inartistic aim at reality'. They were, in fact, like the poets, reacting against naturalism. Moreover what they planned to replace it had, in concept, a great similarity to the highly formalized, symbolic, rhythmical style found so often in the poetic plays of the time. In 1900, a programme note to Craig's *Dido and Aeneas* claimed with succinct pride that the set was 'totally incorrect in all details'. But Craig was not always so succinct. At heart he harboured a thirst for the mysterious, the magical, the intangible. He had 'an almost religious concept of theatre, with the all-powerful Artist as high priest of a cult of beauty'. Small wonder that Symons, the arch-Aesthete, welcomed Craig, the dealer in the visual, with rapt joy.

What words were to the poetic dramatist, the actors were to Gordon Craig. Just as the words were at the beck and call of the poet, fitting into a pattern created by him to express what was to be expressed as aptly and beautifully as possible, so the actors must fit into the total visual design.

. . . Whoever is chosen . . . must move and speak as part and parcel of the design . . . the finer the actor the finer his intelligence and taste, and therefore the more easily controlled.[6]

Craig was a proselytizer for the poetry of theatre. He had tremendous respect for the poet in the theatre, but little confidence in the poet's knowledge of those arts which enable the play to be realized dramatically and to the full bent of its architecture and beauty. In his lack of confidence Craig showed great acumen. The irony is that his work in the theatre contributed significantly to the encouragement of poetic dramatists, but that the results were virtually all unmemorable.

This generalization applies, with some qualifications, to the work of W. B. Yeats. Most of his plays are unmemorable as dramatic pieces but they haunt the memory and the imagination of anyone who reads them because, simply, 'he put better verse into the drama than any writer in English after Shelley'. There is, indeed, an irony here of sharp proportions. Yeats was a prime figure in creating the Irish national theatre, he was the first poet of his era, but undistinguished as a dramatist.

Shaw conquered the literary tendencies of his prose and made himself into the century's greatest prose-dramatist —contributing, directly, nothing to Irish nationalism. His compatriot, Yeats, was always at the mercy of his greatest gift—the gift of a superb poetic imagination and matchless poetic speech—and never succeeded in becoming a dramatist in the true sense of the word. His vulnerability to his own gifts is shared by all those contemporaries of his who so eagerly grasped the nettle of poetic drama. They all failed for very similar reasons.

The impetus given to the poetic dramatist by the theorists and practitioners of non-naturalistic set-design had its own dangers. Craig makes it abundantly clear that the theatre-director (and by this he means someone like himself well versed in the visual language of theatrical communication) should pay little attention to the stage-directions of the poet-dramatist. His belief was that the atmosphere and architecture of the play would transmit itself to the director-designer so that he could then translate what he had experienced from the text into visual terms. What Craig would have done with

118

Widowers' Houses and Shaw's subsequent use of elongated stage-directions and descriptions has to be left to the imagination.

Yeats's plays[7] are written in a variety of forms and verbal patterns, including highly-wrought lyricism, a noble and bare heroic verse (as in *Deirdre*), a mixture of prose and verse, and almost wholly prose (as in *Cathleen ni Houlihan*). He employed the one-act Greek form for *On Baile's Strand* and *Purgatory*, contemporary naturalistic settings as in *The Words upon the Window Pane*, the ritualism of Japanese Noh plays for his *Plays for Dancers*. He experimented with choruses, masks, percussion and stringed instruments, symbolic movement. He mixed Japanese elements with Christian ones, and Christian myths with Irish pagan legends. Whatever the form and whether conspicuously artificed by the resources of poetry or not, all Yeats's plays are the work, most obviously, of a poet. The only distinction of any validity to make is between 'verse-plays' and 'non-verse plays'. Even those without the scaffolding of verse, or the architecture of metaphor and simile, are creations of a poetic imagination—both their strengths and weaknesses are the result of that heredity.

Yeats showed more sense of theatre than many of his contemporaries in his handling of stage-directions, and the considerable revisions to which he subjected a number of his plays show a tenacious attempt to economize on them—so that he would not be seen to do the work of the set-designer for him. Indeed, amidst the bewildering problems of chronology which the revisions set for us, one certainty emerges: Yeats progressively attempted to 'harden' his plays, to rid them of a quality which he once described as 'unmanly'—the roseate and sometimes sentimental lyricism which tints so much of his earlier poetry, and from which in time he ruthlessly released himself. In 1906 he wrote that, 'I have written a good many plays in verse and prose, and almost all those plays I have rewritten after performance, sometimes again and again, and every rewriting that has succeeded upon the stage has been an addition to the masculine element, an increase of strength in the bony structure.'[8] We might put this in another way and declare that it was an attempt to increase the dramatic potency and penetration of the work.

119

This is nowhere more apparent than in the revisions to stage-directions. Less and less do we find, as we come across the revisions and can have some confidence in a chronological progression, that Yeats tried to create 'pictures' out of his stage-directions. Yet he never lost the tendency to create a sort of frieze of action and he was persistently fascinated by light-effects. But, more often as he grew more experienced, he 'naturalized' the directions. In the 1904 version of *The King's Threshold* the King has to submit in company with his entourage. The direction reads 'Kneeling down before Seanchan'. In the 1906 revision the King, influenced perhaps by Yeats's reading of *Richard II,* does not kneel. The stage-direction is much more active—it does not lead to a tableau—'He has put the crown into Seanchan's hands'.

What Yeats attempts progressively to do with his stage-directions is an emblem of a much more important and larger process. Yeats's close association with some of the members of the famous Rhymers' Club[9] during the 1890s (he had shared accommodation with both Arthur Symons and Havelock Ellis—the one a stalwart rhymer, the other an unexpectedly shrewd literary critic) encouraged his attachment to Aestheticism. He set out to write plays which would be a dramatic equivalent of the highly ornate, ritualized poetry he was immersed in. One of the Rhymers, John Todhunter, made a remark which stuck in Yeats's imagination—he had said 'that dramatic poetry must be oratorical and I think now and then I lost courage, as it seems, and remembering that I had some reputation as a lyric poet wrote for the reader of lyrics'. In the confused history of Yeats's revisions of his plays it is at least quite clear that, as he gained more experience from his work with actors, and from observing his plays in performance, he progressively attempted to 'harden' the lyricism. This progression, and his consciousness of it, is simply and clearly expressed in *Autobiographies*:

> When I began to rehearse a play I had the defects of my early poetry; I insisted upon obvious all-pervading rhythm. Later on I found myself saying that only in those lines or words where the beauty of the passage came to its climax, must rhythm be obvious.[10]

Yeats's determination to write poetic drama (although he persistently calls it either 'dramatic verse' or 'verse-drama'), while, at the same time, acceding to the demands of the theatre for directness of communication and the expression of an 'internal life' in character rather than a vague if rich symbolism, was strong. He wished for clear 'manly' expression not only because his nature came more and more to demand it, nor only because the practicalities of theatre demanded it, but for another reason. His plays were to be poetical, certainly; they were to be, given his preoccupations, romantic, but, given his political aspirations, they had to convince and vitalize the imagination of his Irish audiences. They needed, that is, to be calls to action. But his strenuous work to accommodate his aspirations for Irish nationhood without compromising the poetry of the plays was doomed to failure by a number of factors. The primary one is the themes.

T. R. Henn's[11] summation of the four groups of plays together with a note of their central themes is useful. The first group concerns the Cuchulain legend 'with the perpetual image of the "amorous violent man", contending with men, and women, and with an "ungovernable sea"; which might represent "the many" in conflict with the hero'. Of these *On Baile's Strand* comes nearest to objectivizing the theme in dramatic terms.

The second group contains the haunting *The Countess Cathleen* (in which, Henn suggests, Yeats is depicted as Aleel), *The King's Threshold* (with which Yeats himself was well pleased), *Deirdre, The Only Jealousy of Emer, At The Hawk's Well, The Death of Cuchulain, A Full Moon in March* and *The King of the Great Clock Tower*. These involve 'the tragedy of love: the high tradition linked, always, to his own story; with a progressive reduction to its elements in the sexual act, but perceived always ambivalently; and with a constant preoccupation, in the later work, with old age and lost virility'.

Group three—*The Hour Glass, Calvary, The Resurrection, The Herne's Egg*—is mercifully quickly categorized: 'The soul of God: in particular the perversity of the "irrational force", the problems of Chance and choice, and the soul's "war with God".'

And finally, with commendable peremptoriness, Henn

describes group four—*The Words upon the Window Pane* and *Purgatory*. They are concerned with 'Ireland and the eighteenth-century tradition'.

It is always necessary when reading critical works on Yeats to remember that he had a singular ability to induce a kind of density of communication in even his finest, most sympathetic and most scholarly commentators. Even so lucid, shrewd and ironic a man as Louis MacNeice found it difficult to write about his fellow-countryman without some verbal opacity. But in this process there is a clear pointer to one of the main reasons for the failure of Yeats as a dramatist. The plays cannot be reduced to that kind of simplicity by which the reader or audience is convinced of their human credibility. It is simply true that the best drama is, in a very significant way, capable of this kind of reduction. Drama is an art which requires of all authors economy, selection, a basic spareness by which character, plot, incident, even theme, can be subtracted and held, so to say, in the hand for immediate inspection and relation to common experience. No one would declare that *King Lear* is not a profound play, yet there is within it this facility for reduction: the thematic profundity, the symbolic language, the complexities of character can be held in abeyance. They are, in fact, for all their largeness of meaning and implication, held within the basic simplicity we have noted. Yeats's plays are not. Symbolism, ritual, rhythm, 'philosophical' meaning, spill out, engulf the audience and place the reader in a situation similar to that in which Yeats's poems are read—but with this important difference: the poems are not compromised by Yeats's strained desire to be theatrically dramatic. They have their own drama and require only the theatre of our imaginations. The plays strain towards a recognition of the needs of the actor and the auditorium, but are overwhelmed by their own density. The irony is that Yeats seemed aware of this. He expressed the awareness, but the theory never achieved satisfactory practice. Writing of *The Countess Cathleen,* he says that a play passes through a process similar to that by which Christianity passed from philosophy to life:

> At first . . . there is a bundle of ideas, something that can be stated in philosophical terms . . . but gradually philosophy is

eliminated . . . until at last the only philosophy audible . . .
is the mere expression of one character or another.[12]

The very obsession with revision suggests a second reason
for the failure of the plays. We must recall that he wrote in
1906, "I have written a good many plays in verse and prose,
and almost all those plays I have rewritten after performance,
sometimes again and again . . .'[13] He even went to the extent
of allowing productions of his plays simply because he was
thereby enabled to see them and given an opportunity to test
and change them. Only one other major dramatist of this century displays anything similar to this near-obsession to change
his plays after production. This was T. S. Eliot, and it is not
without point to reflect that Eliot was as self-looking, self-
critical about his drama and its deficiencies as was Yeats. In
both writers there seems to be an in-built doubt about whether
drama is a natural means of communication for them. Both, in
their revisions and in their great volume of writing about the
craft and art of play-writing, always seem to be walking the
boundary between self-assurance and complete self-
deprecation. They do protest, perhaps, too much, worry and
hassle too frequently about the why's and wherefore's of
dramatic creation. They both give the impression that Dryden
gives—that the rigours of drama and theatre were too much
for them to grasp, that there was an imbalance in their imaginations, between a comprehension of what was required and
the will and skill to achieve it. Neither (but to very different
degrees) were capable of shutting the door on their massive
poetic selves when they stepped before the footlights.

The revisions, bewildering to the reader, which Yeats
indulged in nearly always succeeded in 'hardening' the poetic
line without in any profound or even significant way improv-
ing its dramatic architecture. Such superstructure cannot be
imposed on an already created basis—at least not to the extent
indulged in by Yeats—without bringing about a sense of
imposition, a kind of added posturing. Was ever a successful
and credible poetic drama written according to the following
plan?

I have finished the prose version of what is to be a new verse
play . . . I am trying to get the prose version typed that I may

123

> go through it with [Mrs Patrick Campbell]. She wants me to
> write, as she phrases it, with her at my elbow. I am rather
> inclined to try the experiment for once as I believe that I shall be
> inspired rather than thwarted . . .[14]

The third element in the chapter and verse of Yeats's failings
as a dramatist has to do with the nature of his imagination.
Creative energy may, to a degree, be self-propagating, but its
form and direction are often ordained by factors outside the
artist's complete control. The fires of the imagination are
banked by the artist's experience of the work of other artists,
both living and dead—but mostly the latter. The true creative
man knows that this process is necessary and occurs often
without being consciously initiated by him. Even the
'revolutionary' artist who wishes to explore new matter and
modes is wise to heed what it is he is rejecting, before he rejects
it; convention, tradition, powerful influence are always ready
to condition even the most avant-garde—and, for the artist
who is quite prepared to seek out their effects, their hold upon
him can be comprehensive.

The triumphal emergence of Yeats as a poet which is apparent in *The Green Helmet*[15] is an event which Shakespeare,
Milton, Shelley, the Aesthetic movement, French symbolism,
Irish history and legend propagated. The triumph was simply
but profoundly that of a creative writer who eventually
achieved an individual voice, which grew stronger and
stronger after he had allowed himself to be nurtured. They
played their part and then, like shadows, departed, leaving
Yeats with his own identity. He became the greatest symbolist
poet of the century; he used language symbolically yet with a
passion and unclouded eye which, in his best poetry, made all
his statements credible to human experience as well as
prophetic.

But, in drama, Yeats never completely threw off his
influences, and though he realized that symbolic language and
drama can so easily become enemies he never succeeded in
reconciling them. Shakespeare, Maeterlinck, the Japanese Noh
plays, Symons, dominated his eyes and ears to such an extent
that he could never find his own identity in drama. Symbolic
writing and pervading rhythm were so natural to his poetic

expression that he never succeeded in giving his plays, except
intermittently, that touch of familiarity with common experience and expression, by which drama achieves credibility for an
audience.

His plays, on their first production, were often enthusiastically applauded and commented upon, but none of them has
ever entered Time's repertory. In fact they are, now, more
likely to find more sympathetic readers, than auditors— who
are, today, less prepared to work hard with symbolic
language, characters and themes. They are, almost literally,
fascinating to read, and not only because of Yeats's immense
skill with language, both poetic, prose-poetic and prose.
Apart from their verbal richness they appeal to any imagination which is willing to accept symbolic, metaphysical and
mythical content. This is neither always easy nor, even to the
keenest mind, clear, but it is often intellectually and emotion
ally enriching and sometimes (as, for example, in *Cathleen ni
Houlihan*) presented with a meticulous regard for form and
logic. Reading the plays, except occasionally, brings a quick
realization that the dramatic nature of Yeats's imagination
(and no one who has read *Byzantium*, for example, can deny
his possession of it) is not really of the kind which works for
theatre. It is nearer to that of Keats (and no one who has read
Hyperion can deny his possession of it). There seems, however, not to have been an imperative need, in the initial motivation, for theatrical embodiment. Yeats, of course, wrote
plays on behalf of the Irish cause—to that extent he was
motivated to convey a message in a public form. But that
motivation seems, in a curious way, quite separate from the
drive behind the text. It is almost as if Yeats, having dedicated
himself to writing plays for a particular (and external) reason
then retired within the drama of his own imagination, often
peopling its stage with creatures who were never quite completely credible enough to support the demands of theatre but
were amply equipped to satisfy the needs of his immense
dramatic inner vision.

Cathleen ni Houlihan provides a good example of this. It has
a specific relevance to contemporary Ireland, which is sym-
bolized by the old woman. The play is a masterpiece of design,
the symbolic figure and the relationships of the other charac-

ters and their actions to it are impeccably clear. It has narrative tension, and the comparative simplicity of its dialogue is an effective emblem of the simple lives of the characters. Yet it seems to be at one remove from truly theatrical credibility. The ending, for example, is very awkward—where the 'message' overcomes theatrical feasibility. Again (and this is a common fault of Yeats—which reaches absurdly gauche proportions in *The Words upon the Window Pane*) it is often over-explicit in the way it provides information—'She turned into the gap that goes down where Mansteen and his sons are shearing sheep'; we may be inclined to say 'so what?' since this piece of intelligence is completely superfluous to the play.

To declare that Yeats's plays—especially those written for 'the cause'—are theatrically effete is to invite the incredulous scorn of those who may remember or have knowledge of some of the reactions of audiences to the first performances. Yeats himself was astonished at the sensation caused by *Cathleen ni Houlihan*. The occasions of these reactions, however, lead to the suspicion that we are here faced with special circumstances. The history of oratory, of drama, of theatre is well endowed with examples of speeches, plays, occasions, whose rapturous reception on the first performance had less to do with the quality of what was performed than with the nature and emotional condition of the auditors. All races are, doubtless, given to celebrating the desired end while seeming to applaud the apparent means. The Irish race is no exception. The test of worth does not lie in the ecstasy of conditioned responses but in the durability of the work itself. It is irrevocably, even ruthlessly, true, that not one of Yeats's plays which were designed for the proselytizing of the cause, has shown much theatrical durability. Even more telling, few of them have shown any 'political' durability. When they were originally rapturously or even violently received it seems now to have been for reasons that had often little to do with their innate quality, or lack of it.

Yeats's plays are, in the final analysis, to be seen as cult-drama. Every one of them is attached, in some way, to a special pleading. Some satisfy the imaginative appetites of those who are stirred by ancient history—half-fact, half-fiction; some appeal to the esoteric devotees of symbolic communication; some quicken the pulse-rates of the romantically-inclined who are patient and perhaps, indeed, civilized enough to respond to exotic narrative and opaque language; some—and these are, dramatically, the best—incite the political and patriotic to emotional responses. All of these responses, except possibly the last, could as well be satisfied by lyrical and narrative poetry. There is very little in the plays, as a whole, of that dramatic inevitability which convinces you that what is said could be expressed in no other way. It is not without significance that even the most perceptive of Yeats scholars (and his poetic eminence has attracted a formidably distinguished collection) laud the plays for all sorts of reasons but very few of them include, in those reasons, any consideration of the relationship between what Yeats communicates in his plays, and the manner of communication. One, for example, falls back on such phrases as 'superb dramatic skill', 'extremely effective on the stage', 'masterpiece of dramatic intensity'.[16] These are emotive and, in the long run, meaningless as explanations or definitions of Yeats's dramatic ability. The clearest view of Yeats's dramatic status is expressed not by his eminent literary commentators but by those who have painstakingly followed his career in the theatre and observed his own doubts about himself. A representative conclusion is this:

> Yeats's whole-hearted dedication to drama for more than five years is impressive . . . But it is difficult not to believe that he felt himself to be still, first and foremost, the lyric poet that he had once been . . . His withdrawal from active participation in the work of the Abbey Theatre in 1910 may have been precipitated by outward circumstances, but it was probably determined also by a conviction that he had recovered his natural medium of expression—lyric verse.[17]

Yeats's poetry was tempered and refined by the rigours of discipline he imposed upon himself in his attempt to write drama. But if he was not a natural dramatist, there are two features of his work which are important and to be emphasized. The first is the immense verbal felicity and beauty and emotional passion he brought to speech that was written to be spoken. The second was his influence. Some, like his near-contemporary, Bottomley, and the younger Stephen Philips, aspired to write on similar themes and could not help communicating in an echo of his manner. Thus, he became partly responsible for a cult of poetic drama in the first two decades of the twentieth century which, even then, hardly found the ear of more than a small minority and, now, seems recherché, bizarre, quixotic, at times quaint. Moreover, the implications of 'cult' have a precise connotation. Many of the plays written from 1919 to the last one, *The Death of Cuchulain*, in 1939 were not only directed towards creating a reaction to conventional theatre in which there was, for him, too little that was as he put it, 'remote, spiritual, and ideal', but had another intention. They were written as closet plays, to be performed not only to a very limited audience (no more than fifty) but only for the 'aficionados'—in a very special sense. He claimed to have invented a form of drama, distinguished, indirect, and symbolic, and having no need of mob or Press to pay its way. He called it an 'aristocratic form'.

But his influence had a firmer aspect to it. He was certainly the first poet of the twentieth century and perhaps the first great lyrical poet ever to express so eloquently, in his essays, letters and prose-pieces, the conviction that the poet had a direct responsibility to his society. If ever a man exemplified the truth of Shelley's remark that poets are the 'unacknowledged legislators' of mankind, it was Yeats. For him, poets could call to action and, for a time, he believed that the form of drama was the best in which to embody the call. The persistence of his attempts to prove this, his authority, quite apart from the nature of the times was, quite literally, an inspiration to many later twentieth-century poets who, at a time of crisis in Western Europe, tried to emulate the ideals of Yeats the dramatist. These were the 'thirties poets'. Like him they were attempting to write an urgent drama of man in his raw environment, but, like Yeats, too, their imaginative sensibilities forced them, at the same time to try and express the inner world of man. As Yeats did, they failed—with a certain nobility.

7 The Interlude of the 1930s—the Poet in Society

For someone born in the 1920s the 1930s was the time when childhood came and went. For someone whose environment and education in the 1930s gave a chance to be aware of that strange, sensitive and often poignant relationship between a time's culture and a time's political and social life, it was a period when what was written seems to have had a special relationship with what happened. Forward-looking teachers of English with memories spattered by World War I contrasted the socially uncommitted felicities of the Georgian poets with the fierce polemics of the new avant-gardists—Auden, MacNeice, *et al*. All decades are conscious of themselves, but the 1930s was unique in the twentieth century in that its self-consciousness very much involved the contribution of the artist to the social and political activities of society. In the twentieth century, in England, there has not been another decade in which the artist was so confidently accepted as an integral and important part of the society:

> All the others translate: the painter sketches
> A visible world to love or reject;
> Rummaging into his living, the poet fetches
> The images out that hurt and connect.[1]

In no other decade have so many artists (and not only verbal ones) dedicated themselves to reflecting and commenting upon the actualities and realities of day-to-day society. The depression, the unemployed, the rise of fascism, the sentimental embracing of marxism, the war in Spain, the inequalities of class, the quest for a new kind of social democ-

129

racy—these formed the material out of which plays, poems, essays and novels were written.

Drama, being the most public of the verbal arts, played an important part in this process. But perhaps most remarkable is that so many competent, and a few remarkable, plays were written, by people whose main literary work was the writing of poetry. What many of the nineteenth-century poets failed at, many of the 1930s poets succeeded in—MacNeice, Spender, Norman Nicholson, Terence Tiller, W. H. Auden.

The most distinguished poet of them all—and the most braggadoccio dramatist, Auden—was on his own testimony excited and influenced by Eliot. Indeed most of the poets with pretensions to the writing of drama were very politically and socially sensitive, but they were also aesthetically very alive. They felt a responsibility to use their craft and art in the service of their society, but it was to Eliot that they looked for guidance.

Eliot seemed to have forged a flexible contemporary poetic language. His influence, chronologically speaking, went further back. Eliot's poetry from the beginning was essentially a speaking poetry. It was poetry meant to be heard. This is one reason why he turned towards drama. In their belief that poetry should speak for and to its own society, the younger generation sought for a speaking language. Many did not follow Eliot slavishly—they often demurred from his theme and style. What they could not and did not do was to escape the example of his speaking words. Auden's first play *The Dance of Death* was produced in a double-bill with Eliot's *Sweeney Agonistes* by the Group Theatre (1935). Auden who, as Francis Scarfe wrote, 'represents a sort of A.B.C. of the poetry of the 'thirties', had an innate dramatic potential. Many of his poems have a persona within them, who often seems to escape from the page to become embodied. Single lines leap out of them as if from the working text of a play—'He walks out briefly to infect a city', ' . . . clutching a little case'.[2] His verbal texture makes much of the element of dramatic surprise and, like Eliot, but with a certain recklessness, he puts the idiomatic and the high-flying to bed with one another. His imagery is intensely visual. Again like Eliot he is basically a cerebral poet, but with the capacity to express his ratiocination

130

in visual terms which are dramatically conceived. This is apparent throughout the whole body of Auden's work and perhaps even more significantly it applies as much to intensely lyrical poems like the famous 'Lay your sleeping head'[3] as it does to longer and more intellectually weighty ones. In fact there is a quality about many of Auden's shorter lyrics which is reminiscent of Shakespeare's sonnets—they tell a story, so to speak, dramatically, with a strong sense of incident and of characterization.

John Lehmann, the distinguished chronicler of the 1930s, says in his book *New Writing in Europe*,[4] that because the 1930s was a period of rapid change, moral conflict and violent action, it lent itself to dramatic expression. The period from 1789 to the end of the century could be described with the same words—but where is its drama?

The 1930s, like the 1590s, was one of those comparatively rare periods when the accidents of individual talent and the pressures of the time came together to produce a distinctive and distinguished body of dramatic work. This comparison holds though no qualitative parity can be claimed. The two periods may be compared in that their dramatists were preoccupied with writing about the theory of drama, they were self-consciously 'poetic' dramatists, and they examined their own craft and art minutely as well as that of their peers and contemporaries. Auden, MacNeice, Spender and Cecil Day Lewis (the latter being the least 'dramatic' of them) wrote, both in book and periodical form, distinguished critiques of the function of poetry, in both its dramatic and non-dramatic roles. The emphasis is on language; indeed most of the thirties' poetic dramatists were as comprehensively deficient in the knowledge of staging as they were fitfully proficient in their creation of dramatic language. Auden and Isherwood's *The Dog Beneath the Skin* shows a quixotic and opulent disregard for the problems of staging—yet what is to be noted particularly is that once the scene has been set in the auditor's imagination, a simple reading aloud or silently of the text, cannot fail to show its rich dramatic nature.

The reliance on verbal efficacy goes to the extent of a quite uninhibited use of highly wrought language—often involving opaque symbolism as in Yeats. Stephen Spender's *Trial of a*

Judge and Auden and Isherwood's *The Ascent of F6* are trapped in a verbal and conceptual prison out of which meaning escapes only with difficulty.

In the theatre the audience has no time (and, indeed, is not prepared to give the time) to chew over concepts and words. The most abstruse and most profound thoughts are of no consequence or relevance to drama unless they can be expressed in a way which is immediately apprehended. To this extent all the poetic dramatists of the thirties suffered from being unable to separate their 'poetic' selves from their 'dramatic' selves. Too often, in their plays, the voices that speak are those of the poet himself or herself. The disengagement of the creator is incomplete. Only MacNeice (and this more particularly in his later radio plays) and Auden (and this fitfully) were capable of the disengagement out of which character is born and drama made active, external to the poet's imagination.

It is much to the credit of the poetic dramatists that their plays, however flawed many of them are, concern themselves with the time's issues. If we read now Anne Ridler's *The Shadow Factory* or Auden and Isherwood's *The Dog Beneath the Skin,* as examples, we are brought up sharp at the graphic and urgent way in which these dramatists show and warn their society—'show their eyes and grieve their hearts'. For this body of poetic drama had no 'absurdist' withdrawal from comment or proselytization, or moral commitment; it was, on the contrary, a fervent body of work dedicated to the task of helping to shore up the civilized values by eloquent warnings:

> Ring all the bells, hang out the flags
> Amaze Europe with proclamatory acts
> Break through the streets like a waterfall
> Armies of men, destroying all
> Twigs and voices of opposition
> With insuperable derision.[5]

Auden, that 'A.B.C.' of the times, can serve, together with his collaborator and, indeed, his stabilizer, Christopher Isherwood, as an example of the inventive urgency of the drama of this time.

132

The Dog Beneath the Skin, the best and liveliest and most verbally pyrotechnic of the plays of Auden and Isherwood, is not entirely written in verse. In fact it presents a kaleidoscope of written forms from conversational prose/speech to superbly lyrical verse, taking in doggerel, blank verse, rhyming couplets and other forms on its way. Auden was as aware as was Eliot when he wrote *Murder in the Cathedral* of the need to avoid the dreaded minefield of Shakespeare's iambics. But the connection ends there. Eliot's changes of style are, on the whole, under very tight control and one has the distinct sense that they are planned. Auden's give an (admittedly) exhilarating impression of being ad hoc. Like a schoolboy in a bumper-car he swerves from one direction to another—sometimes avoiding collision, often describing the most superb manoeuvres and, somehow, avoiding a final catastrophe.

But if the technical control of variety is minimal, or seems so, we have to acknowledge that in every form he uses he displays a versatility of expression. Auden, not Eliot or Yeats, was master of the greatest number of verse forms since Tennyson. The old generalization that equated the thirties, Auden and his poetry solely with *vers libre* is, of course, ludicrous. He was a subtle technician, if a wayward one.

The Dog Beneath the Skin is like a dramatic fairground, an excellent stimulus to the glands and to the emotions. Its intention is satirical and exhortatory, intending to show us our follies and warn us of the quislings inside our own temperaments and society which will help to destroy us while fascism waits to deliver the final blow. The main area of attack is on the decayed and distorted values of Western Christendom, and it is in this area that the most impressive use of dramatic language is to be found.   Auden, in his poetry, reveals a very strong sense of the dramatic, and he uses an impressive number of means to embody this sense in the verse line—surprising metaphor and simile, a 'metaphysical' yoking together of apparently incompatible images to produce a sensational verbal effect, metrical and rhythmical variety, the juxtaposition of the highly literary and the idiomatic. Even at his most lyrical, some elements of the dramatic inform the verse-line.

In the choruses to *The Dog* which are written in a variety of forms varying from a strict metric to a slack prose, the most effective pieces are those in which there is a high lyrical content:

> Now through night's caressing grip
> Earth and all her oceans slip,
> Capes of China slide away
> From her fingers into day
> And the Americas incline
> Coasts towards her shadow line.[6]

There are two kinds of dramatic effect here. The first is the imaginative power which produces the image, and the second is the effect of relentless inevitability produced by the strict rhyme-scheme. The whole is dramatic because we can see what is being told us so vividly and, simultaneously, feel the implications of what we see.

But there is a third effect which becomes apparent only when the lines immediately following are included:

> Now the ragged vagrants creep
> Into crooked holes to sleep.

Such a sudden declension from the general to the particular, from the huge comprehensive sweep to the small detailed observation is typical of Auden's lyrical imagination. This, too, is drama of a kind—the drama of contrast.

Often, the contrast produces irony from mere shock—as if the reader or listener, having been prepared for one kind of experience, finds that it is a very different one that is being expressed. Auden employs irony, not only of this kind, but of the more obvious kind, throughout his poetry and his plays. This conventional kind has its dramatic effect, but this time it is achieved by tone of voice in contest with what is being said:

> Man is changed by his living: but not fast enough.
> His concern to-day is for that which yesterday did not occur.
> In the hour of the Blue Bird and the Bristol Bomber,
> His thoughts are appropriate to the years of the Penny Farthing:
> He tosses at night who at noonday found no truth.

Auden's language, be it formal verse, loose verse, prose, is dramatic in these ways. It is a 'bitter-sweet' language, not unlike that employed by Congreve. In Auden's case the flavour is attained by setting what is natural, beautiful, formal, worthy, important, large, against all the opposites. The experience of life which Auden's language implies is essentially a composite, a bitter-sweet irony, and everywhere he looks he finds this:

> To Red Lamp Street you are all invited;
> Here Plato's halves are at last united.

His language has a remarkable athleticism, but this seems, curiously, to prevent him going beyond the kind of dramatic effects we have noted into a deeper and more comprehensive drama. He is incapable of creating more than a shadow of a character and Isherwood his collaborator may well be responsible for anything more substantial than shadow we may occasionally think we can discern. The reader or auditor becomes fascinated by the way things are said and what is said, but there is no realization of the nature, in human credible terms, of the character who is saying them. In fact what we hear, all the time, is one or other of the many superb impersonations that Auden was capable of—but, underneath, it is always his voice and, indeed, it is always his attitude that we know we are listening to.

In so many ways, and in this instance we must have a care not to underrate the possible contribution of Isherwood, Auden displays many of the qualities of a dramatist while actually achieving a mastery of only a limited number of dramatic effects. The use of the music-hall modes of communication in *The Dog* is both dazzling and often very effective. In the Destructive Desmond episode (Act III, Scene ii) which takes place in a cabaret at the Nineveh Hotel, all the usages are on display at their best. It is one of the most telling pieces of mordant and purposeful comedy in twentieth-century drama. In the scene an inoffensive and unsuspecting Art Expert is called from the audience by the popular comedian, Destructive Desmond, and is mocked, reviled and reduced to despair while the audience progresses from laughter to howling derision. In the meantime their popular idol is hacking a Rembrandt to pieces. The name, Destructive Desmond, the use of a 'victim' or 'fall guy', the style—bantering, hectoring, cajoling, the technique of rhetorical questions,

135

the appeals to the audience by the comic who knows they are his allies because he gives them what they want, the 'jokes' (in this case malevolent, sinister, 'sick') hidden inside a boyish bonhomie—is essentially music-hall. Only Eliot, for very different purposes, employed it, in English drama, with equal success, though John Osborne, in *The Entertainer*, realized its potentiality for polemical drama.

Auden and Isherwood's plays have shared the fate of most of their contemporaries in the 1930s—that is, they are rarely if ever produced. They lie, like so much from that nervous, misunderstood, but culturally prolific era, in that part of older people's memories where the museum pieces of history are consigned. For younger generations they might never have been written. Their plays and those of their contemporaries who devoted much of their writing to verse and poetic drama, are not great plays but they are, as a body, very distinguished pieces of literature, and some of them are theatrically very potent.

But apart from this, the poetic dramatists of the thirties believed, like Yeats, that a poet's duty was to reflect, to comment upon and to warn and to guide their society. They rightly believed that the quickest way to mankind's consciousness is through drama, but they all suffered, like Yeats, from the fatal flaw of being introspective poets first and dramatists second. Like Yeats they possessed, as do most good poets, most of the qualities needed to create dramatic effects, but few of the qualities required for complete drama, and very few of those needed for theatrical representation. Auden, like MacNeice, Spender, Ridler, Nicholson and many others of that generation of dramatists, suffered basically from a lack of verbal economy. For example, they possessed visually fecund imaginations, but no sense that theatrical representation does not require the visual opulence they display. We may marvel and be stirred by Auden's picture of the continents sliding in and out of night in his Chorus, and one or two such opulences of the imagination are easily accommodated by theatre. But the poetic imagination which has no theatrical sense tends to compound such visual splendours. When this happens, true drama slows up, falters, and dies, leaving only vagne memories behind.

136

Shakespeare was well aware of this and he, indeed, is, at times, guilty (as in *Cymbeline*) of exercising his visual imagination at the expense of his theatrical technique. But he, unlike Auden and his poetic contemporaries, had, in any case, one huge safeguard. He was able to abstract himself from his imagination, and people it with credible characters. Shakespeare was neither simply poet nor simply dramatist, but complete poet/dramatist. The poets of the thirties, like all true poets, constituted the citizenry of their own imaginative worlds—and this proved fatal to the credibility of their attempts to make characters and to the movement, pace and variety of their dramas.

There is a very important paradox here. The thirties' poetic dramatists were writing, many of them (like Spender) with an anxious sincerity, about society; they were vitally concerned to write the drama of man in society. But, as poets, deeply reflective, introspective, they could not, at the same time, prevent themselves from involving their own inner world. All great dramatists involve the inner and outer worlds—Shakespeare did—but only exceptional dramatists can create an amalgam of a kind which is truly dramatic and completely credible. The thirties' poetic dramatists failed as dramatists because they could not achieve that amalgam. The wonder is that, within their flawed and sprawling plays, there is a body of poetry which not only evokes the bitter-sweet flavour of that decade but is distinguished and memorable.

T. S. Eliot, a decade older than most of the poetic dramatists who flourished in the thirties, was the one man whose work has survived, even though he has been frequently condemned for being poet first, dramatist second. The younger men learned much from him. Of them all, he was the most profound in his dedication both to inner man and outer man, and he is a focal figure in the movement that poetic drama has gradually taken during the course of the century.

8 T. S. Eliot—the Dramatist in Search of a Language

There are many who believe that Eliot was not a natural dramatist; on the other hand there are many who, having grown up with his poems, cannot shake off their assumption that he was a great poet. There is a connection between the two judgments—a simple but important one. The great poet, always and inevitably excepting Shakespeare, has rarely proved himself to be a natural man of the theatre, though many have tried to be. The self-examining solitude out of which the highest poetic creations seem to be born seems inimical to the extrovertive world of the theatre where ideas and words must seem to express not the creator but his creations—the dramatist has to disengage himself from himself, to a degree, before drama is possible. A poem like *The Four Quartets* is the testimony of a profound quest, most of which is undertaken inside the soul and imagination of the single solitary man—even to attempt an externalization of what has happened inside the man seems a hopeless task.

In consequence even the unarguable testimony to Eliot's continuing interest in play-writing, in his own plays and critical writings, is insufficient, for some people, to establish him as a genuine dramatist—at least not without some pursing of the critical lips.

The 'inner' quality of most of the poems, and the assumption that Eliot was an ascetic (which, in fact, he was not) are, to a large extent, responsible for this. But there are some other, less emotive reasons. Eliot seems, at times, to be doing his utmost to cast doubt on his dramatic work. He was given to (occasionally pernickety) self-analysis; there is some evidence of a tinkering with the plays (particularly *Murder in the Cathedral*) after the first production, of a kind which suggests he had doubts about their dramatic rightness; there is, of course, considerable evidence of his preoccupation—amounting, at times, to a near-obsession—with the problems of dramatic language; as if he doubted his own verbal facility. There is, too, a sense, as we hear or read his plays, of a language-pattern that is 'constructed' to give a particular effect. Spontaneity seems, from time to time, worked at. Sometimes the language and what it conveys seem over-cerebral, and the themes of his plays seem recondite, remote from familiar human association and experience. We feel (with *The Family Reunion* as the obvious example) that some of the characters are rather 'special'—capable of unusual experience, possessed of sense and intelligence which is so extraordinary as to be remote. Shaw's characters occasionally give this impression but, in the long run, they are seen to be as vulnerable as the rest of us to the slings and arrows of outrageous fortune. Some of Eliot's characters seem beyond fortune.

All of this is partly true, but not true enough to uphold the premise that he was not a natural dramatist. We need go no further than one of his poems to sense the man's innate dramatic instinct. Inside that erstwhile 'difficult' poem *The Waste Land*[1] the glorious active lucidity of true drama is to be found. Its most positive appearance is in the 'pub' scene of *A Game of Chess* in Section II.

No 'absurd' dramatist, intent upon aching our conscious minds with ironic futility, could do better than this. We are in a pub; it is the evening, the ladies are allowed by temporarily relenting husbands or 'male friends' to join the immense ritual of the bar. The ladies, responding to an ancient reflex, consort at tables, separated from the menfolk who reside at the bar. From time to time drinks pass, as if computer-programmed, from man to woman. The winter evening maunders on with smells of pickles from the bar, and the women drone. The drama is in the locale, the quite sensational human revelations, the choric shouts, 'Hurry up please its time', of the time-pestered publican, and the pitiless irony of the context against which the whole sordid mess is given us to be judged—'Good night, sweet ladies'.

139

There is a natural dramatist here—in fact *The Waste Land* is a dramatic poem which involves the theatrical imagination to a very high degree. This is to say that the poem is not merely dramatic in the sense in which Browning's dramatic monologues are—where ideas and emotions are made to move excitingly in relationship to one another. Eliot's drama is one which contains the Browning version but has, in addition, that inescapable quality of demanding embodiment in visual and aural terms. The nature of the main changes is, in itself, interesting. What, in the uncorrected typescript is slightly artificial 'common speech' has, after alteration by Eliot become much more authentically demotic in vocabulary and tone: 'If you don't like it you can get on with it.'

We may be thankful that we can see the changes wrought in the poem during the later stages of composition—some of them effected by Eliot alone and others on the advice of Pound and, one infers, at times of his first wife. The picture of 'the young man carbuncular' in the final version of the poem is a splendid example of Eliot's dramatic use of mock, indeed almost pathetic, heroics, but the original version seems to have an even sharper dramatic presence and is, in fact, given one short line of self-revealing dialogue. The early versions of *The Waste Land*[2] which have been preserved are proof positive that the imaginative power which Eliot was exerting during the early period of his working life was not, as so many commentators have claimed, exclusively crammed with the formidable intellectual results of years of intensive academic study, but contained a considerable and lively strain of dramatic and even theatrical potency.

Those speeches, so characteristic of *The Family Reunion*, where a ritual movement can clearly be seen to be counterpointed by unexpected plainness of statement and, at times, of vocabulary, have their early appearances in *The Waste Land*:

> What have we given?
> My friend, blood shaking my heart
> The awful daring of a moment's surrender
> Which an age of prudence can never retract
> By this, and this only, we have existed
> Which is not to be found in our obituaries
> Or in memories draped by the beneficent spider

Or under seals broken by the lean solicitor
In our empty rooms.

The presence of a speaking person, and of an atmosphere of
some tension between this person and an unseen, unheard,
other one, is very powerful here. Even to read it silently does
not diminish an impression that we are hearing embodied
people talking.

The most directly characterized persona in the poem is
Madame Sosostris. Her words not only cry out for speaking,
they ask to be spoken in a certain way—and, if they are replied
correctly, they inevitably create the character. We have, first
of all, the oracular parade of paraphernalia—the display of the
mystery:

> . . . Here, said she,
> Is your card, the drowned Phoenician sailor,
> (Those are pearls that were his eyes. Look!)
> Here is Belladonna, the Lady of the Rocks,
> The lady of situations.
> Here is the man with three staves, and here the Wheel,
> And here is the one-eyed merchant, and this card,
> Which is blank, is something he carries on his back,
> Which I am forbidden to see . . .

But, within this panorama, the shrewd details of the
woman—and indeed of the type—are placed unerringly. The
'special' attention being given to the client is quickly established—'Here is your card'; a hint, a wink and a nod to pull the
client in to a shared knowingness—'the lady of situations'; the
'which I am forbidden to see' fulfils two functions—first it
strongly suggests that the tone of voice is implying the meaning—'which *even I* am forbidden to see'. So the plot thickens,
the awe rises. But, viewed from the outside, by us, as observers, as audience, the line is a comment on the character itself.
To us, not awed, its evasive pomposity is ludicrous. To us, it
has the same effect as Dylan Thomas's masterly, comically
oblique charlatan:[3]

Mrs Dai Bread Two: I see a featherbed. With three pillows on it. And
a text above the bed. I can't read what it says. There's great
clouds blowing. Now they have blown away. God is Love, the
text says.

141

The 'personal' message to the client comes swiftly—'Fear death by Water'—and, we are assured, the outstretched monetary palm is produced just as quickly—'Thank you'. The comfort of satisfactory payment is expressed in the expression of a certain earned intimacy with the client—'If you see dear Mrs Equitone . . .' And, finally, the end-of-session-remark, the hand-on-the-door-knob dismissal—'One must be so careful these days.' An actress courageous enough to place her talent at the disposal of this very short scene—for that is what it amounts to—could achieve a superb embodiment of typed character, of place, and of a slightly dark comedy.

The common critical view of Eliot's dramatic work is that the first testimony of his ability and his quest for true dramatic expression are to be found in the *Choruses from 'The Rock'*. These were published in 1934 one year before the festival edition of *Murder in the Cathedral,* whose style they are said to have considerably helped to form. Without denying the truth of the second premise, we should take note that the evidence of a natural dramatic imagination is amply seen in *The Waste Land* published twelve years earlier. It is true that *The Choruses from 'The Rock'* and *Sweeney Agonistes,* published in 1932, have a more experimental spirit, so far as dramatic expression is concerned, but it is, nevertheless, surprising that *The Waste Land* has been virtually ignored as a very potent evidence of Eliot's highly sensitive awareness of drama, and his ability to create it.

Throughout that part of his working life in which the writing of drama occupied a large section, and certainly in the earlier period, Eliot was searching for a language. But he became obsessed, it would seem, with the need to find a language which would not only speak to its own time with the words and tones and rhythms and associations of its time, but also be capable of expressing deeper and, therefore, less immediately articulate feelings and ideas. In a radio broadcast in 1936 he wrote:

> The verse-dramatist must operate on you on two levels at once . . . It is fatal for a poet trying to write a play, to hope to make up for defects in the movement of the play by bursts of poetry which do not help the action. But underneath the action, which should be perfectly intelligible, there should be a musical

pattern which intensifies our excitement by reinforcing it with feeling from a deeper and less articulate level.

An early and rather blatant example of this occurs, of course, in the section quoted above which involves the pub dialogue. The 'intelligibility' of what is being said about Lil's husband, and indeed Lil's own iniquities, is crystal clear, but underneath this immediate action, this straight speech, there is the irony which needs to be expressed. Eliot does it by grafting immediate speech on a line from *Hamlet*:

Good-night, sweet ladies . . .

There can be little doubt that the more complex irony is gained by the juxtaposition of the crudely prosaic and the finely poetic. Further, we are perfectly aware that the irony owes a lot to the clash of the strident Lil, Bill, goonight, ta ta, with the superb musical pattern of 'Good night, sweet ladies, good night, good night'.

But he soon learned, indeed already probably knew in his heart and mind, that other dramatists' 'musical patterns'—especially Shakespeare's—would lead him nowhere. Eliot, in company with many of his contemporaries who thought about poetic drama, and wrote it, seems to have been very much afraid of allowing his working imagination to be trapped in Shakespeare's iambics. His instinct was absolutely right—and he had only to look at the dismal record of nineteenth-century poetic drama to know that it was.

But although Eliot realized the extent to which Shakespeare had forged for himself the kind of comprehensive dramatic language for which he was searching he never succeeded in sustaining the kind of fusion of disparate elements which is so characteristic of Shakespeare. Perhaps, indeed, he was so concerned with avoiding the iambic trap that he lost his direction.

Shakespeare fused the needs of immediate articulacy and deep communication. In doing this he not only was able to relate his drama to the idioms of his day, to express the inexpressible, but to provide the actor with eminently speakable speech. There are two things which actors have traditionally required from language in a play. The first is the opportunity to seem 'real', actual in speech and therefore in character; the second is to have the chance to display a vocal ability to mesmerize the audience with the magic of spoken music—to express the hitherto inexpressible. Shakespeare's language allows them to do this—the immediate, the apparently actual, the now, are in a constant state of vibrating harmony with the ineffable, the abstract, the indefinable.

If Eliot had paid more attention to the fact that Shakespeare's practice was absolutely in line with Eliot's own principles and less to iambic-dodging, he might have fashioned a more passionately active language structure. And although he was very sympathetic to the problems of the actor, in some of his plays he might have been more helpful in providing them with what they invariably look for.

But Eliot's sympathy was no mere abstraction. The account of his close relationship with E. Martin Browne and others—men involved in the practicalities of staging drama —shows how assiduously Eliot tried to discover the best means of expression for his actors to speak and his audiences to hear. It is almost entirely a matter of speculation as to the effects on his work if he had not relied so much upon the theoretical and practical advice of others. Eliot, curiously for one with a reputation as a lone eagle, was very open to be advised, and, if convinced, to change a text. One may have some doubts about all that Ezra Pound did to and for Eliot's poems, after reading the emendations. It is far less easy to decide about the influence Martin Browne had on the plays. Indeed, the world of theatre is one in which collaboration is the rule rather than the exception. No dramatist is a true dramatist who expects his text to ride through the ranks of actors, directors, even stage-designers unsullied and virgin. The question is—is the play's unity maintained, or is it, in all, a different thing from that which left the author's hand? Unity can still be preserved even if constituent parts are changed, mutated, even, to a degree, removed. The changes incited by Elia Kazan to Tennessee Williams's text of *Cat on a Hot Tin Roof* are a graphic illustration of the implications of what can happen to the author's conception. There is a certain poignancy in Williams's staunch but worried adherence to his faith that Kazan was right to insist upon the changes.

The evidence, largely provided by Martin Browne himself,

for the most part suggests that there were no fundamental interferences with Eliot's plays. What is less easy to accept is that Eliot was always given the right advice, or that the right advice was available. There spring to mind the examples of verbal density in *The Family Reunion,* the slowness of thematic develpment, which Eliot himself comments on in *Poetry and Drama,*[4] the sometimes insipid verbal texture of *The Cocktail Party* and the artificiality of some of the characters' comings and goings. Above all, perhaps, there is the case of the Four Knights in *Murder in the Cathedral.* The intrusion of their prose, the over-explication of their function, has been frequently commented upon. What is the more surprising is that the advent of their prose scene flies absolutely against Eliot's often-stated conviction that a play should not mix prose and poetry. No one seems to have pointed out to him that the Knights' scene and Becket's sermon contradict him.

Nevertheless, on the evidence that we so far have (and we have to remember that Eliot's side of the matter has not yet been published) it would appear that the plays as we have them are the result of careful writing, caring collaboration and agreed compromise on certain changes. It is right to stress this (albeit, in the absence of further evidence, an interim conclusion) because any discussion of Eliot's language has to contend with the quite extensive number of changes between manuscript and typescript, typescript and first publication, first publication and subsequent ones. To record and allocate the source of these changes is a formidable task and one which cannot be safely undertaken until the one-sided body of evidence—largely in the writings of Martin Browne—can be related to any body of posthumous evidence, so far withheld, from Eliot himself. Eliot's plays in their present published form would certainly seem to represent a very valid source for critical comment, since he himself supervised their publication. Only time and revelations will show whether or not they constitute a rationalization which hides precise truth.

A great deal of ink and thinking has been expended on analysing Eliot's metrics—as if metrics were as important as words: the variety of metrical forms in *Murder in the Cathedral,* the poetic line 'of varying length and varying number of syllables, with a caesura of three stresses' of *The Family Reunion,* the loosely accented language structure of *The Cocktail Party* and the flat monotony of pace and stress in *The Elder Statesman.* But, too often, there is a concentration on the metrical bases of his various plays at the expense of other factors that make up the totality of his dramatic language. Metrics support but they do not wholly constitute what we may call the expressiveness of dramatic language. It is as misleading to confine commentary on Eliot's language to his, albeit very versatile, metrical structure, as it is to assume that Shakespeare's language is all iambics.

For instance, in *Sweeney Agonistes,*[5] which is taken by many to be an explicit declaration by Eliot of his dramatic intentions and inventiveness, the *Fragment of a Prologue* has an insidious beat, but it only becomes completely hypnotic in its effect because of the interplay between the beat and (firstly), verbal repetitions and (secondly), the sound of words. 'Pereira' is like a rattle of kettledrums: 'How about Pereira?', 'What about Pereira?', 'You can have Pereira', 'He's no gentleman, Pereira'. Throughout *Sweeney,* this interplay between sound and rhythm—although, of course, it is not always the same rhythm—is both strong and effective. It goes deeper than the creation of a generalized emotional reaction in the listener; it helps to create character. Notice how in Dusty's speeches the repetitions and the emphases on 'I think' and 'I hope' and 'she says' and 'she hopes', and 'mustard and water', not only give a remarkable impersonation of real speech, but help to identify the flapdoodle mind of the speaker. Her lengthened pronunciation of 'Goooood-bye' clinches the over-gushing personality who is speaking.

The most remarkable technical feature of *Sweeney Agonistes* is the evidence of Eliot's ear for contemporary idiom and mode—whether it be in actual speech or in the catching up of the tones and rhythms of popular song. It is important to emphasize this in the face of a persistent notion that Eliot was an ascetic and that his written language (whether in poetry or in drama) came solely from an imaginative/literary source. Indeed there are few writers since Shakespeare who were so conspicuously given to drawing upon 'the dialect of the tribe' for their verbal sustenance. Eliot's interest in vaudeville and music hall is sometimes regarded as a quaint foible; it should, in fact, be regarded as a deep passion.

His sense of actual spoken speech rarely lets him down. It must not be thought that his only contact with it was in Harvard and Cambridge Academe, in Faber's directorial offices, or in some soirée in Bloomsbury. What is so often forgotten is that Eliot's work for the Bank in the second decade of the century took him to many places in England. When he mentions, for example, 'documents c.i.f. London' in *The Waste Land* he has not culled the phrase from some encyclopaedia. He knew what they were, he dealt with them. Neville Coghill clinches for us Eliot's down-to-earthness. The conversation took place at their first meeting:

> Tell, me, Mr Eliot, who is Sweeney? How do you see him? What sort of man is he?
> Mr Eliot: I think of him as a man who in younger days was perhaps a professional pugilist, mildly successful; who then grew older and retired to keep a pub.[6]

This explanation, or perhaps, this context, immediately makes a precise silhouette out of Sweeney, and gives his language, convincing enough even without the context, an extra charge.

Sweeney Agonistes—not intended for performance—is, by comparison with Eliot's later dramatic work, a raw piece. But it absolutely establishes that Eliot had the gift essential to any dramatist. Martin Browne expresses it succinctly and accurately:

> . . . a speech-rhythm which seems natural to actors and audience, and the power to express individual character. These, in addition to what is required of all stage-dialogue, that it should speak with immediately apprehensible point and clarity.[7]

And this is as true of the American idiom as of the English—as the exchanges between Klipstein and Krumpacker amply show. To them, London is 'swell' and 'fine' and, boy, 'Do we like London?' The burr Eliot embodies is impeccably correct.

It is in the *Choruses from 'The Rock'*, written over a decade later, that Eliot shows how far his study of Elizabethan drama and his speculations upon dramatic language have taken him

147

from the raw but acceptable *Sweeney*. Here, for the first time, we are made aware that Eliot had within him and developed other qualities—some essential, others not so essential—of the true dramatist. We have to examine these against the background of something that was not present in *Sweeney Agonistes*. There, all the influences that worked upon him were, so to speak, brashly and effectively but separately paraded—jazz, vaudeville, the voices of people around him. But in *The Rock* he has attempted, for the first time, to put into practice that principle which he never relinquished. In *The Rock* he tried to create a language which would express both the immediate, active and naturalistic as well as what was deeper, less instantly articulate, musical. He tried to fuse the visible and invisible.

Against this attempt we have to see his superb use of irony, his technique of verbal emphasis, of repetition, and its effects, his sometimes cruel wit, and an ability so to 'place' a word that it has, in its very aptness and position in the line, a surprising dramatic effect of its own.

The irony which we find in *The Waste Land* and in *The Four Quartets* is of a kind which attempts sometimes to produce mockery, but always to induce a sense of a richer, complex, even symbolic contrast to that which is set against it. No more telling illustrations exist of this than the superb and dramatically alive description of the 'lovely woman' who 'stoops to folly' in *The Waste Land* and of the music which 'crept by me on the waters' in the same poem.

In other words the intention (and certainly the result) does not have the force of pure satire. Regret, pathos, nostalgia, sometimes hang about it and force our minds away from the sharp judgments and edicts of the satirical spirit.

But the irony of *The Rock* is, to a large extent, sparked off from satirical flint. It is worked without undue remorse, indeed often without any at all. Perhaps the most remarkable feature of it is its social relevance. This 'ascetic' seems as pertinently scathing about the England he sees about him as Auden and Isherwood were to be in their own excursions into poetic dramas in the 1930s—indeed, they might well have penned the jabbing comment—'All men are ready to invest their money / But most expect dividends'. *The Rock* is a 'religious' play, and *The Ascent of F6* [8] is a 'psychological' play, but both are intensely conscious of the realities of the English society which, since World War I, has been in a state of restless and far from always beneficial change. It is not surprising to find Auden and Isherwood adopting a political stance in a decade which was intensely politically-minded. It is astonishing, however, to 'find in *The Rock,* the 'ascetic' religious Eliot writing workmen's choruses with which no true marxist would surely find much to quarrel. The satirical spirit which underpins Eliot's irony does not stop at judgment. It proposes a solution to the iniquity it has uncovered:

> We build the meaning:
> A Church for all
> And a job for each
> Each man to his work.

And Auden and Isherwood seem to say, 'amen' to that:

> *Semi-chorus I*
> Where time flows on as chalk stream clear
> And lovers by themselves forgiven
> The whole dream genuine, the charm mature
> Walk in the great and general light
> In their delight a part of heaven
> Its furniture and choir.
>
> *Chorus*
> To each his need: from each his power. [9]

This eminently practical form of irony is accompanied by a mordant wit, often harsh in its application to man's inhumanity, his dangerous folly. Its effectiveness is strongly nurtured by the incantatory form in which it is expressed—the beat of the line forces the message into the memory:

> Men! polish your teeth on rising and retiring;
> Women! polish your fingernails:
> You polish the tooth of the dog and the talon of the cat.

Sometimes, there is a sort of bemused menace in the witty expression of a self-evident truth:

> And if blood of martyrs is to flow on the steps
> We must first build the steps.

149

More often, however, it is Eliot's ability to place a word which produces both the wit *and* the dramatic effect. He shares with Pope the ability both to amuse and to issue judgment by the exercise of a single word:

> But every son would have his motor cycle.
> And daughters ride away on casual pillions.

Word-placing is not just a matter of the correct word in the pattern of meaning, but of the correct word in the pattern of the sound and pace of the lines. For example, the speaker is given a clear direction for the creation of a dramatic verbal effect in the sound and position of the word 'Ale' here:

> In this land
> There shall be one cigarette to two men,
> To two women one half pint of bitter
> Ale . . .

The implied pause after bitter gives 'Ale' the chance to have its full force—we half expect it to be 'wail'; their cup runneth over.

All these devices quicken and vivify the language—they are the dramatic explosions which keep us constantly on the *qui-vive*. But we must return to the landscape in which the explosions happen. We have to remind ourselves that it is in *The Rock* that Eliot's most conscious attempt to create a unified dramatic language is made. The most significant feature is the avoidance of the iambic and its substitution by a line which accepts stress but is not saddled with rhythmic regularity. This allows it to accommodate both the poetic and idiomatic expression. Martin Browne provides one chorus as a typical example of the way in which Eliot has broken the iambic tradition of Shakespeare:

> The Word of the LORD came unto me, saying:
> O miserable cities of designing men,
> O wretched generation of enlightened mèn,
> Betrayed in the mazes of your ingenuities,
> Sold by the proceeds of your proper inventions:
> I have given you speech, for endless palaver,
> I have given you my Law, and you set up commissions,
> I have given you lips, to express friendly sentiments,
> I have given you hearts, for reciprocal distrust . . .[10]

He comments that Eliot in writing such a poetic line has 'gone back to the basis established by the mediaeval poets, of a fixed number of stresses in the line without any fixed number of syllables'. This is misleading. In the first place we have to guess which mediaeval poets Browne means; in the second place fixed stressing long pre-dated what is generally accounted to be the 'mediaeval' period, and is consistently found in Anglo-Saxon alliterative verse, represented at its most impressive in *Beowulf*. Thirdly, it is very difficult to see (or, more pertinently, to hear) the proof in Eliot's lines of Browne's assertion that the rhythmic structure of these lines is based on 'six or eight stresses'. In fact it is predominantly four-stress (for example, lines one, two, three) closely followed by five-stress.

It is well to emphasize this, at the risk of entering into laboured technicalities, because it is a prime example of the way in which even those most close to Eliot seem to become dazzled by visual metrics and minimize the evidence of the ear.

It is not necessary to deny the obvious—that is, that Eliot worked at his lines with technical expertise—in order to claim that his ear was the final arbiter. The natural dramatist in Eliot fought for supremancy over the precise metricator, and often won. The stresses that he heard in his inner ear were those that men used in speech of urgency, pomp and circumstance, and these were interspersed with those used when men spoke with the speech of the lounge and dining-room. Indeed, *The Family Reunion* is characterized by such contrasts. The stresses and beats which inform Eliot's lines in *The Choruses from 'The Rock'* and continued to, with growing skill and subtlety, in his later plays, certainly have the technical sophistication of poetry, but the most important aspect of them is that their source, or, at least their nearest comparison, is to be found in a prose designed to express both man's uncommon and most common experiences—that of the Authorized Version.

The Waste Land, Sweeney and *The Rock* clearly show that Eliot had a conspicuous dramatic talent for the expression of idiom, high poetry, and, to a degree for combining both with wit, irony and satire. The innate ability to conceive of character through language may be intermittent but it is inescapable.

The greatest test for him lay now in writing a play with a plot and theme which would capture audiences and be credible to them in dramatic terms, and to create characters who would be interesting and equally credible within those terms. Until he wrote *Murder in the Cathedral* Eliot had not faced up to the problems offered by the demands of a full-scale plot and a full-bodied set of characters.

Accounts of the events leading up to the first production of *Murder in the Cathedral* have been copiously and widely disseminated by Martin Browne. Equally, we have been provided with an account of the involved textual history of the play. Until or unless any full record from Eliot himself is posthumously made available there seems little point in speculating upon how far Martin Browne's version is likely to require qualification. There seems no reason why we should not take it that the verbal changes in the play were made, most of them, by Eliot, and all of them with his consent. Every change that Martin Browne has been able to record is a change for the better and a testimony to Eliot's awareness of the needs of the actor.

In addition to what we have relating to the history of the play's making are the many commentaries on the structure of the language. The seekers after metrication never had it so good as with *Murder in the Cathedral*.[11] There is thumping doggerel, four-stressed rhyming, blank verse, three-stress unrhymed; there is a rhythm based upon the *Gloria* of the Mass, and on *Dies Irae*. Not only this but he uses two quite different prose forms—for the Christmas sermon and for the speeches of the Knights. All this is documented, scanned and judged.

Yet curiously, it is the cause rather than the result which seems to have preoccupied most critics. The actual dramatic and theatrical results of his use of so many different forms of expression have been not so much neglected as underexposed. The relationships between sound, beat, placement of word and dramatic effect have not had the attention they so conspicuously deserve. Indeed an examination of Eliot's use of these relationships can embody a powerful proof of the truth that the language of drama *is,* essentially, the drama, and that the language of theatre has to recognize this.

152

T. S. Eliot—the Dramatist in Search of a Language

Eliot's quest for a unified language structure to accommodate every demand to be made upon it seems to have gone into abeyance—the multiplication of metrical forms listed above is sufficient testimony to this. In fact it has not by any means been abandoned, for in the speeches of the chorus—with the exception of those which follow metrics like the *Gloria* and *Dies Irae*—there is a remarkable union of formal and informal, idiomatic and poetic, flight and crawl, elevated and earth-bound. But apart from this, other characters are allotted their own very specific language structure; the Three Tempters, for example, are studiously identified and separated out from one another.

Eliot achieved a major dramatic success with this play and it is the more to be acclaimed because the evidence is that he was, by this copious and exhaustive manipulation of language patterns, experimenting to find the way into the one unified form of expression. But metrics and beats are what affect (or should affect) audiences without attention being drawn to them. It is the words, their colour and pace and place that are nearer to the audience's conscious listening. And it is in this relatively unregarded area of sensibility that we will find the reason why *Murder in the Cathedral* is such a fine play while, paradoxically, it is also such a self-consciously written play.

We can best see it by dividing our examination into three parts. First, to reveal Eliot's technical variety, second to show how his language creates character, third to realize the inter-relationship of language and theme. We are essentially looking at the function of words as they occur, not at the elusive effects of metrics as they exist.

In the first chorus of the play, for example, there is an impressive variety of technical skill, all designed to increase the dramatic activity of the line. Emphasis is achieved by repetition of 'Here let us', and this is given urgency by repeated single words—the hammer-blows, for instance, of 'what'. Contrast is achieved by the change from the dull urgencies of the language of the first eight lines to the pictorial and atmospheric language of what follows—indicating a shift from apprehensiveness to cherished memories of certainty about the inevitable rhythm of the seasons—'golden October', 'sombre November', and the simplicity of natural actions, '. . . the labourer kicks off a muddy boot and stretches his hand to the fire'.

Curiosity is induced by the economical use of questions. Eliot, a devotee of the skills of the music-hall artist in holding suspense and inciting the audience into wondering what happens next, is a master of what, in television and radio drama serials and comedy, is called 'the cliff-hanger'.

> He is at one with the Pope, and with the King of France,
> Who indeed would have liked to detain him in his kingdom:
>
> *First Priest:* But again, is it war or peace?

One example out of context may not convince, but even to read a page or two of the play is to be assured that Eliot is well aware of the dramatic tightening he is achieving by questions:

> Who shall have it?
>> He who will come.
> What shall be the month?
>> The last from the first.
> What shall we give for it?
>> Pretence of priestly power.
> Why should we give it?
>> For the power and the glory.

The plainness of the verbal content of the questions of the second example above is yet another very characteristic technical device. Some of the most effective dramatic moments of the play come not as a result of *what* is said or of *what* happens but because of a quite sensational bareness or terseness, sometimes even banality of statement which is altogether unexpected:

> We have seen births, deaths and marriages,
> We have had various scandals,
> We have been afflicted with taxes,
> We have had laughter and gossip,
> Several girls have disappeared
> Unaccountably, and some not able to.
> We have all had our private terrors,
> Our particular shadows, our secret fears.
> But now a great fear is upon us, a fear not of one but of many,
> A fear like birth and death, when we see birth and death alone
> In a void apart. We

154

> Are afraid in a fear which we cannot know, which we cannot
> face, which none understands,
> And our hearts are torn from us, our brains unskinned like the
> layers of an onion, our selves are lost lost
> In a final fear which none understands.

Sometimes these have the force of understatement, but with,
inevitably, Eliot's typical assumption of irony:

> I see nothing quite conclusive in the art of temporal govern-
> ment.

These accessions of the apparently ordinary gain a lot of force
from being placed, more often than not, either in the midst
of, or immediately after sections of highly wrought language
—the sudden bareness is like seeing a single rock in a field.

In this play Eliot does not commit the error of overworking
this particular device. Indeed he seems to have been much
more concerned with avoiding slackness here than in his later
plays. At times we have a feeling that he senses a need to pull
together the strands of his language. So we have many examples of a gathering up of matters which might become disparate. Eliot, indeed, never lost a predisposition to collect
together qualities or factors which add up to a whole in a tight
Bristol-fashion unity.

Eliot's Chorus in *Murder in the Cathedral* is far more dramatically successful than that of *The Family Reunion*[12] which seems
to form and undo itself on a kind of self-willed ad hoc basis.
One of the reasons for the success is the extent to which Eliot
relies upon it to fulfil a traditional function—a function which
Shakespeare (although, of course, his choruses were not
multi-peopled) gladly employed. It is really quite a simple
matter but it is extraordinary how rarely its importance in
Eliot has been allowed. This Chorus sets the scenes for us, and
is able, verbally, to take us on a visual journey to those areas
which it is necessary that we should see in our imaginative eye.
It fulfils the function of piecing out the imperfections of the
theatre by working on our visual imaginations. Through the
Chorus, we see Canterbury *outside* the cathedral, we experience the seasons, we watch peasant, king and priest at work
and at talk, and we see even great ceremonies—all this germane to what we need to know to experience the play fully.

The second feature of Eliot's language in this play concerns character. Although Thomas uses several different kinds of speech in the play Eliot immediately distinguishes him from the moment he enters into the action. There is a much more gravely formal architectural quality in Thomas's first speech than anything that has gone before:

Thomas: Peace. And let them be, in their exaltation.
　　They speak better than they know, and beyond your under-
　　　　standing.
　　They know and do not know, what it is to act or suffer.
　　They know and do not know, that action is suffering
　　And suffering is action. Neither does the agent suffer
　　Nor the patient act. But both are fixed
　　In an eternal action, an eternal patience
　　To which all must consent that it may be willed
　　And which all must suffer that they may will it,
　　That the pattern may subsist, for the pattern is the action
　　And the suffering, that the wheel may turn and still
　　Be forever still.

And this is a policy Eliot employs for all characters of any consequence. One of the most fascinating and revealing exercises is to examine how Eliot carefully designates each of the Three Tempters. Every sentence of the First Tempter's opening speech is either a specific or an implied question. In the latter respect we should take notice of this implication in the lines:

　　Fluting in the meadows, viols in the hall,
　　Laughter and apple-blossom floating on the water,
　　Singing at nightfall, whispering in chambers,
　　Fires devouring the winter season,
　　Eating up the darkness, with wit and wine and wisdom!

—and, if we mentally insert a question mark after each phrase—one which is almost there anyway—we are immediately aware of the nature of this temptation. The actor who will succeed in this speech is the one who recalls that temptation is something which, in a sense, questions the ability to push it aside.

Indeed one might say that this Tempter is 'histrionically' created—that is, the methods used in the language to designate him are larger-than-life, extrovert, drawing attention to themselves. The use of alliteration is hypnotic in effect, and the use of coiled rhyme gives the sense of cosy self-satisfaction—like a cat curled about its satisfied sleep:

First Tempter: You see, my Lord, I do not wait upon ceremony:
    Here I have come, forgetting all acrimony,
    Hoping that your present gravity
    Will find excuse for my humble levity
    Remembering all the good time past.
    Your Lordship won't despise an old friend out of favour?
    Old Tom, gay Tom, Becket of London,
    Your Lordship won't forget that evening on the river
    When the King, and you and I were all friends together?

But the Tempter is a man whose ability to employ the rhetoric of beguilement is not matched by any ability to hide his shallowness, his insincerity. With remarkable skill, Eliot, having produced him as a dangerous talker, allows him to demolish himself through his own mouth. After the billing blandishments, the empty clichés fall thick and fast, like the tired winks and nods of a faded Pandarus: 'A nod is as good as a wink'; 'I am your man'; 'The easy man lives to eat the best dinners'; 'Leave well alone'. He defeats himself.

The Second Tempter is immediately established as a man of decision, who keeps a good diary:

    Your lordship has forgotten me, perhaps. I will remind you.
    We met at Clarendon, at Northampton,
    And last at Montmirail, in Maine . . .

The language is clipped, it does not have the limpidity of Tempter one. Only in one respect does it resemble it—in its sudden access of alliteration.

    King commands. Chancellor richly rules.
    This is a sentence not taught in the schools.
    To set down the great, protect the poor,
    Beneath the throne of God can man do more?

But the effect is noticeably different from the alliterative language of the First Tempter, where the soft vowel noises between alliterating consonants produced a mesmeric effect:

Spring has come in winter. Snow in the branches
Shall float as sweet as blossoms. Ice along the ditches
Mirror the sunlight. Love in the orchard
Send the sap shooting. Mirror matches melancholy.

One of the most affecting episodes in the play is Becket's
sermon. It grips the emotions in several ways. First, it is a
remarkable sermon, dealing with a particular issue in an
authoritative and graceful manner. Second, it is a splendidly
constructed and modulated piece of prose—it has style without drawing attention to itself, in the manner of all the best and
most memorable sermons. Third, coming, as it does, after the
intricate verse-structure of the first part, it works by contrast.
This does not mean that it is simple in structure but that, by
comparison, it compels the reader's or listener's mind to concentrate without, at the same time, expecting it to contend
with great shifts of pace or mood or style.

From the point of view of its dramatic and theatrical status it
is an important and clear example of the third element of
Eliot's technique—the close relationship between his language
and his theme. It is, on examination, obviously a prose written
by a poet, not in the sense that it is done with a flourish or is
packed with the more apparent poetic devices of imagery and
rhythm; but certain technical resources and the manner in
which they are used bespeak the workings of a poetic imagination. To this extent it is an example of Eliot's conception of a
dramatic style which had no definite break between a poetic
and prose mode, but accepted gradation between the one and
the other.

Three elements—two of which are themes, the other a
concept which is personalized—dominate the sermon. 'Peace'
and 'martyrdom' are the content, so to speak, over which
'God' the Father presides in the sermon. 'Peace' is repeated at
intervals throughout the sermon as the formal theme for the
Christmas celebration. But, at a certain point, the theme of
martyrdom is announced and the word 'martyr' becomes a
noticeable part of the motif. What happens is that the more
subjective theme of martyrdom is always ready to oust the
formal one, but never succeeds. Martyrdom, it says, should
never be sought, should never be allowed to dominate the

158

consciousness—the way in which the word is kept at bay in the speech is itself a demonstration of this persistent note in the play. But both concepts—peace and martyrdom—are under the control of 'He', 'His', 'Our Lord', 'God'. The words are interspersed throughout the sermon and become the third point in this verbal triangle of forces.

It is superbly achieved, and gives an incantatory quality and a tension to a piece of writing which is also an exercise of a kind of logic. The major part of the speech which begins 'consider also one thing of which you have probably never thought' goes from step to step in the proposing of an argument, but the triangle of faces gives the argument both a religious and an emotional impetus.

And, in the last paragraph, 'peace', 'martyr' and the variants of 'God' are suddenly joined by a very personal 'I' (the 'I' of Thomas himself). The effect is a remarkable example of dramatic contrast. The rich and formal architectonics of language have given place to an utter simplicity—Thomas's aspiration for humility in the face of impending death and martyrdom are a poignant dying fall to the robust affirmatives of the major part of the sermon.

A crucial and persistent critical argument about this play concerns the appearance of the Knights, in what Eliot called 'the public meeting' scene, what they say and how they say it. There are extremes of attitude ranging from a belief that their intervention thoroughly allows the play to impinge on the modern consciousness (because both their language and attitudes are 'modern' in content, form and tone) to an assertion that they jar on the ear and fracture the play's unity.

There can be no doubt that the appearance of the Knights is a shock, not only because of their language—which is of a quite different order from that of the rest of the play—but because they directly address the audience. This latter point is often ignored in any assessment of whether they upset the play's elegant design. The shock they give us frequently gives place to a regret that what has been a grand and noble dramatic creation has been both thematically and dramatically compromised for the sake of a coup de théâtre.

It is not easy to dismiss this opinion, but it does not take us very far in understanding what is implied in the appearance of the Knights. What underlies the implications has a good deal to do with language. The shock is verbal and we might say that, in a sense, the language is almost too dramatic. It is well suited for stage delivery, being full of contrasts and modes and moods ranging from the comic to the pompous, and it has a great range of pace. But it is a fundamentally different kind of dramatic language from that used in the rest of the play, including the sermon. It is essentially the language of the temporal, visible, material world—it is the speech of man in his environment and in no way echoes any other world, any other environment. Because of this it can concern itself only with the realities of the visible world, but its presence cannot be justified by claiming that this is exactly what Eliot intended—that we are meant to see how the Knights' raucous speech interrupts the complex rituals of Becket's world as comprehensively as the Nurse's demotic noise crashes into the lyrical designs of Romeo and Juliet's love at their first meeting.

Murder in the Cathedral becomes a different play from what we had been led to expect from its first two-thirds, by the intervention of the Knights. Moreover it is a difference which seems less a result of design than of accident. Whereas the first two-thirds is a sensitively achieved exploration of a man's soul, the coming of the Knights drastically changes the theme to an ironic melodrama about aims and motives. What should alert us to the possibility of this shift being accidental is the fact that what the Knights have to say about aims and motives has already been covered by the Tempters. The attitudes of the Knights, the permutations of why and wherefore and if, have been more subtly conveyed already. No dramatic reason therefore exists for their interference in this scene—they are essentially a theatrical happening.

The play recovers as ritual language re-establishes its claim on Eliot's theme and communication and, in the final analysis, the Knights' scene has no lasting damaging effect. They are, nevertheless, interesting because they make us inquire into the reasons for their appearance. Martin Browne, who seems to have had a good deal of responsibility for the allocation of speeches to the various Knights, is of no direct help. But it appears that Eliot was not short on suggestions from outside sources. Ashley Dukes[13] had something to say about characterizing each Knight by an introductory phrase, for example. Perhaps Robert Speaight, who played Becket originally, and those who actually played the Knights also contributed their opinions.

The tone of the scene, the theatricality of its presentation, the fact that it does not really contribute much to the theme, all suggest the possibility that Eliot (or someone) felt that some kind of relief from the high tension of the preceding events was necessary. Perhaps the existence of this scene is proof positive that Eliot's frequent doubting of his own dramatic instinct and capability found expression in practice as well as theory.

What *Murder in the Cathedral* amply shows is that Eliot's doubts about his own ability were unfounded. He went on to write plays of progressively less dramatic credibility because he seems, on his own testimony, to have doubted whether the language of *Murder in the Cathedral* was viable for any other kind of drama. What he seems not to have realized is that far from any other play requiring a quite different language-pattern, what he had created for *Murder in the Cathedral* might very well be capable of infinite variety. He moved, however, further and further away from a mode which allowed of both a high degree of poetic resource as well as a judiciously calculated amount of low-tensioned prose, into a prose medium which eventually lost all sense of contrast, variation of pace, colour, as it desperately tried not to seem 'artificed', dependent, in any way, on those resources of poetry.

In *The Family Reunion* the process has begun, although there is still a great deal of versatility and inventiveness in the use of language. This play gives an overall impression of having been written in prose, whereas *Murder in the Cathedral* gives an overall impression of a poetic mode. This is a simple measure of the change that has begun to take place. In fact, in *The Family Reunion* it is possible to see both the relics of his method in the earlier play and the forerunners of modes he was later to use. The choric ritualism is still present,

> The agony in the curtained bedroom, whether of birth or
>   dying,
> Gathers in to itself all the voices of the past, and projects them
>   into the future.

> The treble voices on the lawn
> The mowing of hay in summer,

though the line lengths are, generally, shorter, more clipped. The familiar rubs shoulders with the highly-charged poetic mode,

> Men tighten the knot of confusion
> Into perfect misunderstanding,
> Reflecting a pocket-torch of observation
> Upon each other's opacity,

but the vernacular, either in phrase, or in association, is more obtrusive, altogether more brash, than in the former play.

Repetition, question and answer, rhyme, alliteration, are employed in *The Family Reunion,* but sometimes instead of seeming to be, as in *Murder in the Cathedral,* deeply integrated into a larger and planned pattern, they seem to be quirks of design, self-conscious, not so much ad hoc as de rigueur.

But if the past is in the language in these modified ways, the future seeds are already planted too. Martin Browne records that Ivor Brown had prophesied in *The Observer* that Eliot might write an excellent light comedy. He wrote *The Cocktail Party*[14] which is a comedy of sorts, *The Confidential Clerk* merits the description (Browne says that it has a smack of W. S. Gilbert or Oscar Wilde) and *The Elder Statesman*—a seriously-intentioned play which leaves the reader puzzling as to whether it be melodrama, satire or morality. What is less open to argument is that the style of all these plays is dominated by one characteristic which began to make its appearance in *The Family Reunion.* W. A. Darlington encapsulates it in a comment on *The Cocktail Party*. He refers to it as being full of 'philosophy, wit and epigram'.[15]

This is the ingredient which is to be found gaining its strength, ready, later, to oust much of the poetry, in *The Family Reunion.* Some of wit's appearances are embryonic, in the most primitive sense:

Gerald: I might have been staying with Compton-Smith, down at his place in Dorset.
Violet: I should have been helping Lady Bumpus, at the Vicar's American Tea.

Some epigrams are neo or sub-Wilde:

Harry: Changed? Nothing changed? how can you say that nothing is
changed? You all look so withered and young.

And a good deal of the 'philosophy' is old Eliot writ sometimes with stark ritual:

This way the pilgrimage
Of expiation
Round and round the circle
Completing the charm
So the knot be unknotted
The crossed be uncrossed
The crooked be made straight . . .

and sometimes writ plain:

Gerald: Why painful?
Violet: Gerald! You know what Agatha means.
Agatha: I mean painful, because everything is irrevocable.
Because the past is irremediable.
Because the future can only be built
Upon the real past . . .

With variations this is a pattern which increasingly
monopolizes the language of the plays, but with an equally
increasing emphasis on the reduction of the obvious poetic
elements. These do not disappear—indeed in the last, *The
Elder Statesman,* there are strains of a grave and stately poetry,
particularly in the latter part of the play:

Age and decrepitude can have no terrors for me,
Loss and vicissitude cannot appal me,
Not even death can dismay or amaze me
Fixed in the certainty of love unchanging.

—but they become fugitive.

What seems to have happened to Eliot—who, in his first
play, may claim to have given evidence of a great poetic
dramatic gift and who, in *The Family Reunion* gave evidence of
being able to manoeuvre it with a contemporary theme—is a
loss of nerve, resulting from his dissatisfaction with his
attempts to reconcile the imaginative and verbal demands of
poetry and those of drama.

In an interview he gave to *The Glasgow Herald* on 27 August 1949, Eliot referred to *The Cocktail Party* as if it were a poem. He said:

> No explanation in the ordinary sense of a poem is adequate. If you can completely explain a poem, with an exact correspondence between the deliberate intention of the author and the reception of the idea by the reader, then it just is not poetry.

All Eliot's plays are poems in the sense that their themes and characters are conceived within a complex world of the imagination, and that what is required even to attempt to communicate their meaning must, of itself, match their emotional and intellectual intricacy. Total explanation is impossible; the best a poet can do is to try and give his readers as much as possible of the experience he had himself of his inner world or, at least, to enable him to enter into the world and use his own sense and sensibility within it. But Eliot was also well aware of the special demands of dramatic communication, which involve compression and simplification in order to introduce an immediacy of understanding and response from the audience. So, in the same interview, he commented:

> All that one can aim at in a play of this type . . . is to provide a plot and characters and action which are on the immediate theatrical level intelligible . . . the characters should not be on the surface unusual or different from ordinary human nature, and there should be perfectly intelligible things going on, with a reasonably intelligible conclusion.

Eliot's intense desire to make his deep and poetically conceived themes (all of them, to a degree, with religious implications) 'available' was matched by a drive to find a language to communicate them. In *Murder in the Cathedral* he discovered it; in *The Family Reunion* he got near to 'domesticating' it, but a negative attitude, perhaps a fear, entered in at this point. The rest of Eliot's plays—'philosophizing', 'witty', 'epigrammatic'—seem, in language, to be often an amalgam of Wilde, Gilbert, Coward. There is a kind of 'West Endery' about them. The serious content, the true poetic ring they intermittently have, alone allows them to escape a kind of weary and flippant sententiousness.

Eliot, far from being a true poet and a dramatist manqué was, in fact, a great poet and a true dramatist who became over-conscious of his audience. The early experiments, *Murder in the Cathedral* and, to a degree, *The Family Reunion,* show evidence that, if he had allowed himself to forget that, at some point in the creation of a play, there must be an avoidance by the dramatist of too close a scrutiny of ways and means, he might well have become a great dramatist.

9   Harold Pinter—the Deceptive Poet

Harold Pinter has attracted to his works what seem to be unbreakable critical reflexes which have eventually produced verbal clichés. His work is festooned with critical tags, each inviting the reader to categorize him. But one does so at the risk of a loss of touch. 'Pinter's world' is the world of 'the absurdist' in which you find 'characters incapable of communication', but who nevertheless seem to achieve the impossible by using 'Pinter's language'. Of these the references to his language are the most prevalent; critical discussion of this dramatist is concerned to a quite unusual extent with the means by which the plays express themselves.

The most surprising feature of this discussion is that it is in itself so unusual. Modern critics are not often given to more than cursory examination of the details of a dramatist's language. The extent to which generalization replaces close particulars is graphically indicated in the words of E. Bentley:

> As to Britain, drama is there reduced to the status of opera; all the best energy goes into revivals of classics. . . . One might be tempted to say that the theatre . . . fulfils only one precondition of renascence: it is dead.[1]

If we seek, in twentieth-century criticism, for anything approaching the extent of the detailed verbal analysis of Pinter's plays, we find it only in commentaries on Yeats, Eliot and Christopher Fry.[2] In short, we find it in poetic dramatists in whose language the technical and aesthetic resources of poetry and verse are used to a very high degree. In each example, a special case can be made out for the level of attention paid to

166

language. Critics took their cue from Eliot himself—he seemed so possessed with concern not only about poetic language but his own particular forms of it that he incited his critics to emulate him. Fry's case was phenomenal. After the long quietus of war, the catherine-wheel glamour of his language seemed an earnest that colour, richness, a licence for imaginative indulgence, had returned. There was an intense curiosity (very short-lived) in how Fry generated this incandescence. Yeats shared, up to a point, the fate of Eliot—inciting critics by personal example. But his case is more complex overall. There was, and still is, a curiosity about how the language of his plays and his poems are related.

Pinter does not seem at first sight to be a special case. He is the most reticent of men about his work and his language does not *seem* to have special poetic qualities. Why then the intense searching and theorizing and speculating? There are two possibilities. Either there is something unique about his language which cannot be ignored, or his language shares a quality or qualities with that of poetic dramatists—who have attracted more critical dissection than their prose colleagues.

Pinter's language is generally regarded by the intelligent theatregoer and by some perceptive critics as a remarkable evocation of 'real speech'. It is often declared to be the embodiment of the way *we* speak—half-inarticulate, stumbling, leaving questions completely or half-unanswered, lacking clarity—generally of meaning, often of articulation. Both 'real' language and Pinter's version of it, are a long way from that of the 'well-made' play and even from the studiously-constructed naturalistic drama of, say, Galsworthy and Shaw. Indeed it is easy to conclude that Pinter's language is a particular antithesis of Shaw's, having nothing of its sinewy articulateness, its directness, its wit, its socratic poising of question and answer, statement and counter-statement, its almost embarrassing lucidity. In Shaw, phrases are rarely if ever left to fall off tightropes, never allowed to stand alone, unrelated, but placed square-footed to achieve the maximum effect of balance and presence.

At face value, certainly, Pinter 'sounds' like people speak, and Shaw sounds like the way many think they speak; that is, the one sounds like a rough faute-de-mieux, the other like a fait-accompli. Significantly, when Shaw attempts dialect, he still contrives to sound literary, and when Pinter (as in *No Man's Land*) writes 'educated', balanced, apparently intellectually superior characters, they still manage to sound inconsequential.

The obvious way to test this notion of the Pinter speech is to listen to the 'dialogue' of a group of real people and to examine how consanguineous it is—or not. This is a procedure which would be quirky were it not for the persistent and widely current assumption that Pinter's dialogue is barely a step away from 'real' speech. One may, a little covertly, attempt it with a hidden tape-recorder in an unsuspecting drawing room.

A: Don't disturb him.
B: Who?
A: Him. He's trying to write.
     Pause
B: What?
A: Write.
B: No. What's he writing?
A: He's writing . . . they're going again.
     Look.
B: Every night.
     Pause
A: Wonder it isn't tired. It must be eight.
B: Eight for a dog is fifty-six.
A: Why every night . . . four miles?
B: Don't disturb him . . . I don't know, fifty-six.

It certainly doesn't have the noise or shape or sense of Shaw—or indeed of Barrie, or Coward or Priestley. But it *does* seem to belong to 'Pinter's world'. Does this mean that we must firmly put aside any possibility that Pinter, in some way, belongs among the poetic dramatists? Not at all, for if we listen, more carefully, any resolutely affirmative answer has to go into cold-storage. The real speech does not seem to be going anywhere—why should it? We cannot know what the end of this 'real' play is going to be, any more than do the speakers. But isn't this unknowing itself very redolent of the effect of Pinter? Is there not a strong sense that his plays, at any given point, do not seem to be going anywhere—that there is, and can be, no destination? Compare the language of a well-made play with a Pinter play, and a contrast is apparent—verbal purpose, direction as opposed to apparent ad hoc verbal activity. We may, indeed, push the matter a little further and declare that his plays do not, in the conventional sense, 'end' at all. They stop.

But although we seem to recognize, in the real speech, the Pinter timbre, we should, if we listen carefully, also realize that it lacks, unquestionably, a kind of tension which Pinter habitually possesses. This, in itself, should warn us against a too close association between the real and the written. Pinter's language is as taut as a bow-string—it contains a potential that the real neither has nor intends. At this point we must remind ourselves of the special quality of true dramatic language —its containing of the elements required to enable the actor to awaken it. The testimony of actors about dramatic language is always valuable—in the case of Pinter's, it is crucial.

We begin to draw away from a confusion between Pinter's language and real speech when we learn that actors who have appeared in Pinter's plays do not find this confusion. To the non-professional the apparent inchoateness of a Pinter script would seem to make the task of memorizing alone extremely difficult. But this is not so. Actors, time and time again, testify to the resemblance between a Pinter script and a piece of music; if anything is left out in the process of memorizing, its absence is felt like a vanished tooth. A precise design is disturbed when even the smallest element is removed. More than this, a precise notation of vocal pausing is given by stops—a pause may therefore be . long or . . or . . . .

Pinter has

> . . . a linear structure and a formal structure which you'd better just observe—don't learn it wrong, don't speak it wrong, you can't, you mustn't . . . once the play is beginning to live you cannot be too meticulous. What Pinter wrote is always better than what a lazy actor will come up with. Now this may seem a very small and pedantic point, but most of our actors have a fairly easy-going, not to say contemptuous attitude to what a dramatist has written, and for the average playwright writing the average colloquial flim-flam, it doesn't much matter whether you say 'but' instead of 'and', or put in a few extra

words. It does in Pinter . . . But *when* you get it accurate then the rhythm—and he has the most astonishing ability to write rhythms—begin to work . . . If you sing a Mozart aria correctly, certain responses begin to be necessary inside you. Now, you could say that's beginning to put the cart before the horse, but that's the way it is—you're not improvising something of your own, you're singing some notes of Mozart. It's much the same with Pinter.[3]

This extemely enlightening and perceptive comment on Pinter's language comes from one of his most sensitive and successful interpreters—Peter Hall. It confirms the intricate design of Pinter; it implies, with its musical analogy, the distance of Pinter's language from real speech; it tacitly accepts the prime importance of his language.

We can now take up the question of Pinter's uniqueness. One very important facet of it is that the language is eminently written for the actor—he is a player's playwright—as a kind of code. This is not to say that other dramatists, using very different modes, are not aware of the requirements of the actor. However, Pinter is unique in expressing his awareness in this extraordinarily precise way.

Yet, however much a close examination of Pinter's language reveals a sophistication of concept and technique, it is difficult still not to feel the tang of 'real' speech in it. 'Real' speech—but whose? We do not all speak like Davies or Aston or Goldberg. Yet, curiously, we think we recognize each species of utterance as it comes along.

Davies's sniffy attempts at bonhomie as he talks about the knick-knacks that are in the room 'all right'; Aston's wistful attempts at gaining his confidence as he speaks of the way he can work with his hands 'you see'; Goldberg's romantic fancy as he recalls the girl who lived down his road, a remarkably beautiful girl with a voice like a nightingale's on 'my word of honour': Pinter is no more and no less successful in depicting the speech patterns we recognize in the disaffected, the underprivileged, as in Davies, than he is with the sophisticates in *Old Times,* or the pompous (with a trace of Jewish incantation) in Goldberg. We recognize them all. We swear we have heard people who sound like this.

But 'Pinter's world' is a strange world. We may very well

have heard, in our own world, similar noises, but how often can we say that we have ever seen or been truly in the presence of such people? The truth is that we have overheard the speech of Pinter's characters in trains, buses, pubs, shops, museums, lecture-rooms, living-rooms, lounges, libraries, income-tax offices, but if we chose to become acquainted with, committed to, the people whom we overhear, we would find that *only* the speech (and, in the final analysis *only some* of the speech) reminds us of Pinter. Little else does—especially appearance. It is extraordinarily difficult to visualize Pinter's characters; they are, until an actor becomes them, particularly disembodied. No one on this earth looks like a Pinter character.

The difficulty of visualizing them or assessing what they are like or what motivates them is due to the fact that a Pinter person is not complete—it is a piece of ore that we experience, and a small piece at that. Our experience in the theatre does not bear out one critic's claim that Pinter's plays cover such a wide social and emotional range. In fact the range of emotions covered is very small and though he uses the speech-characteristics of different social and professional classes, the characters who speak this speech are too partially-formed to represent their class—they sound as if they come from this or that class, but they do not in any other way relate to it. What Pinter has done has been to endow very fragmentary dramatis personae with the apparent characteristics of totally-rounded characters, and he has done it by creating a language which to a degree 'impersonates' the real, but which very often has its own ritual and rules, its own life. There are, for example, occasions in Goldberg's and McCann's dialogue in *The Birthday Party*[4] when the language seems to express nothing but itself, as if a computer had become half-demented in a staccato way.

And, indeed, even when we are, in the hands of this supreme verbal magician, lulled into believing that what we hear is 'real', inside the speech a certain stylization is at work. Davies's description in *The Caretaker*[5] of his mate at Shepherd's Bush who runs the convenience and gives him free soap is a strange piece of ritual, neatly bracketed by 'Shepherd's Bush' at beginning and end; it has both rhyme and rhythm in the repetition, in the first part, of 'convenience', and, in the second part, of 'soap'. The design is almost, but not quite, symmetrical, but is near enough to confirm the sense of formed ritual. Davies's litany pathetically consummates the importance he gives to having a mate in a specific place, who not only runs a convenience, but the best one, who not only has soap, but good soap.

Such faith in the religion of possession and status requires a ritual observance. Sometimes it occurs within a single speech, but, more often, involves two characters whose relationship to one another while the ritual is created always involves the dominance of one over the other—priest and acolyte, teacher and pupil, predator and victim. In *The Room*,[6] Riley calls upon Rose (whom he calls Sal) to 'come home'. The short, clipped, half-lines sometimes responded to by 'yes' and 'no' seem, at first sight, incontrovertibly naturalistic—but a subtle and poetic technique is at work.

What is immediately noticeable is the bracketing of the scene by the phrases 'come home, Sal' and its slight variation, 'come home now, Sal', and the repetitions of 'come', 'home', 'now' and 'Sal' which produce a hypnotic rhythm. Indeed the rhythm has a very important function in the development of the episode. Up to the second pause Riley's phrases have a slightly non-realistic quality, a kind of chilly quaintness in 'so now you're here' and 'I wanted to see you', 'now I touch you'. This quality is the more apparent when the phrases are read or heard in the context of Sal's flat reponses—'Don't call me that', 'Don't touch me', 'I can't'. But after the second pause the verbal roles seem to be reversed—as if Riley's hypnosis has worked, and Rose has become of his world. It is now he who can relax into a familiar staccato—there is nothing odd about his 'Yes', 'No' and 'Come home now, Sal', while she begins to sway into a verbal incantation—'I've been here', 'Long', 'The day is a hump, I never go out', 'I've been here'. The religion of acquisitiveness has claimed, in its ritual, another victim.

The effect, in reading the text, is as if you were coming across or, more accurately, being led into, a short or extended poetic image. It is poetic because of the technical resources of rhyme, repetition, rhythm and out-of-the-ordinary verbal resonance; it is an image because although the impersonation of real speech is always, to a degree, present, what is being said is a key which unlocks a door to what is unsaid. In even short phrases, as, for example, Meg's and Petey's staccato confrontation about the merits of his breakfast and the contents of the newspaper,[7] an image of 'character' becomes eloquent.

The development of Pinter's expertise and sensitivity with language has not meant a departure from this basic 'metaphorical' writing but a subtilizing and complicating of it in structure, tone and implication. In *The Homecoming*[8] there occurs not the first but, up to that point, the best manifestation of that development, for in it there is a complete and superb integration of dramatic language with the language of theatre. Throughout his career Pinter has been acutely aware of, and has utilized, inanimate objects, stage-furniture, and made them into extra dramatis personae. The newspaper, the spectacles and the electric light in *The Birthday Party;* the shoes (reminiscent of *Waiting for Godot)* and the Buddha in *The Caretaker;* the coffee cups in *Old Times.* Even when there is no one dominating object, the reader and the theatregoer are made to feel, every time an object is handled or even mentioned, that it means significantly more than mere touch or mention. Nothing, so to speak, is wasted—the realistic bric-à-brac of the well-made play seems, by comparison, museum'd and inert: in Pinter inanimate objects seem always on the point of coming to life: 'She butters the bread'; 'She goes to the sink, wipes a cup and saucer and brings them to the table'; 'She pours milk into the cup'. Each time, in *The Room,*[9] a stage-direction occurs, an extra dimension is added not just to the action of the play, but to the elusive meaning that lies behind the words. In *The Homecoming* the conspiracy of words with inanimate object is graphic and alarming. We may note the very much more sophisticated use in this play of repetition and rhyme, and the bracketing by single phrases, as in the repetition of 'glass' and 'I'll take you' in the extraordinarily tense scene when Ruth attempts to seduce Lenny.

The customary notion of a Pinter play is that it sidles inconsequentially from an unimportant point A to an indeterminate point X, Y or Z—it does not matter which. In fact the verbal image-building which has been noted produces an episodic structure. It is very noticeable that a Peter Hall direction of a play exposes this episodic structure without in any way producing a staccato or stuttering effect which might happen in less sensitive hands. The movement of a Pinter play on stage is very much one of ebb and flow. The extended images represent points of crisis, but between their appearances there lie areas of relaxation.

It is misleading to say that Pinter shows us human beings in certain states of mind or feeling. The proposition is only correct if it is turned on its head. Pinter's plays are 'about' certain states of feeling (rather more, indeed, about feeling than thinking) which are presented to us in human embodiment—it is a kind of allegorical writing. The feeling *is* the character just as surely as, in a mediaeval play, the vice or the virtue *is* the character—the message *is* the medium. These are resemblances between Pinter and mediaeval dramatists which, in their theatrical appearances, take us further than mere academic speculation.

Many of Pinter's plays are, to a degree, concerned with one or other of the seven deadly sins and these are embodied in characters, though he does not, like the earlier playwrights, often depict or assume or imply the existence of virtue. Good Deeds, we may say, has little to do with Pinter's Everyman, but Lust, Pride, Avarice have.

It is, therefore, as wrong to assess a Pinter 'character' and the language it uses in customary psychologically realistic terms as it is to conceive of a dramatized mediaeval Vice or Virtue in those terms. Moreover, the dramatic use of inanimate objects that we have noted in Pinter is also to be found in his ancient colleagues. The tense oscillations between words and things are as apparent both when the language is twentieth-century demotic and the objects teacups and tumblers, and when it is fifteenth-century vernacular and the objects the cross or a saint's bones.

In literary criticism the rigid distinction which used to be made between 'what is poetry' and 'what is prose' has relaxed considerably, and, as we shall see, the work of a number of American dramatists has been a significant contribution to this process. By the mid-point of the twentieth century the traditional image of an iron partition which separated prose from poetry had begun to fade. Now, it seems incredible that we were once taught that a prose communication was 'suitable' for some subjects and a poetic for others. Even the working materials—metaphor, simile, rhyme, metre, alliteration, and so forth—which were said to demonstrate conclusively the differences between the two—now no longer seem to be exclusive. We have ceased asking the question—'What is the difference between prose and poetry?' The sceptical may believe that this is due less to an access of sophisticated and profound reasoning than to a decay in the individual exercise of both forms.

Yet, whatever the cause and effect, it is still surprising that a writer so apparently intimate with the rough usages of the vernacular should have the word 'poet' used so frequently to designate him. Indeed, the measure of the change in attitude towards poetry and prose communication is in this very fact.

A further surprise awaits for anyone examining the claims made for Pinter as poet—he passes, in several respects, a number of the old and traditional tests. Older critics would claim that his work is poetic because it uses, though in ways that are often covert or disguised, many of the conventional resources of poetic communication—rhythm, associative value of words, image-making, tonal effect. He is poetic in the deeper sense that no specific and clear literal meaning can be abstracted from the majority of his plays. In a very obvious sense you not only change a Pinter play if you try to translate it into different terms, you destroy it in the way you would destroy any work of art and, moreover, you find you are no nearer the heart of a mystery. You can no more explain *A Slight Ache*[10] than you can *Hamlet*. You can make an accurate précis of any one of Shaw's plays (except possibly *Heartbreak House*) but Pinter's defy you to do it.

The allusive and the elusive predominate in Pinter—unlike naturalistic prose-drama where it is either non-existent or of marginal effect. Unlike so many of his contemporary prose-naturalistic colleagues Pinter neither seems in any sense to want to lead men to action nor to relate his events and characters to explicit contemporary actualities; he exhibits no anger, looking either backward or forward, about the establishment, and he seems not to have considered the social causes of underprivilege and tried to root them out.

Pinter incites the imagination, troubles the spirit, and

175

excites the emotions. None of his plays, while we are actually watching them, engage us in any 'issue', moral or otherwise—the 'experience' given us with dramatic subtlety, verbal sophistication and a complete awareness of theatrical possibilities is too strong to allow us to engage ourselves with anything else. It is only afterwards when, in any case, we are often trying to pin down meaning, that the question of 'issues' may arise—as, for example, the 'morality' of *The Homecoming*.

Pinter is not concerned with the actualities of man in society but, taking on the traditional function of the poet, with some of the realities of what man is. He uses, as many poets have done, the sense-data of the contemporary world as a sharp salt, but it is no more.

When we enter into a Pinter room we have to accept a format which embraces states of feeling rather than impersonates the real world, which is self-sufficient and has very much more the status of an image rather than of an actuality. Our experience of this is very different in quality but it is very similar in kind to that which we get from Shakespeare's *The Tempest*—a play which seems constantly to be aspiring to the condition of a poem.

Part IV
The Language of Cousins and Contemporaries

10   American Connections—O'Neill, Miller, Williams and Albee

In any conspicuous sense the history of American drama begins in the twentieth century, though its theatre has a robust and rich tradition which extends well back through the nineteenth century. Drama, of all the art-forms, flourished latest in the New World and though many reasons—social, intellectual, even ethnic—may be put forward to explain this, it is a little surprising. Americans are very theatre-conscious, they respond very quickly to the histrionic; the growth of America and the expansion of its territories are, in themselves, dramatic events. Above all, the American language is a wonderful instrument for the expression of the grand and grandiloquent occasion, gesture, situation. But whereas both the novel and poetry in the twentieth century have been fed by the virile ancestry of the past, the drama has had to gain its substance from more recent sources. Eugene O'Neill, very much a man of the twentieth century, is at once America's first and, so far, its greatest dramatist.

He, and all of his contemporaries, both of his own generation and those born later, have turned to Europe for both intellectual and technical inspiration. Ibsen, Chekhov, later Brecht, then Beckett, have been dominating influences on a number of American dramatists—but most notably on O'Neill and Miller. With something of a start we recognize the snapped-chord musical reminiscence of Chekhov in *Death of a Salesman*[1] and the self-conscious assumption of a European myth is constantly apparent in *Mourning Becomes Electra*.[2]

The effects and detail of European influence have been well and comprehensively written about, almost always with a

177

sense of regret or frustration that the American dramatists have found it well-nigh impossible to be free of that European grip so that they could create a characteristically American culture. But what the Americans could not take from Europe (because they had, long ago, already brought it with them and transformed it) was the English language. One of the unique features of American culture is the language. Among the indigenous features in American society—the emergence of Yankee and Southerner, the looming fact of black and white, the 'classlessness' which is so full of layers and snobberies—there are others which seem more familiar. But it is often dangerous for a foreigner to try and interpret them in his own terms or to presume too much upon what, so often, turns out to be an illusory familiarity: There is, for instance, no exact equivalent in England of the Willy Loman type, in the sense of Willy's status in society and society's assessment of his professional expertise, or lack of it. We can, it is true, feel and see the truth of Willy's 'tragedy', as surely as we are able to experience Blanche Dubois, but the tensions which create the tragedy are, to a degree, the product of a social environment and a history which is alien.

It has become a joke to point out the difficulties which too glib an attitude towards the American language can lead to—'garters' and 'braces' and 'lifts' and 'elevators' all bear with them a jocose confusion. But the jokes hide important matters. The resonances of many words and phrases in American speech are in themselves—like 'give me a rain check'— inexplicable to us, as indeed are 'hwyl' or 'small beer' to an American.

The English are, indeed, in a specially difficult position in any attempt to assess American verbal culture, simply because the compulsion is always to assume that the same words mean the same thing in the two different languages—a 'cow-poke' is as innocent in the United States as a 'knock up in the morning' is in the United Kingdom, but geographical transposition is not without stern hazards.

A conceit of knowledge is both protected and increased for the English (the Americans are far more cautious about assuming they know what English words mean) by the hypnotic pervasiveness of American films. Because the English hear so much American they think they know. Indeed, quite often, they not only think they know, they sometimes affect what they believe is an American way of speaking. It is no idle fact that it seems to be far more difficult for Americans to 'take' English regional speech in plays and films than it is for the English to accept American. In a very real sense Tennessee Williams is a regional writer, but his plays have been infinitely more successful generally in England than have the plays of Arnold Wesker in the United States. In a great many Western films there is often a strong regional accent used or 'mixed in' with something near a 'standard' custom-built verbal product—the vinegar of Virginia with oil of Hollywood—but we never baulk at it. It is partly because we have become used to it, partly because we are ignorant of the mix, and partly because, indeed, we only listen to the noise it makes, without really attempting to understand the specific meanings and nuances of its verbal patterns. The latter factor may very well play a more important part in our experience of the American language than we think. The success of the Western film in England may be because it is overheard rather than listened to. As the film's visual splendour, rangy psychology, graphic story, unfold, our interest mounts and is sustained against a context of speech 'noises' that are unusual and, for most people, attractive.

And so, as with Eliot's famous belief that poetry should be having and has an effect on audiences without their being conscious of its presence, American speech in films has its effect without too great a straining on our part. We do not have to grasp for every detail of meaning, every nuance, in order to be beguiled by the tonal virility of it, and the magic it exerts is reinforced by the fascinating attractiveness of certain words and phrases. The scalp lifts a little when we hear—'I knew a guy down in Wichita', 'What d'you know', 'Reach for it', 'I've got you covered', 'Sure thing', 'Yeah'. It is the noise, perhaps first of all and perhaps most of all, that arrests our attention and corrals it.

The 'noise of the American language' is, of course, a contradiction in terms—since there are many accents, many noises. But just as there are a number of unmistakable characteristics from which we can recognize an 'English noise', so there are for the American. Perhaps the most conspicuous characteristic of American speech is to be found in the wonderful variety of the use of vowels. To hear a Southerner pronounce 'Tallahassee' is to experience a kind of lilting delight. On the other hand, a Bostonian rendering the same wonderful word is an expendable experience. In no English dialect is there to be found the strange kick before 'a' in the pronunciation of 'man', in many American accents, so that it becomes 'myan'.

Perhaps it is Hollywood that has produced the prevailing impression that the American 'voice' is deeper than the English one. Whether it is or not, it so often seems to be, giving a sense of purpose, strength, decision, standing-on-its-own-feet power. Whether or not we are here dealing with fact or invention, it is remarkable how often in American films and plays, a high-pitched voice is associated with all the opposite qualities. To speak high is to be weak.

There is stronger ground for fact to rest on in another aspect of 'Americanism' in speech. Certain quirks of utterance are demonstrable. For example, the ubiquitous habit of the unspoken question—the uplifting of the voice at the end of a statement which is really asking (very politely) if you are hearing or understanding or will remember what is being said—or, indeed, if you agree with what is being said—'My name is Cicero Jones Junior [?] and I've come to stay with you' [?]. There is, too, the very frequent use of 'uh huh' as an implication of question or of agreement. This has crept into the English mode of common expression but is still not so widespread in use as in America.

Again, 'please' is a word more often honoured in the breach in American expression, though 'thank you' is often fulsome, or apparently so. The polite and deferential 'sir', often used interrogatively, is beginning to die out, but is still very characteristically American. The English 'sir', now almost defunct, had a much more formal usage and was often used as castigation not deference.

No doubt very comprehensive differences in grammatical structures between the English language and the American could be noted, but what is of great significance is that most Englishmen's experience of American is through the ears not

180

the eyes. It is film, radio and television, far more than the public library, which bring the American verbal realities home to us. This is a fact which should form part of any assessment of the dramatic language of American plays.

There is an element of 'thrill' in listening to a language which is apparently built of the same materials as one's own but which has strongly unusual features—noises, rhythms, words, phrases, nuances. Without pushing the notion too far, we may perhaps consider that there is an analogy here with the thrill of listening to poetry. It, too, uses the raw materials of our own common stock of speech, but its attractiveness and power come from the unusual usages to which that common stock is put. It may indeed be that the experience of listening to the familiar/strange American language is the nearest many people, not otherwise given to exploring the unusual in verbal communication, get to an experience of 'poetry'.

There is a need to be careful about the analogy we have made. We must not find poetry where it does not exist. What is thrillingly unusual to us may well be familiar, ordinary and dull to the Americans. What our imaginations see as strange may to them be a commonplace domesticity. And yet, both non-literate and literate Americans seem to have an astonishing self-consciousness about language. They sometimes may use it badly, but they rarely use it dully. They are inventive with it; they like, enormously, to write and talk of style and manner and expression. They often speak their words with an undoubted ear to the frisson which their pronunciations and associations have.

If, then, we are to be careful not to overstate the 'poetic' qualities of the American spoken language, and, by inference, of the dramatic language of American plays, we must still not underrate the American sensitivity to verbal expression. Yet the record of strictly poetic writing for the theatre is both sparse and unremarkable. The American theatre has been, in fact, almost wholly bereft of any body of verse drama. Distinguished men of letters have tried but have not succeeded. Wallace Stevens was a considerable poet but no dramatist. Maxwell Anderson was a distinctive playwright but an unconvincing poet. Archibald MacLeish[3] was neither a good dramatist nor a satisfactory poet. We are almost forced to look

181

elsewhere in drama for the literary evidences of the American way with language.

And everywhere, in the work of prose-dramatists, both in incidental comments and in their plays, the evidences are plain. The aspiration to write a 'heightened' language is common to Eugene O'Neill, Arthur Miller, Tennessee Williams, and is implicit in Edward Albee and others. However much they may write of their 'naturalistic' or 'realistic' motivations or of the 'language of man in the street' their work is by way of being a kind of contradiction. The idea of drama as the unusual expression of unusual people is nearer to being true of American than of English twentieth-century dramatists—particularly in the last three decades. English naturalism and its language of man in society is altogether more raw than its American counterpart. The characters of English naturalistic drama are generally of a diminished or even mean stature when seen against them. Stanley Kowalski is as psychologically violent as Jimmy Porter but he is a 'bigger' persona. Willy Loman is as much 'failed' as Archie Rice but his failure has a greater eloquence of expression and, as a consequence, his status is both individual and typical—as, indeed, are Shakespeare's characters.

No writer of American drama was more conscious of language than Eugene O'Neill. He wrote of his own deficiencies and aspirations with candour and insight. The play which, ironically, most of its admirers would term his most 'poetic' —*Mourning Becomes Electra*—fell short of his own standards because 'it needed great language' and, he added, 'I haven't got that'. By way of consoling himself, perhaps, but certainly expressing an important truth, O'Neill declared that he did not think 'that great language is possible for anyone living in the discordant, broken, faithless rhythm of our time'.[4] This remark, vivid in its truth, is the more impressive in that it was written before the frightful onslaughts made on the English language by mass media. But his belief that he was living in a time of decayed language did not lessen his aspiration to write above the time: 'The best one can do is to be pathetically eloquent by one's moving, dramatic inarticulations.' Putting aside the emotive and largely personal implications of 'pathetic' the significant words in the sentence are 'eloquent' and 'moving'. It would be very hard, perhaps impossible, to find any English dramatist of the twentieth century and certainly not since the war who would be prepared to admit those words as emblems of his aspirations. Even Clifford Odets[5]—who is the nearest version of an English 'social-realist' dramatist in American drama, in the sense that his language positively embraces the vernacular, the raw, the idiomatic—rises to a pitch beyond naturalism. 'Do not hesitate to use music wherever possible. It is very valuable in emotionally stirring an audience', he writes in his production notes, and his language, in its final effect, soars towards rather than aims at its subject. Wesker, alone, seems to have the American aspiration to eloquence, in recent English drama. Kenneth Tynan, with something of contradiction, only confirms this aspiration as a general characteristic in American prose-drama when, having declared *Death of a Salesman* a 'triumph in the plain style', he adds that it 'rings with phrases'; he concludes that Willy's wife's rebuke to her sons in memorable and that Charley's words about his dead neighbour have the 'half-articulate power' of an epitaph. His final judgment is that, although 'Miller's prose slips into a sentimental rhythm of despair' and that there is some 'otiose breast-beating', it has 'an emotional effect unrivalled in post-war drama'.[6] One is inclined to ask how 'plain' can eloquence be?

The question is the more pertinent in view of the nature of the disapproval which Miller's play *Death of a Salesman* attracted. Its supporters hailed it as a modern tragedy, its detractors seized upon its language and the 'ordinariness' of its hero to support their contention that tragedy requires unusual expression by unusual personages. George Steiner dismissed Miller with a sentence:

> The brute snobbish fact is that men who die speaking as does Macbeth are more tragic than those who utter platitudes in the style of Willie Loman.

Miller himself seemed to be an advocate on behalf of his detractors in some of the statements he had made about drama and language. He claimed that it is 'necessary to separate drama from what we think of today as literature'; he declared that although it 'uses words, verbal rhythms, and poetic image' it should not be looked at 'first and foremost from literary perspectives'.[7] But this is quite different from saying that dramatic language should not be eloquent in the sense that it should resonate beyond the mere surface tension of its statements. What Miller wished to avoid was, simply, artificial and literary speech. His detractors believed that, to do this, he deliberately wrote a language completely devoid of anything but the most banal expression.

Tynan has already alerted us to have a care with our definition of what is plain. It remains to examine whether Miller's language in the play most generally agreed to be one of his most realistic, and which some regard as one of the finest American plays of the century, confirms or denies the general premise that American prose-drama embodies the naturally 'poetic' condition of the American language. *Death of a Salesman* is a crucial test-case. It is man-in-society Miller is writing of; it is 'unexceptional' man in every sense he is dealing with. The play succeeds or fails in relation to the extent to which it is credible not only within its own context but to the social context of its times. It must, therefore, speak a language its times can relate to. What kind of language is it?

The first, and general impression given by *Death of a Salesman* is that it is a carefully designed piece of artistic expression. There is nothing avant-garde-ish, nothing anarchic, either about its theme or its communication. Miller is obviously writing within a cultural framework which includes Ibsen and Expressionism. It is a piece of art which has a prefabricated design on our emotions and our social awareness—though the relative degree of Miller's emphasis on these is not clear, and may be different for a non-American. The second impression is that the play is compulsively readable; it has the grip of good narrative, interesting characters and tense atmosphere. It is important to emphasize this since Miller is on record with his abhorrence of plays which are meant to be read, and are readable. He shares this feeling with Tennessee Williams. But neither of them can escape their fate—their plays both read and act well. Miller, in fact, positively flies against his own principle in some of his stage-directions, where, one might guess, he has taken a leaf out of Shaw's book. A number of them have that fullness and extra-dramatic quality we have noticed as characteristic of Shaw. Miller, for example, in *Death of a Salesman*, personalizes location:

> The leaves are gone. It is night again, and the apartment houses look down from behind.

He emulates Shaw's character-analyses in his stage-directions:

> —she more than loves him, she admires him, as though his mercurial nature, his temper, his massive dreams and little cruelties, served her only as sharp reminders of the turbulent longings which she shares but lacks the temperament to utter and to follow to their end.[8]

Inexorably, Miller pushes the reader and the theatregoer into an experience which is naturalism plus. To put it crudely, no one can believe that Willy Loman is just a depiction of a failed salesman and that the location in which we see his life played out is a mere naturalistic framework for a naturalistic character. To sit in a darkening auditorium or, less tensely, in one's study, as the Miller play unfolds is to be taken into a world which has, about it, a kind of incandescence; there is a strangeness about the place, the people and the language they speak:

Willy: First thing in the morning. Everything'll be all right.
   (*Biff reaches behind the heater and draws out a length of rubber tubing. He is horrified and turns his head towards Willy's room, still dimly lit, from which the strains of Linda's desperate but monotonous humming rise*)
Willy: (*Staring through the window into the moonlight*) Gee, look at the moon moving between the buildings!

Banal phrases of dialogue, certainly, but the confluence of visual and verbal is not without emotive force.

Two usages of Miller's increase the force and momentum of the play's advance from plain naturalism. One is the use of music which, when it is called for, always accompanies speech. The other is the oscillation between time-present and time-past. The language of the play slips in and out of tenses as its characters slip in and out of different time-scales. A ritual is gradually built up, and, within it, the characters, particularly

Willy Loman, are exposed to its mercy. We have to assess what the characters say, and what is said about them, not through any banality we may detect in specific lines of dialogue, but in the function and nature of that dialogue in the ritual. Close examination shows it to be complex rather than crude.

The use of repetition, particularly in Act I, is too persistent to be accidental. The first piece of dialogue we hear is dominated by it:

Willy: It's all right. I came back.
Linda: Why? What happened? (*Slight pause*) Did something happen, Willy?
Willy: No, nothing happened.
Linda: You didn't smash the car, did you?
Willy: I said nothing happened. Didn't you hear me?

'Happened'—it is not merely a rhythm which is hypnotic, it holds a fear and a frustration. There is a sickening dying fall in the disposition of prefixes—'What?', 'something', 'nothing'. Indeed, the repetition of words is used with consummate skill to convey a quirk of speech of Willy's (shared, to a degree, by his family). But, always, the repetition adds up, so to say, to a reflection, usually ironic, on the character himself:

Don't make any promises. No promises.

. . . and you're very young, Biff, you're too young to be talking seriously to girls . . . Too young entirely, Biff.

Happy: Go on to sleep. But talk to him in the morning, will you?
Biff: (*Reluctantly getting into bed*): With her in the house. Brother!
Happy: (*Getting into bed*) I wish you'd have a good talk with him. (*The light in their room begins to fade*)
Biff: (*To himself in bed*) That selfish, stupid . . .
Happy: Sh . . . sleep, Biff.

Soon as you finish' the car, boys, I wanna see ya. I got a surprise for you, boys.
Biff: (*Offstage*) Whatta ya got, Dad?
Willy: No, you finish first. Never leave a job till you've finished.

Wouldn't that be something? Just swingin' there under those branches. Boy, that would be . . .

The unfinished condition of the last example reinforces the effectiveness of the device of repetition. Indeed, although both Williams and Albee also use the device, none do it with such consistency and variety as Miller, particularly in this play. We have seen the ways in which it is used to surround naturalism with an aura in which emotion, rhythm and impressionism can flourish, but there is one other usage which takes us further into the domain of the poetic.

It has long been recognized that Shakespeare's plays contain dominant and repetitive images. Critics have disagreed on many of the implications and meanings of particular image-groups or clusters, as they are called, but their existence and their theatrical effect is generally agreed. Miller repeats key words. The effect has little of the potency and extreme subtlety of Shakespeare, but, inevitably, they give to the language a characteristic style and shape, and they create moments of intensity when some aspect of character or situation which otherwise lurks unsaid comes to the surface of the play. 'Like', 'promises', 'job', 'terrific', 'lonesome', 'anaemic', 'boys', are, as they repeat themselves on Willy's lips, as much windows into his own soul as they are reflections of his relationship with those around him. Although he is given the major amount of repetitions, they are not exclusive to him. There is a most touching example of a more subtle form of repetition in the scene between Linda and Willy before he goes off to meet Biff at the restaurant. 'Glasses', 'handkerchief' and 'saccharine' become pathetic emblems of what Willy has become – perhaps what he always was:

Linda: . . . You got your glasses?
Willy: (*Feels for them then comes back in*) Yeah, yeah, got my glasses.
Linda: (*Giving him the handkerchief*) And a handkerchief.
Willy: Yeah, handkerchief.
Linda: And your saccharine?
Willy: Yeah, my saccharine.

Another version of repetition produces a wry irony. In this example there is a gap before the key word is repeated. When that gap is closed it is found to contain a kind of emptiness— which is Willy's character:

Linda: . . . You see how sweet he was as soon as you talked hope-
   fully? (*She goes over to Biff*) Come up and say good night to him.
   Don't let him go to bed that way.
Happy: Come on, Biff, let's buck him up.
Linda: Please, dear. Just say good night. It takes so little to make him
   happy. Come. (*She goes through the living-room doorway, calling
   upstairs from within the living-room*) Your pyjamas are hanging in
   the bathroom, Willy!
Happy: (*Looking towards where Linda went out*) What a woman! They
   broke the mould when they made her. You know that Biff?
Biff: He's off salary. My God, he's working on commission.
Happy: Well, let's face it: he's no hot-shot selling man. Except that
   sometimes, you have to admit, he's a sweet personality.

There are times when Miller tries too hard to achieve a
reverberation of language. But here we are again in that area
where we must caution ourselves about the difference between the American and the English language, and the
acceptability or otherwise of the usages of one by the other
country.

The United States, both in written prose and in public
oratory has a distinguished record in the employment of
rhetoric. The Gettysburg Address, the Declaration of Inde-
pendence, some American presidential addresses to the
nation, have a grandeur, a stylish and stylized shape, an emotional ebb and flow which perhaps only Winston Churchill
(who glorified in his American connections) in this century
could emulate. Miller, O'Neill and Williams in a descending
order of extent have this quality of rhetoric. To Welsh ears it is
reminiscent of preachers long dead—and indeed, its sources
may have had pulpit oratory mixed with them—and is acceptable. English ears often find it embarrassing, over-bold in its
calculated artistry, its assault on the emotions. Churchill was
effective not because his speeches were brilliantly constructed
alone, but because the times and the dispositions of his listen-
ers were temporarily able to accept them. Linda's sudden and
famous rhetorical outburst on behalf of Willy sounds like an
American defence lawyer's summing up in a prestigious film
about political scandal. The speech contains the words:

> Willy Loman never made a lot of money. His name was never
> in the paper. He's not the finest character that ever lived. But

he's a human being, and a terrible thing is happening to him. So attention must be paid. He's not to be allowed to fall into his grave like an old dog. Attention, attention must be finally paid to such a person . . .

On stage, in the United States, well delivered, it might well achieve its purpose which, presumably, is to indicate Linda's depth of love and, perhaps, to raise Willy's character into a representative status—all small men might take heart, so to speak. But, as so often with rhetoric, it is over-generalized. 'Something' or 'somebody' must pay attention, but who? Again, rhetoric tends to depersonalize language, as if the withdrawal of the personality of the person speaking is likely to lift the words into a higher plane of communication and make them more portentous.

The use of rhetoric, of which this is one example only, is highly characteristic of American drama. It may be suspected that it is a deliberate attempt to raise 'poetry' out of the soil of 'prose'. The irony is that, as both Miller and Williams and O'Neill show, the American language itself, in its idiomatic state, contains enough of the stuff of poetry without recourse to the kind of high inventiveness rhetoric displays. Thus it gives an impression of contrived eloquence, the more so since it comes from the mouth of a character to whom it seems singularly inappropriate—Willy Loman's wife.

This is neither the only example in this play (though the most obvious) nor in Miller's other plays nor, indeed, in other American dramatists. Indeed it is a characteristic of the dramatist who, committed to a naturalistic mode, nevertheless wishes to increase the lift of associativeness of his language so that it rises above the 'common cry' of ordinary language. Naturalistic dramatists (whether they be English or American) who on the one hand want the immediacy of idiom and on the other cannot help recalling that it is heightened speech which carries drama beyond the implications of the mere present tense, are wont to use it. Wesker and Osborne are prone to it, even Galsworthy shows a tendency towards it. But no English dramatist has anything like the oratorical tradition to embolden him to use it with quite such embarrassing largesse as do the Americans.

The conclusion cannot be escaped that it is a surrogate for
'poetry' since it is so often used for those moments of heightened consciousness which, as Eliot said, ask for poetic utterance. Ironically, however, the Americans do not require it
since they have, in their everyday language—and very much
nearer to the surface than in contemporary English
speech—the stuff out of which poetic statement can be made.

Tennessee Williams not only gives the impression of being a
'poet' of theatre, but, in some ways can justifiably lay claim to
being the most consciously poetic of his generation of American playwrights. All his plays give a strong impression of
meaning more than is conveyed by their surface appearances;
all of them, to a degree, have what E. Martin Browne has
referred to as a 'luminous' quality—as if the characters were,
so to say, on loan only to this clay-ey earth and brought with
them, for their temporary stay, a colouring of some other-
where. In their different ways, Blanche Dubois, Chanie
Wayne, Big Daddy and Rosa, are all citizens of a country
whose nature we can only half guess at. What we experience of
them is what is revealed when they are planted in the explicit
naturalistic situations of the plays.

And this is the paradox. Whatever of poetry we may find in
Williams's dramatic imagination and in his theatrical technique—and there is a great deal of it—its intention is to shar-
pen the naturalistic truth of his themes. What he says of *The
Glass Menagerie,*[9] in the production notes, is true in one sense
or another, of all his plays: 'Expressionism and all other
unconventional techniques in drama have only one valid aim,
and that is a closer approach to truth.' We should be clear that
the 'truth' he speaks of is no abstraction, but is concerned with
man's battle with the environments he discovers or creates for
himself. Williams uses a poetic vision and technique in order,
as he says, 'to find a closer approach, a more penetrating and
vivid expression of things as they are'.

The verbal medium he generally uses is prose and, in most
of his plays, it is not a heightened form of expression but relies
a good deal on the vernacular. Miller achieves his effects
largely through his manipulation of language and, in fact, he
has a far more subtle way with words than Williams. The
latter pushes his plays through the naturalistic barrier and into

more evocative and resonant areas by a combination of different techniques in which words are only a part not the whole.

The play by which he became known outside the United States—*A Streetcar Named Desire*[10]—has suffered the greatest amount of misinterpretation of any play since World War II. It was serialized in England in one of the more spectacular Sunday newspapers and advertised as calculated to 'shock' its readers. It achieved a reputation as being sexually permissive—a fate curiously withheld from Williams's *The Seven Descents of Myrtle*,[11] with its very explicit depiction of the oral sex act. The play was vilified by many and over-adulated by some. It was regarded by a few as an allegory of the North–South complex in the United States and claimed by others to be a study in nymphomania. While all the contrary opinions and judgments were aired, the play was steadily being enjoyed by millions of theatregoers.

The most remarkable feature of *A Streetcar Named Desire* is that, after thirty years, it has not only not dated but seems, now, an even better play than even the most immoderate of its supporters believed when it first appeared. Even more, now that time has provided a context, a landscape filled with other figures, it is possible to see how this play had an influence, not only in the United States but in England. Arthur Miller's technical problems, especially in space and time, in *Death of a Salesman* must surely have been eased by his reading and seeing of Williams's play. Stanley Kowalski seems not only an ancestor of Jimmy Porter but the prototype of the half-baffled creature of anger which has inhabited so many 'realistic' films and plays both in this country and overseas. If ever one were forced to be explicit about dramatic history—a subject where certainty is an elusive thing—the significance of Stanley Kowalski might well provide the opportunity. The day of the passionate non-hero dawned when Kowalski yelled 'Stella'.

But Williams's play has other claims on our attention. He wrote others set in different places and occupied with different themes, but *Streetcar* contains within itself the essence of a particular technique of writing which is not exclusive to the United States, is not unique to Williams, yet is employed there and in him with far greater confidence and by more dramatists

191

than in England. Williams's play is a fine example of the technique.

Martin Browne was not sure whether to call Williams a poetic realist or a realistic poet and, in a sense, his uncertainty is less important than what his use of the terms leads us towards. 'Poetic' suggests words, 'realist' suggests attitude, but it also suggests the technical means by which the dramatist makes that attitude clear. As we have noted, Williams's poetry does not, in fact, lie all in his words, neither does his realism lie all in the way he looks at and constructs character, his theme, his plot. We are faced with a curious mixture of creative effort in which the verbal and the technical react upon one another.

Perhaps Martin Browne's uncertainty about his terms is influenced by his belief that Williams is 'a visual writer'. This is true, and Browne is right in declaring that Williams's successful stage-pictures of the apartment house in *The Glass Menagerie* and the 'see-through' house of *Streetcar* extended the visual range of theatrical effect. But Williams has a very strong aural sense, and is outstanding among American dramatists for the contrapuntal effects he is able to achieve by a putting together of 'heard' and 'seen' material. Williams's poetic qualities come, unlike Miller's, from a sense of design in which the verbal is only an element. Indeed, when Williams occupies too much of his energy in squeezing effect out of language—as in *Camino Real*—the result is artificial-sounding, contrived, unrelated to character. In *Streetcar* his language is given the place in which it can best fulfil its role in the overall design.

Like Miller, he uses, but much more sparingly, the device of repetition. Partly because of this spareseness, when it occurs it sometimes seems a little forced:

Stanley: He must have had a lot of—admiration.
Blanche: Oh, in my youth I excited some admiration.

Its function, unlike Miller's is, on the whole, to emphasize a trait of character, rather than to create a rhythmic effect. Stanley is given to repetition and, through it, his relentless determination is emphasized:

> Genuine fox fur-pieces, a half a mile long! Where are your fox-pieces, Stella? Bushy snow-white ones, no less! Where are your white fox-pieces?

192

Williams also employs occasionally a device which produces an immediate ironic effect. It is important to distinguish between irony used as a suddenly imposed device for a particular moment and as a tone, a style, and therefore an attitude, throughout a play. Few modern dramatists have this overall ironic quality; most, like Williams, use only the sudden catapult effect which strikes its target but delivers neither a great nor a lasting wound:

> Blanche: . . . and there has been a continued round of entertainments, teas, cocktails, and luncheons—
> *(A disturbance is heard upstairs at the Hubbels' appartment)*
> Stella: *(Crossing to the door)* Eunice seems to be having some trouble with Steve.

Williams, in common with Miller, seems to have a compulsion to compress 'messages' into set-piece speeches—a device which acquired obsessive proportions in Wesker and Osborne and Delaney and which has continued into contemporary English drama. In these speeches Williams, like Miller, and their later emulators, gives us the core of a character's personality or attitude; it is a kind of important summing-up and almost invariably is communicated in a way which draws more and more attention to itself as the message unfolds. These speeches have the effect of emotive perorations. In *Streetcar* Blanche has a monopoly of them and, from her, they seem natural. Her personality is one long peroration, her training as an English teacher has taught her the ability to use words emotively. Sometimes we have minor examples—too small in length to achieve the emotional build-up of such a speech as Blanche's on Stanley as cave-man, but making, so to speak, a splash in the auditor's imagination by use of simple symbolism:

> Blanche: What you are talking about is brutal desire—just
> —Desire!—the name of that rattle-trap street-car that
> bangs through the Quarter . . .
> Stella: Haven't you even ridden on that street-car?
> Blanche: It brought me here . . .

In these ways Williams gives his text a patina. It is often effective, it is occasionally obtrusive, but it never seems to be more, in terms, that is, of verbal effect alone, than a gloss on a basically simple and demotic style. What any foreigner must realize, however, is that in *Streetcar*, and in *Cat on a Hot Tin Roof*,[13] that demotic style in itself carries with it a tremendous associative quality. Anyone who reads *Streetcar* or those plays of Williams's which have Southern characters without hearing the Southern accent in his head can completely misjudge the effect of the play. The Southern accent gives *Streetcar* its music, its irony, its lyrical plangency, its curiously decadent tone. These are not to be found on the page, silent. They are in that pervasive, strong, clinging accent which has so much of dispossession in it. Williams's plays are full of dispossessed people who we feel were once gentle but who find the jungle has caught up with their gracious clearings and spaces and the animals with their civilized pursuits. We hear in it, too, a kind of self-defeat, self-delusion, a weakness, so that we wonder what lies behind the gentleness, the civil behaviour.

But Williams does not rely just on the Southern accent and a few technical devices to produce his quite remarkable dramatic language. He ensures that the naturalism of character, location and plot ascends into poetic dimensions by placing his verbal effects within a larger theatrical design. The details of this design are true for all his plays, but it is *Streetcar* which employs them with greatest clarity and, on the whole, with greatest impact.

There are three aspects and all involve both visual and aural. The first is the creation of visual set-pieces, reminiscent of Shaw's 'gathering-together' of persons for moments of dramatic significance. The very form of expression of certain of his stage-directions emphasizes this:

> There is a picture of Van Gogh's of a billiard-parlour at night. The kitchen now suggests that sort of lucid nocturnal brilliance, the raw colours of childhood's spectrum . . . (For a moment there is absorbed silence as a hand is dealt.)

And, when groups move, they move as if in an ordained frieze:

> Eunice descends to Stella and places the child in her arms. It is wrapped in a pale blue blanket. Stella accepts the child, sobbingly. Eunice continues downstairs and enters the kitchen

where the men except for Stanley, are returning silently to their places about the table . . .

But, second, and unlike Shaw, these visual effects are almost always accompanied by very strong, calculated, aural effects:

Eunice goes back to the portières. Drums sound very softly.

Two women, one white and one coloured, are taking the air on the steps of the building . . . Above the music of the 'blue piano' the voices of people on the street can be heard overlapping.

Throughout *Streetcar*, and reaching dominance towards the end of the play, there is a contrapuntal effect between visual and aural. In one section (Scene vii) aural and aural are the ingredients. The stage-direction reads:

Blanche is singing in the bathroom a saccharine popular ballad which is used contrapuntally with Stanley's speech.

And, thirdly, there is a frequent use of actual noise, as distinct from speech, to symbolize states of mind, or to heighten atmosphere. In *Streetcar*, the sound of a locomotive, the squeal of cats, a piano, voices whose words cannot be discerned are as potent as the wind and the whistling in *Camino Real*, the music in *The Glass Menagerie*. Always, the noise is accompanied by visual reactions to it by characters, or by some change of light—sound and shadows on a wall are a constant motif in Williams's imagination.

The importance of Williams's use of the language of drama and of theatre, often with complicated subtlety and, it must be admitted, often with forced contrivance, is that it is an emblem of what seems to be an American search for a form of dramatic communication which will have the effect of poetry without losing the immediacy of naturalistic prose. There is no such thing, in any significant sense, as a tradition of American dramatic verse. Many reasons have been put forward for this, but the deepest may lie at the heart of a paradox. For a country so committed to the cultivation of individual initiative it is remarkably gregarious and capable of corporate action; for a country so fond of preaching the gospel of material wealth it is wonderfully responsive not just to the acquisition but the appreciation of the abstract; for a country that seems sometimes neurotically determined to project the image of rugged rationality, it shows vast evidences of sentimentality. A nation like this and whose language can be both terse, clipped, monosyllabic and rich in imagery and inventiveness is one torn between the desire to seem down-to-earth, of the present, decisive, and the yearning to be aerial, unhampered either by space or time, reflective. It wants both to spend its gold *and* turn it into 'airy thinnesse'. It commits itself completely neither to the pursuit of the one nor the other. It cannot, by the same token, harbour a drama that is either unequivocally 'poetic' or totally 'prosaic'. Its dramatists still search for a language—in the widest sense of the word—which will embody both. In their own ways all modern American dramatists try to solve a paradox. Tennessee Williams is the most typical and the most assiduous of them.

But the most brilliantly effective user of the American language in drama is Edward Albee. He has achieved as much fame in England as have Miller and Williams. In his case there might seem to be a special relationship with European drama for he has frequently been dubbed an 'absurd' dramatist. The claim of his alleged affiliation to this essentially European cult was based largely on the play *The Zoo Story*. On the evidence, however, of a more substantial and longer work—*Who's Afraid of Virginia Woolf?*[4]—the claim seems to have an uncertain validity.

Absurdism, in so far as it relates to drama, has two main aspects—the point of view expressed in and by the play, and the method and means of expression. Perhaps the purest if not, in a sense, the best absurd dramatist is Ionesco and, in him, the two aspects are very clearly to be observed.

No reader or audience of an Ionesco play can fail to be aware (whatever else may puzzle them) of an overwhelming presentation of an attitude, a vision, a 'philosophy', related to the writer's apparent experience of life. There is a sense of futility, often becoming despair, there is a wry, sometimes even savage presentation of the inadequacy of human thought, feeling and action, there is an often baffling demonstration of the failure of human relationships and of human communication. Above all, in these plays mankind seems lost and alone in a present which terrifies him and oblivious to a past and a future which may or may not have any reality. The vision is 'absurd' because there is so much that is incongruous, incompatible, inexplicable to be seen in man's existence. Simply because of this absurdity the action that is presented in such plays can be both comic and pathetic, savage and inert. There is no moral judgment, or any other kind of judgment, involved—these plays and the characters who inhabit them just 'are', and that is all. The audience is not requested to make any decisions about what he experiences except the decision to 'accept' rather than attempt to 'explain' the play, and whatever conclusions he makes or questions he asks are his own affair—nothing is asked to be laid at the door of the play. 'Is "Godot" God?', someone is supposed to have asked Beckett, and received the answer—'if you like'. The interviewer, emboldened to ask Pinter what one of his plays 'meant', is said to have been told that it meant what it said.

The language of an 'absurd' play is just as distinctive as the vision which one senses or observes in it. Indeed what marks off Pinter, Ionesco, Beckett, in particular, from their non-absurdist colleagues is the amount of attention the language they use demands (because of its uniqueness) from the playgoer and the critic. To a very high degree, the language is the focus of the vision. To try and separate meaning and speech in an absurd play is to enter far into misrepresentation or into bafflement. In absurb drama language is used poetically, in the sense that however much it may seem to be a naturalistic version of real speech, closer examination shows that it is using the resources of poetry, to a degree. Beckett and Pinter, in particular, demonstrate this superbly. However, while it does this, in the way it uses inconsequentiality, idiom, pause, repetition, it gives speech to the essential quality and the details of the author's 'absurd' vision of existence.

An absurd play is, therefore, an image of human existence. It uses the sense-data provided by the so-called everyday world (even *Waiting for Godot*[15] does this) but, in the long run, the spatial boundaries of an absurd play are not to be found in 'real' life, but in an inexplicable universe and a relentless eternity.

Edward Albee, in *The Zoo Story*, seems to partake of some

of the characteristics of absurdism. The language is apparently inconsequential at times; the relationships are unsure or inexplicable; motivations both for speech and action seem governed less by rational processes than by a meaningless spontaneous reflex, the 'meaning' is elusive and, like so many absurd plays, there is 'no beginning, no middle, no end'.

This seems a formidable collection of evidence, but it may be suggested that, qualitatively, it is spurious. Almost every item seems too mechanically arrived at, contrived by a 'clever' writer. All the figures are correct, but the answer is not the right one. There are two main reasons for placing doubt on the claim for Albee's absurdism.

The first is the absence of the characteristic absurdist vision. This is absent from all of his plays, including the chief candidate for acceptance—*The Zoo Story*. In that play the frenzy, the change of mood, the menace, seem to be less an attribute of character than an exercise of quixotic theatricality. Apart from this, we find ourselves eventually wondering whether this sort of episode happens often in Central Park – in other words the play is less an image than a brilliant piece of quasi-naturalistic guignol.

The second arises from the degree of 'naturalism' which is present in Albee's plays and which, finally, separates him from the absurdists. Both the degree and its extent is rooted in Albee's sensitive, almost nervy feeling for contemporary American society. He is a superb demonstrator and explicator of certain aspects of Americanism. In order to align him with Pinter we would have to say that in Pinter we find the best mirror of certain aspects of British society today—and nothing else.

It is Albee's commitment to a surgical analysis of certain aspects of American society which debars him from acceptance as a complete and pure absurd dramatist. It is easy to see why he has been associated with these dramatists, because some details of attitude which he takes up towards his society are reminiscent of the typical absurdist vision. *The American Dream*,[16] *Who's Afraid of Virginia Woolf?*, *The Zoo Story*, in particular, exhibit the meaninglessness of certain habits of behaviour, speech, *mores*, cults, myths. Again, all three plays, to a degree, brilliantly dissect certain sterile usages of speech.

The Zoo Story, especially, is redolent of Pinter's concern with human isolation and the dark wastes of non or partial communication. It might be said that Albee's apparent preoccupation with an inability to beget children (in *The American Dream* and *Virginia Woolf*) as an image of sterile futility is, in itself, an 'absurdist' point of view.

But, in all this, there is not the characteristically absurdist miasma of menace, sometimes terror, the sense of unfathomable contexts behind the immediate world of the play, the implacable atmosphere of a-morality, the curiously paradoxical use of language in a 'poetic' fashion to demonstrate, often, the futility of language itself. Indeed it is in the use of language that we can find the distance from European absurdism and the closeness to Americanism. In Albee, too, is perhaps the clearest proof, if not the deepest, that the American language is not the same thing as the English language.

He is amazingly versatile in his deployment of language forms and styles, but there are two broad areas in which he excels—they occupy (and this alone is a proof of versatility) extreme positions from one another. The one may be called literary/dramatic—an eloquent, rhetorical, philosophically inclined mode, the other is demotic/dramatic—in which the usages of contemporary American speech are employed with exciting variety and effect. In *The Zoo Story* he uses both types, in *Who's Afraid of Virginia Woolf?* he concentrates, though not exclusively, on the second, *A Delicate Balance*[17] is almost monopolized by the first. His handling of the demotic/dramatic is much surer, and the results are decidedly more dramatically and theatrically credible than his attempts in the other mode. There, echoes of Eliot, traces even of Charles Morgan[18] and a ghostly assembling of literary forefathers petrify the drama:

> I wonder if that's why we sleep at night, because the darkness still . . . frightens us? They say we sleep to let the demons out—to let the mind go raving mad, our dreams and nightmares all our logic gone awry, the dark side of our reason. And when the daylight comes again . . . Comes order with it. (*Sad chuckle*) Poor Edna and Henry. (*Sigh*) Well, they're safely gone . . . and we'll all forget . . . quite soon. (*Pause*) Come now; we can begin the day.

It has eloquence, it always suggests the operation of sophisticated mental processes, but it is essentially a literary language —it does not so much embody character as describe it or make very articulate the workings of the mind and the emotions.

Albee is revealed as a dramatist of stature in his use of his 'alternative' language. He owes something to Miller in his deployment of certain characteristics of American speech but, in the long run, his is a more precise and searching mode. The most obvious affinity to Miller is in the use of repetition, but the effect is different. With Miller we feel that repetition is used in order to heighten the effect of the language—to take it one degree over naturalistic statement. With Albee we are aware that the repetitions fit more closely into the matrix of characterization; indeed they are often used, as in *Virginia Woolf*, self-consciously by characters with that kind of brittle, conscious verbosity apparent when the scotch-on-the-rocks set has reached the cocktail hour and its tongue is becoming loose.

Nick: Bourbon on the rocks, if you don't mind.
George: (As he makes the drinks) Mind? No, I don't mind. I don't think I mind. Martha? Rubbing alcohol for you?
Martha: Sure. 'Never mix—never worry.'
George: Martha's tastes in liquor have come down . . . simplified over the years . . . crystallized. Back when I was courting Martha—well, I don't know if that's exactly the right word for it—but back when I was courting Martha . . .
Martha: (Cheerfully) Screw, sweetie!
George: (Returning with Honey's and Nick's drinks) At any rate, back when I was courting Martha . . .

It should be remarked that this characteristic is to be distinguished from the equivalent English class speech—the gin-and-tonic professional—set. Their communication is equally wordy, inconsequential, self-conscious, but it is less outright, tends to be blander, it gives far less an impression of speech used as weaponry in which repetition is advance and riposte.

One of the most conspicuous characteristics of absurdist writing is the extent to which dialogue—often using repetition—mirrors emptiness and futility. That emptiness separates and isolates the participants in the dialogue as certainly as a thousand miles of ocean. The audience's experience is of two, occasionally more, individuals being aware of that ocean or trying to comprehend, even, sometimes pitifully, sometimes comically, seeming to consider attempting to cross it. The emptiness is, largely, imposed upon the participants, first and foremost by the nature of existence, but also by the particular situation and by their respective personalities. The crucial factor, however, is the first one—the strong sense of a blank force beyond control.

Albee very rarely gives this impression. The gaps and emptinesses that fall between his characters when they speak habitually convey the impression that they could be filled but, more often, they are filled almost as soon as we are aware of them—not by words, but often as efficaciously in the circumstances. Albee, unlike the absurdists, is less dominated by 'mal d'existence' than beguiled by 'mal de psychologie'. His silences and gaps are filled very quickly by material which comes straight out of the personality of the participants, goaded by the situation or event. In this passage there is a Pinteresque ring to the dialogue, but we are not in one of Pinter's limbos—on the contrary we are with George and Martha, very much with them in their American lounge:

Martha: You laughed your head off when you heard it at the party.
George: I smiled. I didn't laugh my head off . . . I smiled, you know? . . . it was all right.
Martha: (*Gazing into her drink*) You laughed your goddamn head off.
George: It was all right . . .
Martha: (*Ugly*) It was a scream!
George: (*Patiently*) It was very funny; yes.
Martha: (*After a moment's consideration*) You make me puke!
George: What?
Martha: Uh . . . you make me puke!
George: (*Thinks about it . . . then . . .*) That wasn't a very nice thing to say, Martha.
Martha: That wasn't *what*?
George: . . . a very nice thing to say.
Martha: I like your anger. I think that's what I like about you most . . . your anger. You're such a . . . such a simp! You don't even have the . . . the what? . . .
George: . . . guts? . . .
Martha: PHRASEMAKER! (*Pause . . . then they both laugh*) Hey, put some more ice in my drink, will you? You never put any ice in my drink. Why is that, hunh?

George: (*Takes her drink*) I always put ice in your drink. You eat it, that's all. It's that habit you have . . . chewing your ice cubes . . . like a cocker spaniel. You'll crack your big teeth.

The difference between this and true absurdism is neatly confirmed in the sentence that ends the episode—'I can't see you . . . I haven't been able to see you for years.' This throws the whole emphasis upon the relationship between the participants and, so to speak, domesticates the emptiness and futility. Moreover the stage-directions themselves direct the attention towards particular tones of voice and mood which people the gap in the conversation with familiar, naturalistic responses.

Albee's métier as a dramatist of society and man's self-created tensions within it, and his versatility with words are shown, too, in his remarkable manipulation of the language of situation. Again, he uses repetition, but with a very much greater sense of using a technique; at times he reminds one of the Restoration penchant for drawing attention to the very fabric of language and to the cleverness with which it is spun. *Virginia Woolf*, again, provides the best evidence.

Nick and Honey have just arrived, very late, at George and Martha's. The latter are near-drunk and contentious and don't expect visitors. George is prickly. The unfinished sentences, so expertly contrived by Albee, not only precisely echo what so often happens in such a situation when relative strangers are thrown together but, in particular, they directly reveal George's attitude, and in their very incompleteness give an edge to the atmosphere.

Nick: (*Indicating the abstract painting*) Who . . . who did the . . . ?
Martha: That? Oh that's by . . .
George: . . . some Greek with a moustache Martha attacked one night in . . .
Honey: (*To save the situation*) Oh, ho, ho, ho, HO.
Nick: It's got a . . . a . . .
George: A quiet intensity?
Nick: Well, no . . . a . . .
George: Oh. (*Pause*) Well, then, a certain noisy relaxed quality, maybe?
Nick: (*Knows what George is doing, but stays grimly, coolly polite*) No. What I meant was . . .

Albee, generally, seems to be very much more deliberately conscious of the technicalities of using words and takes more delight in employing them for dramatic and theatrical effect than other twentieth-century American dramatists. He seems to have a fastidiousness in his make-up which impels him to look at and to listen to the way his countrymen speak with a rare attention to detail. For example, he uses questions liberally in that affirmative way which is so characteristic of American speech. He makes telling use of the word 'Sir' with its customary attendant question mark, which can, depending on tone of voice, imply either respect or a kind of incipient aggressiveness. He has noted what no other dramatist save J. B. Priestley[19] has observed—that intoxication passes through a stage in which clarity of speech rather than incoherence is dominant. So often dramatists commit the error of making incoherence stand for drunkenness. Albee manipulates repetition brilliantly to reveal the stage where the intoxicated mind is just winning the battle for a kind of exaggerated clarity:

Martha: You bet your sweet life.
George: (*To Nick . . . a confidence, but not whispered*) Let me tell you a
    secret, baby. There are easier things in the world, if you happen
    to be teaching at a university, there are easier things than being
    married to the daughter of the president of that university.
    There are easier things in this world.

In his deployment of American speech Albee, especially in *The Zoo Story*[20] and *Virginia Woolf*, shows that same compulsion towards the rhetorical which we have seen in Miller and Williams and which seems to be a characteristically American predisposition. Albee seems more aware than his colleagues of its dangers—of sentimentality and sententiousness—and he attempts to disguise these in different ways. In *A Delicate Balance* where he uses a sophisticated language which has the flavour of the more cerebral long speeches in *A Family Reunion*, he tries to moderate the effects by the occasional use of an idiomatic phrase. In *Virginia Woolf* there is a speech by George which has all the marks of a set-piece statement which the author wanted to get off his chest. George is under the influence of drink and Albee, at one and the same time, tries to convey this and to lessen the possibility of its seeming set piece and rhetorical by breaking up the lines to give the impression of a faulty delivery. It does not work, however. Only a sudden insertion of the idiomatic breaks a certain falsity which has begun to creep into the play:

> George: (*At Nick, not to him*) You take the trouble to construct a civilization . . . to . . . to build a society, based on the principles of . . . of principle . . . you endeavour to make communicable sense out of natural order, morality out of the unnatural disorder of man's mind . . . you make government and art, and realize that they are, must be, both the same . . . you bring things to the saddest of all points . . . to the point where there is something to lose . . . then all at once, through all the music, through all the sensible sounds of men building, attempting, comes the *Dies Irae*. And what is it? What does the trumpet sound? Up yours. I suppose there's justice to it, after all the years . . . Up yours.

Albee, like Miller and Williams, is at his best when he is not attempting to create a 'literary' language. The American penchant for over-dramatization, over-explicit statement, sentimentality of expression, overcomes them all when they try to invent a poetry of language. All three, but particularly Albee, succeed when they exploit the resources of American spoken speech, not when they try to make one up. This can be put in another way. When American dramatists, either consciously or unconsciously, try to achieve an English classicism they fail. When they write out of the dialect or dialects of their own American tribe, they succeed.

American dramatists, unlike some of the poets and novelists who inherited their nationality and language, sometimes seem to have been too timid to enter fully into either. The great siren song of European culture and the huge centaur of English dramatic history seem, at times, to have both lured and scared them. The irony is that English dramatists, so many of whom nowadays, seem bent on using nothing but the lowest common denominator of English spoken speech, could learn much from the versatility, sensitivity and imaginative richness of their American cousins. These, when they choose to remember that they have their own language, always find in it a strange, indigenous hard poetry.

11 Drama in Contemporary Britain —Verbal and Non-Verbal

John Russell Taylor in his book on the new dramatists of the 1960s and 1970s writes that, 'Again and again, these dramatists are attracted to such subjects as child murder, sex murder, rape, homosexuality, transvestism, religious mania, power mania, sadism, masochism'.[1] This is indeed an impression that many people have of contemporary drama; for these people the dominant characteristic of the drama of our times is its obsession with the seamier side of life.

The reasons they give are various. Some find the culprit in what is usually described as the general permissiveness of contemporary life, involving a decay of religious faith and observance, a disregard for discipline, a dismissal of authority, and a gross slackening of personal and general moral standards. The drama is said to reflect all this and, by implication, is defined as a drama of despair, described by David Mercer in graphic terms and reported by Russell Taylor:

> [Humanity] has been in the wrong bloody boat ever since Plato . . . it's too late to roll back the whole history of Western civilization, to get back to sources and start again.[2]

Indeed, it is not difficult to conclude that there is a pervading joylessness in contemporary drama. All the fun seems confined to a small if virile enclave—as it were, a kind of innocently naughty commune led by the toothy English farceur, Brian Rix, or the snub-nosed American jokester, Bob Hope. Generally, comedy seems to have lost its bright eyes and become black in look and mordant in temper. Farce, too,

205

has apparently lost its athletic naiveté and become sinister. The word puritanical—with its implication of the savouring of sin while it is condemned—might be used to describe a good deal of contemporary drama; so much of it seems to be saying, particularly to any member of society who shows even slight signs of affluence or élitism—'Dost thou think because thou hast cakes and ale that thou shalt not suffer for it?'

Television is claimed by some as the root cause of most of society's ills, including the alleged permissive state of our drama. Yet television cannot, of itself, create a permissive society. It can only exhibit it, report upon it, embody it, and gratify a ready audience—the causes lie deeper than in the eye of the camera. The theologians and philosophers and sociologists may well argue the cause, but television cannot entirely be dismissed from a certain reckoning. What it has created is an acceptance of a greatly increased amount of time devoted to, and experience of, common denominators rather than special ones. Its impetus has been towards removing the element of élitism in, among other things, politics, religion, art, philosophy, even psychology.

This does not mean, so far, for example, as drama in the medium is concerned, that there is no 'serious' drama. What it does mean is that the notion of minority tastes has been abandoned. There are television productions of the classics, adaptations of famous novels and there are, from time to time, new plays of merit. But the typical TV and radio play almost seems custom-built to avoid any accusation of appealing to a special denomination—in any sense. In a way, there is an element of paradox in the typical TV play in that there seems to be an assumption that its values and style are those of all viewers. The truth is, of course, that typical TV drama is a reflection of the vast shift in the location of power, in political and other senses, in society. Privilege, élitism, cultivated speech are far less passports to influence than they were. In fact the opposite is often true. The typical TV play has a 'trade' or regional accent, its characters more often than not are from the lower or lower-middle wage group, the *mores* are those of that group and so are its values. The plays are essentially naturalistic in both plot and location and speech. The themes are often related to a 'social' or 'personal' problem that is immediately recognizable. The media have literally broadcast what, before, was private—particularly sexual and marital problems.

In some ways the typical TV play is a version, albeit sometimes a superior one, of the ubiquitous TV 'soap-opera' serial. Not only is life serialized, it is conceived of as a serial thing. At times it almost seems as if the TV medium has created its own quite characteristic language of drama and theatre—TV people (tele-persons, we may call them) TV situations (tele-life) and TV language (tele-speak). There is an immense predictability in the typical TV play, a frightening opportunity for the viewer to transpose characters, speech, plots and themes from one evening to another as play succeeds play—but nothing ever really seems very different. Both in the United States and in England television drama seems more and more to aspire to the predictabilities and familiarities of soap-opera though, in the States, this depressing process has reached a very advanced stage indeed.

TV continued then finalized the process which eventually emerged in the 1960s and for whose proselytization the so-called 'kitchen-sink' dramatists must take some responsibility. The basic characteristic of the vast majority of naturalistic plays since the early 1960s has been the assumption that, in a very certain sense, no one is 'special'. Time and time again we read in commentaries to the effect that Jimmy Porter 'spoke for his generation', that Beatie in Wesker's *Roots* 'articulated for the hitherto inarticulate'. It seems to be taken as axiomatic by many critics and by even more television viewers and theatregoers that unless a play contains some element of the 'representative' then it is suspect (on grounds, often, which confuse political with artistic judgments). Locations of plays are held to be 'typical' of 'our environment'. In one play, *The National Health*,[3] the ward of a state-controlled medical ward (for that is what it amounts to) 'stands for' Britain as a whole. In fact the play was lauded mainly for its representativeness—a description sometimes dignified by the word 'symbolic' (a word frequently misused in contemporary criticism). Whatever the word used, the 'representative' characteristic is common and it is often assumed that any member of any audience will accept its relevance to himself and his own environment. Thus Michael Croft, the director, writing of Peter·Terson,

assumes that a particular play about a particular environment
stands for or equals 'the quality of life in England':

> His ironic commentary on urban society says more about the
> quality of life in England today than most plays of our time.[4]

And this is the representative piece of urban society which is so
telling:

> This is about a boy who leaves school, with wasted years
> behind, with nothing in front of him except a fuck and a family,
> and the only immediate present.[5]

The collapse of heroic drama (and Ibsen's *The Masterbuilder*[6]
alone can remind us that we do not have to equate 'heroic' with
'royal' or even 'noble') was completed in the 1950s and 1960s
when the concept of 'specialness' gave place to the acceptance
of 'representativeness'. It is partly because of this that it is
customary to forget the names and any specific characteristics
of protagonists in contemporary plays. The truth is that their
names do not greatly matter as an appellation of individual
men—but their general dispositions matter a great deal, and it
is these we remember.

Again, relationships between individual characters are frequently conducted on a basis which emphasizes less the uniqueness of the relationship than its typicality. Indeed, perhaps
'relationship' is too bland a word to use; often, 'confrontation'
would be more applicable. Confrontation seems to have
become the hallmark of the most common and everyday
intercourse of an increasing number of people in society. The
sad advent of wariness, watchfulness, suspicion, an en-garde-
ism has made itself felt in all aspects of life. The softer attributes—kindness, tenderness, trust, affection—are, it seems,
not dead, but, curiously, so often when they appear, both in
everyday existence and in drama, they are presented as a kind
of bonus—not as a natural welling-up, spontaneously, of feelings of warm compatibility. In so many plays lovers seem to
be fighting a resistance to love itself, and, when the outcome is
happy, surrender with astonished surprise to any kisses that
are given as well as roughly taken, to any words that are
offered, not flung, to any gestures that are gracious not militant. The surprise is the give-away.

But the drama of our time has its own heroical aspects—of a kind very different from the traditional. It may best be isolated and identified in the extent to which so much contemporary drama, in character, plot, language and location is expressly designed to be 'a slice of life'. The documentary factor in naturalistic drama is not only dominant but accepted as natural. Television has exploited documentary plays, so·has film, and the genre is a potent influence on stage-naturalistic plays. Documentary has two aspects of importance. The first is either the fact, or the impression, of actual events and characters used as the basis for a creation of a fiction. The degree of 'fact' in contemporary drama is extensive. All drama, of course, draws upon actuality, but rarely have dramatists been so explicit in informing us of it or of using it sometimes so 'near to the bone' of actuality. Peter Terson may speak for many—'I drew my characters from different periods of my life and bundled them together in that factory yard.' In truth it is often difficult to disentangle the fact and the fiction, the actuality and the impression. The proximity of actuality to the fictional format of a play often damages any sense of form or design that may be present. But equally (and this shows in television drama) the fictional element can often detract from the impact of the 'actual' material being employed. Sometimes, indeed, it seems as if the use of a fictional form like a play is an attempt merely to dignify actuality with the illusion of 'artistic creation'—as if perpetuity is more likely to be granted by this process than by a straightforward narration of events and characters. But not always, for there is no doubt that skilfully contrived, the embodiment of actuality in a dramatic form of expression increases the impact on the auditor and viewer. The realization that actuality can have an impact upon an audience often of more telling effect than fiction seems to lure some dramatists into employing it with what seems to be a reckless disregard for any pattern or direction their drama is taking. The account of the way in which Terson kept on adding to the original draft of *Zigger-Zagger*[7] material taken from actuality is, again, emblematic of a process that is not uncommon if we are to believe the statements and comments of dramatists. When the motivation, as it so often is, is to draw attention to some social

209

iniquity, we can applaud it while deprecating the frequent formlessness it engenders. Nevertheless, salutary factory legislation, perhaps the social services themselves, might well have appeared decades before they did had Dickens's work been thus treated at the time. The desire to make as strong an impact on an audience as is possible is, of course, common to all true dramatists, but where documentary drama is concerned (and this is the second major aspect of the genre) the motivation is complex. In the nature of this complexity lies the new 'heroic' spirit in drama.

By far the major number of plays written in England in the 1960s and 1970s seem (often strenuously) determined to deal with man in his environment—man in his prose and usually prosaic worlds. But the motivation is not merely to impress upon the audience the facts of that environment but, more often than not, the iniquities of it. The motivation is not merely to 'show their eyes and grieve their hearts', but, if possible, to incite to personal and public action. The heroic has become, so to speak, institutionalized, in the sense that in so many plays we are moved (the more commonly used word is 'disturbed') by the sight of an individual or a group at war (in confrontation) with a threatening system. That system is the Evil against which Good is to take up arms. But Virtue is represented not in terms of an abstraction, far more as an emblem of a set of attitudes, beliefs, even prejudices, assumptions, deriving from a socio-political faith. The heroism lies in the extent to which the individual addicts himself to this faith which, as the play will show, is to overcome or, at the least, uncover the foe. So, this kind of heroism is institutional in that, though its derivation has much to do with individual response, the response, in itself, is dictated as much by environmental as by psychological stimuli. Heroism in contemporary drama is cognate with the simple archetype—riding out to meet the foe—with the very significant difference that no special attributes are given to the hero. He, or she, is heroic only in the sense that they have recognized and accepted what is for the greater good—the institutional nirvanah. But the contemporary 'hero' figure has, if in watered ways, a number of the constituents of the traditional version: the posture of defiance, the release of passion, the ability to evoke

210

sympathetic responses and a disposition to sudden accesses of eloquence. But, now, the defiance is often less noble than ugly, the passion not so much profound as destructive, the sympathy exacted more sentimental than emotionally rich, the eloquence when it occurs a self-conscious decoration rather than a natural attribute. The 'hero' is, indeed, often a covert figure in contemporary drama whose significance has to be guessed at because for him or her to be too obtrusive would be to deny the typicality, the un-élite posture by which 'virtue' is measured. Perhaps the protagonist in Bond's *Saved*[8] best represents the covert contemporary hero. Even Bond singles him out for a kind of post-play salvation in his references to his status and destiny in the introduction. In Pinter's *The Homecoming*, the Uncle is yet another example. Besieged, half-articulate, with some strains of compassion in them, vulnerable, sentimental, and trusting, they hang about contemporary drama and we often overhear them and catch glimpses of them rather than find them forced upon us.

And so, Good and Evil have been redefined, drastically so, as the presence of the hero has been, in a sense, emasculated. The redefinition has had one of the most profound effects on the history of contemporary drama, and we are not at the end of those effects.

The reduction of the conventional hero has been accompanied by the decay of the traditional tragic villain-hero. Macbeth has no place in a society which has abjured God and banned élitism. The most obvious reason for the disappearance of the 'larger-than-life' and his replacement by the 'slice-of-life' villain-hero is the changes wrought in the structure of society. The relationship of the old layered, hierarchical structure to the great heroic type (villain or not) was crucial. But when kings ride bicycles Aristotle must think again. Far more penetrating in its effect, however, has been the change in the concepts of Good and Evil. They, like Virtue and Vice, have been completely redefined. A clear, if over-simplified though not distorted idea of how this redefinition has occurred can be realized by thinking of society in a pre-Freud and a post-Freud condition.

Before his penetrating if, as now seems likely, not always judicious safaris into human motivation and habit, there was a broad acceptance in the Western world of conceptions of Good and Evil which were part of religious faith and belief—God was the source of Good; a man who was good was automatically assured of redemption. There was a distinct reward for virtuous behaviour. The Devil was the source of Evil and he who was evil was punished by damnation. The reward and the punishment were immutable and were supernaturally ordained.

Yet, post-Freud, these clear distinctions between Good and Evil and reward and punishment became confused. The individual's responsibility was removed—largely because both God and the Devil were removed. Evil is now largely regarded as a sickness for which the individual is not responsible. Wrongdoing is often attributable to deprivation, sometimes by environment, sometimes by neglect, not to any personal shortcoming, and as a result the onus does not lie with the wrongdoer.

Some of the potency of the traditional tragic hero lay in his being torn between Good and Evil. But there can be little moral debate in a society which believes neither in Destiny nor individual responsibility, and whose conception of free will is so restricted that the hero can only 'do his own thing' as far as he is allowed or prevented by his material environment alone.

Tragedy's power over audiences lay in its ability to show unusual individuals becoming involved in matters which, at least in essence, were capable of being experienced by anyone—'there, but for the grace of God, go I'. Moreover, tragedy's extra potency, in the fact that it trafficked with Death and depicted what seemed to be an example of the eternal battle between Good and Evil with eternity looking on, has withered. Death, alone, remains as a sole survivor of the traditional tragic experience. And even Death, in contemporary drama, has lost its association with damnation and redemption. It is all, one might say, on the National Health.

Areas of sensibility have been removed from mankind's experience of the universe—indeed the universe has become a matter of scientific speculation, and supernatural soliciting about its meaning is at a premium. The possibility even of anything external to mankind, as a spiritual reality, is under siege. The belief that man can relate to anything except himself has been dented.

From the point of view of the material amelioration of the greatest number the contemporary obsession with man in the world has much to commend it. If we believe that our life on this planet is the only one we have it is not difficult to argue a case which would sacrifice a thousand *King Lears* for the sake of starving children. This indeed is no theoretical argument, for the more raucous is the push towards institutionalism and egalitarianism, the nearer, inevitably, is the moment when art itself will be stridently requested to show its hand, and to abjure any evidence that it should be concerned with anything other than the actions of man in society and the recording and embodying of the struggle against the iniquities of his environment. Kings, either in fact or fiction will not only ride bicycles. They will lose the name of kings and be asked to explain how they came by the bicycle.

One of the most obvious symptoms of the decay of the old areas of sensibility and experience appears in language. It must follow that a shrinking of the sense-data will involve a shrinking of the language. At its most simple level, many words are just not needed any more or are reduced to ugly functionals. A huge number of words, often of Latin origin, are now either not used at all, or used wrongly. There has been what is now called a 'deteriation' in the use of language in the media (including the newspapers, and in middle-brow periodicals) and this deterioration, while it has such obvious indications as wrong usage, incorrect spelling, complete neglect of many words, has one overriding characteristic which leads us directly into the heart of the way in which the vast majority of contemporary dramatists use language.

This characteristic is a reduction of associativeness to that which can be recognized by a common denominator of intelligence or appreciation. It may be argued that if words are to be associative and evocative they should be so to the greatest possible number of people. This is true—so long as two conditions are fulfilled. The first is that it is certain that the associations to be aroused really are possible to the greatest number. Now, in this latter half of the twentieth century, it is far from certain that this is so. Minority associativeness is sometimes assumed to be majority associativeness. For example, the jargon of Trade Union public language—even the use of the word 'Brother'—is a minority usage which, for other powerful reasons, is regarded as a general usage and employed as such by the media. To a less extent, this is true of the jargon of management. Football is only a 'national' sport because, marginally, more people attend it than attend other sports, but its language is regarded by the media as being of general associativeness: in fact, millions of people are baffled by some of the usages.

The second condition that must be fulfilled is that minority associativeness when it is employed is not consistently an assertion of discrimination or élitism and therefore to be derided or condemned. The university don is as much given to associative jargon as is the factory worker. It would be as tedious and frustrating if literate associativeness came to be regarded as a generally acceptable norm as it is now that other minorities rule the language-roost. An imposed associativeness (which is what, by practice if not yet by injunction, we now have) is yet another symptom of the institutionalization of existence and the triumph of representation and typicality over individuality.

Undoubtedly, the dominant impression to be gained from a reading of contemporary drama is that, with certain exceptions, literacy and form are of less importance than immediacy. Depending upon one's attitude one can view this either joyfully or sadly as the removal from a great deal of the language of contemporary drama of 'art'—indeed, at times, it seems as if 'craft' has also disappeared.

The phenomenon of 'mid-Atlantic' English is well known to those who listen to the gabble of disc-jockeys on a number of British radio stations. This, in itself, is another symptom of imposed associativeness. The employment of what is obviously fondly believed to be an American accent (usually it is a ludicrous amalgam of a decimated English regional accent and a nasal clipped noise) is obviously intended to associate the disc-jockey, his works and his auditors with a generalized image—probably derived from the lower reaches of the Hollywood film industry. This image is supposed to stand for a virile, get-up-and-go, stand-on-your-own-feet, ruggedly

214

handsome, decisive, no-nonsense, up-to-the-minute persona. One suspects that it is compounded of wisps of mixed-up memory of films of James Cagney, Davy Crockett, Cary Grant, the frontier, tobacco-chewing cowboys, smooth executives with voices of creamed gravel and wives bought from some Tiffany's that specializes in human flesh as well as fox-furs. It is intended to associate the British listener with a tough, affluent, with-it glossiness. The pathos of its failure is ruthlessly exposed by its artificiality, its paucity of vocabulary, its inaccuracy of tone, and in its terrible, fruitless hybridity. The 'art' of language is, so to speak, allowed to take care of itself but, in any case, 'formed' language is not a thing that is much encouraged or sought for—what is frequently called 'naturalness' of speech is the ambition. At times this 'natural' ambition extends to the whole matter (concept is too inflated a word) of writing a play. Peter Terson proclaims:

> I don't think I have any ideas, any statement I want to make. I just seem to keep on writing plays.[9]

The persistent and cheerful immunity to deliberate control which this seems to imply (what else can it imply?) is perhaps characteristic of that particular dramatist, but an impression of slackness is common to a great many contemporary dramatists. It extends to, perhaps actually influences, the way in which even the most mentally adroit commentators express themselves about this body of drama. Writing of Bond's *Saved*, John Russell Taylor says:

> In a very tense, funny scene Len nearly seduces Mary, Pam's mother, or she nearly seduces him.[10]

Which is it? It's surely important to be sure. Time and time again in contemporary drama, as in life itself, it is not easy to know where the facts or the emphases of a situation lie—it is, we might say, as natural as that, or, it can be put in some further words of Peter Terson writing of his plays: 'I don't know why I do them.'[11] Nothing could be more natural than that!

But many contemporary plays, quite apart from the overwhelming necessity to emulate the 'naturalness' of life, seem haunted by a need not to give words very much more than a functional job. Thus the associativeness is either confined to a minority or it does not exist at all; indeed the words might well be replaced by action. The dramatists seem haunted by the pressure of non-verbal drama which has grown from being a fringe activity to occupy a significant place in the theatre life of the country and an astonishingly large place in educational theory and practice. As Taylor says:

> . . . verbal drama, as opposed to improvised and non-verbal theatre, is almost by definition, however outlandish its style, taken to be establishment, on the side of the squares.[12]

With certain notable exceptions, and even these are not consistent, language in the drama of the sixties and seventies seems so often an embarrassed element in the play. The dramatists seem self-conscious about using it at all—and in their efforts to hide their feelings they resort either to an unformed ugly vernacular or an awkward manipulation of language which stops short of a full committal to full-blown evocative speech and, at times, even of fully dramatic speech. Sometimes it seems as if the very emphases which true dramatic speech must have—in rhythm or sound—must be avoided in case the language gives the impression of singularity and, therefore, becomes too untypical, too unrepresentative.

The use of vernacular speech as the basis for dialogue is the dominant general characteristic of the language of contemporary English drama. This vernacular, unlike that of Galsworthy or Wesker or Pinter is not, however, the starting point for a process of verbal creation but, in many cases, the be-all and end-all of the dramatic speech. In short, in some dramatists, the language used is barely distinguishable from that of the streets, the bar, the semi-detached. It sometimes does not seem to have passed through any rigorous process of refining or selection or integrating with an overall sense of verbal pattern and design. A typical example of such dialogue goes thus:

> It's parky when the passion wears off.
> This is all the tea we've got.
> I got a quarter yesterday.
> We drink a lot this weather.
> Yes. Have you got your—thing?

What do you mean, my thing?
I mean, have you . . . brought your . . .
My whatsit?
Oh no.
Come along. Two is it?
Yes please. Two.
Thank you, son.
eh?
I dunno how you can do a job like this.
What's wrong with it?
I wouldn't fancy it cooped up in here all day.
In winter you mustn't never see the daylight.

The vernacular sources of that language need no comment. But a sleight of hand has been performed in order to underline a matter just as important. The extract, in fact, is not from one play, but from four by different authors. Lines 1 to 4 are from the much-hailed *Zoo Zoo Widdershins Zoo* by K. B. Laffan, first produced in 1968. Lines 5 to 8 are from *Lovers* by Carey Harrison first presented in Manchester in 1969. This was published in *New Short Plays* (2) in the prestigious Methuen Playscript series. Lines 9 to 13 are from Alan Ayckbourn's *Ernie's Incredible Illusions* published in 1969. Lines 14 to the end are, again, from the Methuen publication, but from a different play—Maureen Duffy's *Rites*. Miss Duffy was, at one time, regarded as one of the most original and exciting of a young generation of playwrights.

The same trick could have been performed without difficulty by taking sections from another set of contemporary playwrights. While it is perfectly true that a similar effect could be obtained by lacing together small pieces of dialogue from a specific thematic genre in the 1930s or the 1920s, the number of playwrights available who used a mode of writing so extraordinarily similar to one another would be strictly limited. This applies as much to American drama as to English, with, possibly, one proviso. An examination of that very popular genre of American plays of the 1940s and 1950s typified in film versions, seen in England, by the preserve of Cary Grant, Fred MacMurray, as professional men in both marital and family predicaments, and represented best by plays like *Junior Miss* by Chodorov and Fields and *The Male*

217

Animal by Thurber and Nugent, might yield some interesting results. It might very well be that at least the film versions of such plays would show a very strong tendency to this stylistic institutionalization. Since the 1960s, however, the number of playwrights employing a vernacular style in England is legion. And, again, while it is not necessarily a complete test of the overall flavour of a dramatist's dramatic idiom there is a most marked absence of individuality in the style of those contemporary dramatists who are addicted to the vernacular. It would seem that the institutionalism and representationalism which we have noticed in other aspects of drama is characteristic, too, of much of the dramatic language of our time.

The extent to which the institutional style has become dominant in contemporary dramatic language can be measured in other ways. The old traditional devices and usages of dramatic expression—wit, irony, contrast of pace, rhythm —are still to be found but yet again, with astonishingly little variation from one dramatist to another.

The contemporary equivalent of wit (defined as a demonstration of mental and verbal agility) is a kind of banter. The retreat from intellectuality in vernacular drama has removed from wit that essential sense of mental power, fine judgment in concept and in expression. What is left is, on the whole, nothing more than an explicit, occasionally blundering 'verbology' of a kind which will be familiar to those who recall music-hall, but which is now presented in a modern form and given currency largely by television. It is cross-talk speech, and it has a number of variants.

It is prone to attempt laughter by absurdity or incongruity—sometimes between verbal and visual. For example: the scene is a public lavatory—'Sound of cistern flushing. Pause. The others listen. A loud rustling. Ada: "It's like having mice . . ."' [13]

More often the effect is entirely verbal—'If y'sed t'Dafford, "A've just been elected President o' t'United States", e'd reply, "I 'ave the shallowest armpits in Islington".' [14]

Quite often it involves punning—which is the most sharp symptom that a surrogate for the truest wit is being employed. 'You look like a nun, Mr Bradbury. Nun but the purest.' [15]

218

And, very often, it has the 'capping' style so typical of
music-hall and, indeed, characteristic of the aggressive, confronting style of 'conversation' which social change has
pushed to the forefront of society's tongue.

Zigger: . . . Hi, we're new boys. Will you take us in?
Glenice: No. You've got to sign the visitor's book and it's a bit
embarrassing if you can't write.[16]

And, habitually, it uses the rabid simplicity of the reply
direct—without much mental resource, but with the speed of
lightning:

Len: . . .Yer got a fair ol' arse.
Pam: Like your mug.[17]

The range of emotional effect possible when the vernacular is
used with such persistency is very limited. In fact it consists of
sudden jerks between the extreme of confronting banter and a
half-shy sentimentality. There is little or nothing between an
attitude of fending-off and one of cautious embrace. The
technique by which the latter posture is conveyed is again
derived from, or seems to derive from, music-hall in its tele-
vised second coming. Repetition and line-lengthening, often
accompanied by a song, are the almost inevitable means used
to achieve it.

It is analogous to what happens when the stand-up comic
stops his crackling jokeyness and changes his mood prior to
singing his ineffably sentimental love-lyric or one which
glutinously announces the astonishing good-fellowship to be
found everywhere in the universe:

Mill: What about them beans?
Gary: (Off) What?
Mill: Do you want the rest of them beans?
Gary: (Off) Might as well. Got to keep my strength up now.
Mill: Awful, you are.
Gary: Awful, yes. Oh, Mill!
Mill: Hullo?
Gary: (Closer) Keep the tin.
Mill: What?
Gary: That tin, keep it, like I said. There's no point wasting nothing.
(*Another train begins to approach. Mill begins to sing—any pop song
will do . . .*)[18]

Indeed 'any pop song will do' because the emotion is so
generalized, so predictable. The repetitions, the lengthening
of phrases, announce the change of relationship. The pop song
is, in fact, merely a sentimental anointing of a ceremony
already completed.

The most assiduous employer of the vernacular in its most
apparently untreated form is Edward Bond in his notorious
play *Saved*. Both its strengths and limitations are very well
demonstrated by his work. Bond has a remarkable ear for the
noise that language makes. Some might say that it is less the
noise of language that we hear in *Saved* than that made by
human animals in vain attempts to communicate with each
other. But the verisimilitude he achieves is remarkable:

Len: Wass yer name?
Pam: Wass yourn?
Len: Len.
Pam: Pam.
   . . .
Pam: Ow!
Len: D'yer 'ave the light on?
Pam: Suit yerself.
Len: I ain't fussy.
Pam: Ow!

Bond is ruthless in avoiding the pitfalls into which so many of
his vernacular colleagues fall. The music-hall technique does
not obtrude, the sentimentality is an indigenous part of character not a mere function in the story line, the jokes are natural
and not, as so often, a substitution for true dialogue. What is
more, Bond, in a manner which is reminiscent of Pinter,
conveys the inconsequentiality of ordinary speech and its lack
of pattern without losing control of his dramatic intentions.
The seduction scene in *Saved* between Mary and Len is a
remarkable example of how the vernacular can be made to
have a controlled if narrow associative effect when the
dramatist is entirely aware of his direction.

But Bond, in company with other intelligent and techni-
cally highly accomplished dramatists, seems, in *Saved*, to have
fallen into the trap of expecting the vernacular to 'carry' much
more of meaning than it is capable of doing. Undoubtedly fine

220

artist as he is, his dedication to the principle of the common denominator of language has apparently made him forget that great art is not and never has been expressed in common denominator form. The old and much-rejected dictum remains true—the highest art remains special until mankind catches up with its meaning and its language, or learns how to live with it. No catching up is necessary with the kind of vernacular that Bond uses in *Saved*. The language itself teaches us nothing, acquaints our ears with nothing that we have not already heard a thousand times from sources far less inventive than Bond's imagination. The proof of the inadequacy of this language to 'carry' what it is meant to carry is starkly found in the preface to the play and in the fate of the play. He declares he did not write the play 'only as an Oedipus comedy'. He tells us in great detail what the point of the last scene is. The play apparently involves science and religion. He asks us to believe, in the preface, that the protagonist (the word must be used, since the theme is Oedipal) does not know what he will do next at the end of the play, 'but he never has done'. But none of this is embodied in the play! We know to a remarkable degree what Othello, Iago, Macbeth, even Hamlet, do or do not know about themselves and their actions. We know this because they are articulate enough to tell us—and to tell themselves. Bond's vernacular is not the language for all seasons, it is only for one season, one place, one time. It has little ability to reach into areas beyond the immediate environment in which it is expressed. It is largely a thing of convenience, a shorthand. Even treated by his imagination it lacks the stamina for art. The measure of this vernacular play's paucity, ironically enough, is to be found in Bond's richly verbal *Narrow Road to the Deep North*. Because there was no connection between meaning and language *Saved* was generally deemed to be about baby-stoning. Bond's eloquent explanation of the depth of the meaning he intended it to have can only lead us to conclude that a catastrophe happened between intention and execution. It is as if *Measure for Measure*, for want of proper communication, is considered to be about nun-groping.

The second main type of language employed in contemporary

drama is essentially prose, but although it makes use, as a secondary element, of the vernacular, it is very much an invented thing. It is very much nearer to being 'literary' than is the vernacular idiom. Some of the most distinguished plays of the contemporary period have employed a prose-literary idiom—*Rosencrantz and Guildenstern are Dead, 'Afore Night Come, Equus, Entertaining Mr Sloane, Narrow Road to the Deep North*, [19] and a substantial number of others. The ones listed are sufficient alone to warn us that we have to make careful reservations about defining the idiom used. At first sight there would seem to be little connection between the verbal pattern and content of, say, *'Afore Night Come* and *Rosencrantz and Guildenstern are Dead*. The one, at a glance, seems nearer to a dialect source than the other, whose progenitor seems to be some erudite philosopher aided by the ever-convenient William Shakespeare himself.

Yet there are sufficient common denominators to the language used in these apparently very different plays to merit the suggestion that what we are faced with is a recognizable alternative to the common vernacular—élitist and particular. This alternative is not used by the dramatists to demonstrate an opposite political or social attitude but rather, it would seem, because they either tacitly or consciously realize that the vernacular, widespread as it is in contemporary drama, just is not capable of carrying all that needs to be said—even about the very class from which it derives. It must be emphasized that the alternative we are discussing is not a poetic but a prose one. From time to time, within it, we find the resources of poetry being used, but there is no dramatist of note now apparently prepared to commit himself completely to the idiom of verse-drama.

The first and overwhelming characteristic of non-vernacular prose-drama is its seriousness. This may seem a curious contention in the light of the kind of jokeyness, whimsicality and verbal antics that are to be found in *Rosencrantz and Guildenstern, Narrow Road* and in Joe Orton's plays.[20] But the seriousness is, often, less of tone and nuance than of an underlying sense of deep purpose. There is, about so much of this drama a relentlessness—as if the dramatist were determined that we should be aware that for all the beer and skittles along the way our route is planned and our destination certain. What is more, most of these plays make it plain to us that what we will be aware of at the end is a statement about the 'human condition'. Vernacular drama tends to dig itself into its own specific situations and characters and we are not always aware that a general statement is being made. The alternative drama hardly ever allows us to make this mistake. Second, for those who believe that violence and permissiveness are significant general characteristics of drama today, this prose-literary genre can provide an enormous amount of confirming evidence. *Entertaining Mr Sloane, Loot, Belcher's Luck, The Killing of Sister George, The Mighty Reservoy, 'Afore Night Come, The Ruling Class*[21]—all plays which, for a time, held public attention, some acclaim, and had commercial success, are all in this category. Most of them, whatever other comments were directed at them, were subjected to some condemnations of their plots and themes.

It is important to make a distinction between the kind of violence and moral permissiveness of the prose-literary play and that of the vernacular play. The latter's verbal equipment is used to display and embody violence as naturalistically as possible. The genre now under discussion normally achieves a far greater impact by the very eloquence and indirectness it employs. There is nothing more calculated to increase a sinister effect than an oblique verbal technique in which hints and portentous vocabulary and an apparent, but only apparent, calm rationality are employed. In the prose-literary drama verbal density is used to widen the emotional reverberation of violence and permissiveness and to deepen the intellectual associativeness. Moreover, the moral implications of what is being described, discussed or embodied—though more often it is reported happenings—are often suddenly brought to the surface only to be dismissed with a surprising and shocking cynicism:

Christ: . . . Their cleverness has become cunning, their skill has become jugglery, their risks have become reckless gambles, they are mad. How can I suffer for men, what are my sufferings compared to theirs? How can one innocent die for the guilty when so many innocents are corrupted and killed? This is a hell worse than anything my father imagined.

. . .

Magician: I have it! I have it! I'm sure my figures are right! Yes! I can make a bomb out of dust! We're saved![22]

Within this framework of literary prose, in which violence and permissiveness are embedded, the characters take on what is, in a sense, a limited kind of dramatic existence. It is not that they fail to make an impact upon the audience either in terms of what they say or what they do, but that they seem to be conceived less as impersonations of actuality than representations of points of view, attitudes. They are given a stance rather than allowed to develop a personality. An extremely good example of this process is to be found in Edward Bond's play *Bingo* which uses William Shakespeare as its catalyst for the development of a very eloquent though, finally, somewhat puzzling, dramatic essay on the nature of man. Every character in the play, and this includes minor ones, seems to 'stand for' some attitude, or is a variation on an attitude of some other character. In *Narrow Road to the Deep North* the allegorical posture of the characters is increased by its remote setting in time and place. In Stoppard's *Rosencrantz and Guildenstern,* the two characters are conceived in an intensely intellectual way—in a very certain sense their superbly athletic use of language is the only 'reality' they definitely possess. They exist on the fringes of everything, even on the edge of being 'characters' in the accepted sense of the term:

Player: Once more, alone—on our own resources.
Guildenstern: (Worried) What do you mean? Where is he?
Player: Gone.
Guildenstern: Gone where?
Player: Yes, we were dead lucky there. If that's the word I'm after.
Rosencrantz: (Not a pick up) Dead?
Player: Lucky.
Rosencrantz: (He means) is he dead?
Player: Who knows?
Guildenstern: (Rattled) He's not coming back?
Player: Hardly.
Rosencrantz: He's dead then. He's dead as far as we're concerned.
Player: Or we are as far as he is.

With the possible exception of David Rudkin's,[23] Joe Orton's plays afford the most sensational, exciting and clear examples of the way in which prose-literary drama deals with its characters. Orton's method, in fact, is to use language relentlessly to build up an apparent normality of human behaviour; it is only at a very advanced point in the play, or even after its close, that we realize that not only are the characters not 'normal' (either as conventional 'characters' or, sometimes, in the psychiatric sense) but that the language is only apparently the language of people speaking. It is, in the closest analysis, a verbal methodology of the author cunningly and relentlessly building up a serious statement. In *What the Butler Saw* a not uncommon human decision—to hide from one's wife certain guilty little secrets—leads to a farrago of incident and activity, in which sexuality, nymphomania, lesbianism, blackmail, mass seduction, transvestism, are compounded. The manner in which the language seems to set up a 'normal' verbal structure, only, so to speak, to be contradicting itself as it proceeds, is skilfully achieved. Indeed, it might be said that language itself, seeming so rational, but with serpents of contradiction, madness, irrelevance, farce, despair lurking beneath, is one of the most vital characters of the play.

Joe Orton is a comic dramatist with a serious purpose. John Russell Taylor's claim that he wrote the most glittering artificial comedy in English since Congreve is well taken. Orton takes the implications of some of his comic situations and characters further than Congreve—into regions where a fierce moral judgment has to be made by the audience upon the nature of what is happening and what is being said. To this extent Orton's comedy is 'black'; but it is essentially, like Congreve's, a verbal comedy. It does not avoid ludicrous situation but it is happiest with vocal expression.

Many of the prose-literary plays are comedies in the sense that they engage our laughter, but most of them require us to qualify the word 'comic' in that they are grimly purposeful as well. Their comedy always tends to be mocking, mordant, wry, sarcastic—that is, it is essentially verbal. Violence, or discomfort, or unease, or outrageousness, or despair, always seem to be lurking beneath the surface of their words. At times, in different dramatists and for different reasons, we are very conscious of a prevailing atmosphere of danger—as if the very civilized pattern of the words themselves was only just holding back chaos. One is indeed often reminded of the cool, mocking deliberation of the poet Ted Hughes's preoccupation with the consanguinity of man and the jungle when one reads these plays.

John Osborne's first stage-direction in his play *A Bond Honoured*[24] says—'We English are more violent than we allow ourselves to know.' Since Osborne wrote that, our intellectual dramatists have, we may say, let the cat out of the bag—and it has all the characteristics not of domestication but of naked violence, made the more terrifying by the urbanity with which it is done.

There is a sense in which the use of the words 'literary' and 'intellectual' to describe such plays might seem to be a contradiction. Some of the dramatists, almost certainly Bond, would vehemently reject the descriptions, and possibly turn the point of what he would consider to be the sword back towards the heart of the critic. For, indeed, few writers seem to want to be associated with what is deemed the élite conceptions of 'literary' and 'intellectual' (and we can add the word 'academic'). The image of the sword is a true one—writers feel a sense of attack when the words are used.

But what else should we call a body of drama in which the verbal emphasis is not on the recapitulation solely of vernacular speech but on created language in the traditional sense? And what other word exists for drama, or any art, in which the writer has not only engaged his own but strenuously engages the audience's cerebral as well as emotional life?

What one calls the drama, however, is less important than other considerations. It cannot be overemphasized that literary prose-drama is a positively different genre from the monolithic and near-monopolistic body of vernacular drama which is the dominant verbal expression in our contemporary theatre. Literary prose-drama accepts the vernacular, including its dialect forms, but that does not make it a naturalistic drama. It is a drama which expresses concepts arising from the author's contemplation of man's inner and outer life rather than merely impersonates his behaviour. The word 'concepts' in itself suggests the strong philosophical or quasi-philosophical flavour of much of the manner in which these reflections upon man are made.

226

There is more than one way to explore, in art, the nature of man in society and man within himself. The literary prose-dramas are only the most recent confirmation of this. What is important about them is that they constitute a genre with a minor place in drama, yet their importance far outstrips this.

The drift of our times, the shift in political power, the pressure of social change has created a society in which an idiomatic vernacular derived from the lowest common denominator of speech has been elevated to a pre-eminent status. There has been an accompanying growth of suspicion and rejection of the special, the intellectual, the academic—all grouped as élitist. The pre-eminence of the commonplace seems likely both to increase and continue. In vernacular drama, which is the most public showplace of the annunciation of the commonplace, there is a virility of speech, frankness of statement, honesty of communication and a frequent earnestness of purpose in theme and characterization. All these qualities are not only often open-hearted they are also, in themselves, to be applauded. There may be much that is frank and direct but there is rarely much that widens imaginative experience in language that so inexorably reaches for its energy in the speech of the least articulate. The inarticulacy may be due to a deprivation for which society must find a solution by social action, but neither the inarticulacy nor the need to announce social action can create true and memorable art. In any case great and true art has neither to impersonate the language of its times nor to proselytize causes expressly in order to demonstrate its commitment to human amelioration and ennoblement.

There is little point in echoing Beatie's cry that, as one formerly dispossessed, she has learned to speak, unless the speech she utters is, in itself, an emblem of her new dignity and pride. Few American dramatists in the last twenty-five years have missed this point. Nor have they missed its corollary—that even weakness, degradation, despair needs a certain eloquence; Blanche Dubois testifies to this. Yet in England it is the fashion to deride language that echoes beyond its immediate environment. Indeed, it seems that even art has now to be defined as the satisfaction of a creative urge without necessarily resorting to any rigorous intellectual, emotional or technical discipline. Immediacy has taken the place of dimension—we seem to be taking everything out of language, thoughts, feelings even, except the ingredient of instant response. Memory, comparison, context are 'lost leaders' and form is broken and untended. The virility of that huge area of vernacular contemporary drama is attractive enough at times and it is certainly always apparent, but virility is a very temporary thing.

Prose literary-drama represents some kind of bastion to prevent the complete hegemony of the vernacular. Its language represents some care and retention of values outside and beyond those of the present, the immediate, the 'now'. Joe Orton and Bond and Peter Shaffer notably display this care. What Taylor says of Orton underlines what drama lost by his death but it also implies the significance of the other two and others like them.

> Orton was, perhaps first and foremost, a master of verbal style . . . One is always aware in Orton that he is using a convention.[25]

'Style' and 'convention' are terms that can be extended to few of the vernacular dramatists—'posture' and 'antic' are as near to a sense of formality as one can get. Style is a point of view which governs the relationships between language and character and theme and plot; convention is the recognizable method by which that point of view is held and exerted. Both can be innovatory and highly individual (as was Orton's) or they can be derivative and yet still contain the authoritative stamp of the particular writer (as is Bond's in his neo-Brechtian *Narrow Road*). But in order to achieve both, the writer must be conscious of what he is doing and not just let the play come—as seems the case, by their own avowals, with more and more of the vernacular dramatists.

To drift, merely, into language—and the easiest language to pick up as one drifts is the vernacular—is to begin a journey into a situation where language may become of secondary importance and, eventually, of no importance at all.

No comment on contemporary drama can ignore the non-verbal forms which have proliferated since the early 1960s.

Their nature is such that they cannot be critically analysed in any detail simply because no texts exist to allow the critic to confirm his appraisals or enable the theatregoer to contend or agree with the critic. In a very practical sense, therefore, non-verbal drama is the apotheosis of instant response—this is borne home to us the more strongly when we remember that in many of its forms a great part is played by improvisation.

The critic and commentator has to rely for his appraisal of any example of non-verbal drama on the exigencies of memory. All dramatic experience which is to be critically appraised makes demands on recollection but, in non-verbal drama, the problems thus raised by the form itself are compounded by the fact that, often, these plays have very limited runs; memory, therefore, cannot easily be refreshed.

The genre has two main divisions—that which is entirely physical and that which, though it employs vocalized words does so largely on an unplanned or virtually unplanned basis. The control exercised by a working text is not present, so that the verbal element is ad hoc or improvisatory and therefore, to a degree, without form—it is, essentially, 'non-verbal'.

Both forms are to be found in so-called 'fringe' theatre, and in street and local community theatre on both sides of the Atlantic. This, in itself, has a number of variations. Sometimes it is a small building with quite unsophisticated equipment and facilities which operates on either a temporary or permanent level. A recent version is travelling theatre in which a small company of players have shares and which subsists by performance in rented or free locations—village halls, schools, pubs, churches.

The most bizarre form is street-theatre where the ad hoc, improvisation and lack of sophistication in equipment are often slavishly pursued. Street-theatre often attempts to create the illusion of spontaneity—as if a folk-happening had suddenly blossomed out of the ruck and reel of everyday drudgery; as if, for a short time, man found his soul sprouting out of his nine-to-five beat on the incessant highway of existence. Sometimes, street-theatre forms part of an organized event—a city or town's annual carnival or specially conceived festival of the arts. However organized the context, street-theatre contrives to maintain the posture of easy-come, easy-go spontaneity and a sense that art springs fully-armed, as it were, out of the environment —however dull that may be.

The first main division of non-verbal drama—the physical—may, conveniently, be described first since a good deal of what it contains and what it aims at—or seems to aim at—has influenced the verbal improvisations and vocal ad-hocery of the second type. The physical is the be-all and the end-all of the specific dramatic content of this type of theatre. A little man in a polo-neck sweater and baggy trousers and a bowler hat will arrive on a pavement or a field, or a schoolyard or a city centre precinct and sit for an hour on a suitcase in an attitude of Rodin's *Le Penseur*. Sometimes he will shift his stance or his gaze. He attracts watchers like a hole in the ground does. He attracts reactions as a hole in the ground does not—for he is unusual in this chosen place of his, and what he is doing seems unnecessary but compelling. Or a group of weirdly-attired men and women—spangled, piebald, woaded, crowned, tinselled, will antic in a churchyard, laying dead fish meticulously nose to tail, drawing on the pavement, sitting in a circle. Or two or three young men will, again in outlandish dress, begin to gibber and leap and thump a tumbril and stop and stare and buttonhole passers-by, and offer artificial flowers. Whether it be in San Francisco or Birmingham, England, the effect is startling and the result, ironically, usually indeterminate. The internationalism of this kind of physical theatre is wryly demonstrated by the fact that audience-reaction on both sides of the Atlantic can not only be forecast but shows no difference between one country and another. Observation of many performances in the United States and England leads to a definite conclusion: audiences take up defensive attitudes in which are compounded incredulity and disinterest. There is an almost pathetic paradox here, too. It consists in the astonishing difference between the sensationalism of the theatrical activity attempted and the relative apathy of audiences. The variations on physical presentation are, of course, endless. What is to be concluded, however?

This form of theatre is based on the principle that man in an industrial age is slowly losing the ability and the opportunity to express himself. He is losing the use of many of his senses as he is conditioned by the demands of technology and organization. This theatre is, therefore, proselytizing on behalf of the human being to be uninhibited in seeking himself. But why should this be effected in public? Because the first principle is involved with a second one—nearer to being a political one. It is that art is something we all have inside us; our bodies 'are' and contain art. It is not something that is the gift of a few individuals—it can be called up, at any time, by any one by the exercise of a desire to express. It has to be public in order to spread the gospel. It is political in its fierce denunciation of élitism and in its implication of a total 'democracy' of artistic inspiration and expression. This is compounded—in physical theatre, audience-participation is the rule rather than the exception. Sometimes, indeed, as a spectator, one finds oneself involved, or cajoled into involvement, against one's will. To refuse seems, and is sometimes made to look, like an act of social treachery. The irony of physical theatre is the paradox that it encourages individual self-expression only to subject it to a collectivization which is fiercely held to be the goal of an individual's experience of himself.

Street-theatre in the physical sense is often improvised, but elsewhere the improvisation is a calculated matter. Nowhere is this more true than in schools, colleges and universities and in some of the more nearly-permanent theatres whose companies have a high degree of professionalism and, therefore, a disposition not so much to avoid improvisation as to subject it to as much formalization as is possible without losing the illusion of spontaneous creativity. Indeed, the more permanent the location then the more professional the company, and the more 'conventional' what is presented becomes. The great enemy of all that improvisation (in the widest usage) stands for is an element of permanence and any species of professionalism which cannot forgo discipline, preparation and form.

But it is in the education of the age-group from five years old to pre-college or university that the greatest breeding-ground for the theory and practice of physical theatre is to be found. Obviously, the social quest in the United States is different from that of the United Kingdom where the search for individual expression is more likely to be equated, in a politically socialist society, with the needs of collectivism.

231

Nevertheless, the emphasis on the efficacy of dramatic embodiment in teaching a number of subjects is just as strong in the United States, and the retreat from the verbal just as pronounced. Many unsuspecting parents might be astonished either with delight or despair to learn to what extent their children—particularly in the so-called formative age-group of twelve to fourteen, and often older—are taught subjects which, formerly, were regarded as self-contained, through the medium of what is called 'drama'. Very often, and particularly in the earlier stages, this drama puts a strong emphasis on the physical.

The principles are similar to, indeed derived from, those of physical theatre proper, especially that branch of it (in permanent locations) which uses the physical both as a kind of spontaneous demonstration of free-expression and as a means of fulfilling the ancient function of dramatic art—to tell a story. Thus, history, geography, literature are amenable to illumination and vivification by dramatic embodiment in which movement plays a large part. At the same time what is held to be an essential need in young people—to learn confidence in themselves and to express it in a group-situation (jargon spawns in education)—is satisfied. A probable bonus is, of course, that physical action can breed physical well-being. The socio-political (the spawning is incessant) results are confidently expected to be beneficial both to the individual and to the child. Again the paradox appears—the quest for self-discovery is meant to lead to collective consciousness, action and experience.

A very detailed examination of physical drama in all types of schools in England over a number of years and in different parts of the country yields some conclusions.

First, that there can be little doubt that the majority of children find the activity involved more immediately rewarding than the traditional teaching methods.

Second, that there seems to be no correlation between the enjoyment of the child and the educational results achieved. Certainly there cannot be any doubt about the physical results—healthy well-being, the possibility of discovering potential ballet-dancers, physical education teachers—all on the credit side. But there is no evidence that the facts and realities of history, geography or literature (the subjects most frequently involved) are retained in the child's mind, or that relationships within the child's imagination are sensitized any more efficiently than by traditional methods.

Third, that there is no evidence that the socio-political ideals of physical drama theorists are fulfilled. The enthusiasts for physical drama often seem unable to grasp that a substantial minority of children do not find physical activity, especially in public, natural to them. In fact, for some, far from freeing them it seems to hog-tie their personalities. The achievement of individual freedom within the incompatibility of collectivization turns out for all children to be another form of authoritarianism and, for a minority, a painful and embarrassing illusion.

Fourth, that the best results, in terms of an equality between energy generated, enjoyment gained and education implanted, are achieved when improvisation in physical drama is subsumed in a disciplined and formal and planned pattern of activity and intention.

Fifth, that most children are not only amenable to being asked to respond to disciplined form and pattern, but that they welcome it.

It is perhaps apt, at this point, to turn to the second main type of non-verbal drama—that which either has noises instead of words or in which a verbal element is almost completely improvised. The physical drama that has been described and commented upon above is often soundless or accompanied by music or invented noise.

Improvised physical drama in both schools and fringe theatre is often accompanied by vocalization (when it is not 'backed' by music or invented noise) that is itself improvisatory. The nature and extent of this verbal improvisation bring about a different relationship between actor and actor, and actor and audience.

The greater the reliance on both physical and verbal improvisation the more does the actor come nearer to 'self-expression' rather than the agent by which a fictional character is expressed. So that, in this situation, actors X and Y have a relationship with one another upon the stage which partakes very much less of the characters b and c which they are supposed to be embodying. It is said that improvisation unlocks the inhibitions which prevent personal expression, but the art and craft of true acting is operating only when personal expression has been locked up inside the cage of a fictional character.

In an improvised play the actor searches within himself for words which, normally, are given to him (in his role as a character) by the text of the play. The words that come out of him in an improvised situation and the responses that are made to them by another improvising actor may, indeed, be following a theme and plot roughed out or blue-printed before performance, but the element of verbal freedom means that what is expressed and the relationships set up are likely to have a very high degree of the personal, the subjective, in them. But the more often an improvised play is performed the nearer it will relentlessly get to being a conventional play. Tricks of phrase, a telling word, a good sentence, a riposte that worked last night may well reappear tonight. Improvisation falls a victim to formalization; a 'text' begins to be created. But if there is a rigorous refusal to avoid this, and a strong element of true improvisation remains over a period of time, the result is that different relationships (to a degree) between actors and theme and text, and between actor and actor are created in each performance. The element of 'personal expression' remains a dominant one in the presentation of the play. The extent of this will vary, but it will also affect the relationship of actors to audience. One of the most prevalent characteristics of theatre with a large amount of verbal improvisation is the frequency with which the audience is directly addressed. Sometimes it is part of a planned effect, sometimes it is in response to an actor's sense of the mood of an audience, sometimes it is a panic move as the actor loses the thread of the improvisation, cannot find the words; when this occurs he cries for help.

Ideally, improvised drama should have no audience because the existence of one presupposes that, having paid money, it has to be satisfied by a product which, by testing or rehearsal, is guaranteed to please. The existence of an audience is another of improvisation's greatest enemies, because it brings with it—indeed by its very nature it implies—a sense of form, of pattern, of prepared ritual. In the classroom, when verbal

234

improvisation is used, there is no audience, except the teacher or, sometimes, that part of the class for which no participation can be arranged. Classroom drama is a purer form of improvised drama than anything that can be found in the professional theatre—though it is, inevitably, less efficient.

The enthusiastic supporters of verbal improvisation point to the way in which, like physical improvisation, it allows the child to free itself, to express, to make its imagination into words. But the enthusiasm seems to ignore the significant minority of children to whom verbal expression is less natural, less desirable, less capable of destroying inhibition than something else. Many children, and indeed adults, who find themselves jostled and jockeyed into saying something in a theatre hell bent on audience-participation, suffer torture through the mistaken belief of theorists that through their mouths will they be incited to find themselves. The absence of an audience makes no difference—in fact it may compound their fear and mental stress.

. What exists in both fringe physical and verbal improvisation theatre and in education is a very curious and very disturbing confusion of what constitutes freedom of expression and what constitutes any cohesive conception of art. The frightening increase in classroom violence may lead us to think that part of its cause may be the fact that the inducement to find freedom of expression has not been accompanied by an answer to the question—freedom for what? What is presented in a good deal of physical theatre, thankfully, as yet, not accompanied by violence, may prompt the same reflection.

Again, we may ask of verbal improvisation why it is necessary to assume, as it is assumed, that free expression and liberated imagination can only be achieved by language which is an immediate response and has not undergone any process of reflection or care for felicity? If this were true we should have to look elsewhere than to the rigorous labours of their schoolmasters to explain the astonishing verbal fecundity of the Elizabethans. But where should we look?

Language should be not merely an indication that mental and emotional activity is taking place, but an embodiment of that activity. Why is it, in a 'planned improvisation' (the hybrid has to exist in an educational system which has not yet

statutorily abandoned the formal teaching of English literature) where pupils are asked to present physically the meeting
between Macbeth, Banquo and the Witches, that it is thought
that free expression (and Will Shakespeare) are best served by
one child muttering to the best of his bent, 'Here are some
witches', three others are 'freed' by mumbling, 'We've made
some poison' and yet another saying 'Go away', when await-
ing these children is the frisson of 'So foul and fair a day I have
not seen'—and so on? The question is pertinent because this is
one example of a process that is common in school drama. The
answers usually given are that Shakespeare's language is too
difficult or (in more enlightened schools) that, eventually, the
children will be led to Shakespeare's language after, so to say,
involving themselves in the fiction of the play.

But the second is losing ground to the first, simply because
of the growth of the notion that 'specialness' (and Shakespeare
is nothing if not special) in verbal communication over and
above a certain denominator is not only 'undemocratic' but is
too difficult—and is likely, if it is allowed its head, to help to
distinguish between children's sensibilities and make too
apparent a hierarchy of ability and perception.

An acceptance of language as one of the few indications that
mankind is not only a cut above the beast, but can express an
awareness of this in a manner which ennobles and thrills, has
given place to something else that regards language as a convenience for the expression of common denominators of
human experience. The next step from this is to relegate
language to a position where it must play a minor role in
human experience. To adopt Pater's phrase—'not the fruits of
experience, but experience itself'[26] may well express the
motivation of a civilization which, in order to gratify the
demands of instant response, will be prepared to sacrifice one
of the few attributes which distinguish man from the animal—to which instant response, and that alone, is a natural
function. .

A society whose drama and theatre exhibit such a degree of
dedication to the common denominators of language, to the
physical, to improvisation has already, ipso facto, begun this
process of relegation. The same society which encourages or
permits its education, incited by ferociously sincere theorists,

to regard language as merely therapeutic and functional is increasing the process. And that society which finds what is aesthetic and intellectually rigorous an affront to its sociological or political expediencies is not only hastening the process but hurling itself towards a terrible kind of silence. There it will be deaf to everything except the huge grunts of mankind as it satisfies its animal instincts.

Notes

INTRODUCTION

1. A. Artaud, *The Theatre and its Double*, 1938. Quoted in E. Bentley, *The Theory of the Modern Stage*, London 1968, p.55.
2. H. Pinter, *The Caretaker*, first performed, London 1960.
3. W. Shakespeare, *Macbeth*, I.vi.1-3.
4. ibid., I.v.35-7.
5. ibid., II.i. 56-60.
6. H. Pinter, *The Homecoming*, first performed, London 1965.
7. G. Steiner, *Language and Silence*, London 1967, p.13.

CHAPTER 1: The Word and the Play

1. A distinction should be made between the process by which a playwright and director (as in the case of Elia Kazan and Tennessee Williams or E. Martin Browne and T.S. Eliot) either collaborate or disagree or compromise and the procedure (as with Joan Littlewood and Shelagh Delaney, so it appears) where the director unilaterally changes a text.
2. I. Kott, *Shakespeare Our Contemporary*, London 1964, p.73.
3. Quoted by I. Jack in *English Literature 1815-1832*, Oxford 1963, p.178.
4. A. Symons, 'A New Art of the Stage' in *Studies in Seven Arts*, London 1924 (2nd edn), p.223.
5. P. Brook, *The Empty Space*, London 1968, p.37.
6. ibid., p.38.
7. Quoted in A. Nagler, *A Source Book of Theatrical History*, New York 1952. The comment is made by the Knight of Malta in Smollett's *Peregrine Pickle*, 1751.
8. R.C. Sherriff, *Journey's End*, first performed, London 1928.
9. S. Langer, *Feeling and Form*, London 1957, p.68.

238

CHAPTER 2: The Twentieth Century and the Language of Drama
1. V. Woolf, 'Modern Fiction', in *The Common Reader*, London 1925.
2. Letter from W.B. Yeats to John Quinn, 1908, quoted in S.B. Bushrui, *Yeats's Verse Plays*, Oxford 1965, p.154.
3. R. Brustein, *The Theatre of Revolt*, London 1965, p.15.
4. T.S. Eliot, *Poetry and Drama*, London 1941, p.34.
5. ibid., p.35.
6. See J.W. Dunne, *An Experiment with Time*, London 1927.
7. J.B. Priestley, *I Have Been Here Before*, first performed, London 1937; J.L. Balderston and J.C. Squire, *Berkeley Square*, first performed, London 1926 and based on Henry James's unfinished novel, *The Sense of the Past*.
8. J.M. Barrie, *Mary Rose*, first performed, London 1920.
9. J. Bridie, *Tobias and the Angel*, first performed, London 1930; S. Vane, *Outward Bound*, first performed, London 1923.

CHAPTER 3: Bernard Shaw and the Language of Man in Society
1. G.B. Shaw, *Bernard Shaw, Collected Letters 1889-1910*, (ed Dan H. Laurence), London 1972, p.945.
2. ibid., p.957.
3. ibid., p.461.
4. Shaw, in the 1898 preface to *Widowers' Houses*.
5. ibid., p.72.
6. ibid., p.73.
7. Shaw, *Letters*, op. cit., pp.294-5.
8. A. Symons, 'An Apology for Puppets' in *Plays, Acting and Music*, London 1928, p.9.
9. A. Wesker, *Roots*, first London performance, 1960.
10. Shaw, *Pygmalion*, first performed, Vienna 1913.
11. Shaw, *Captain Brassbound's Conversion*, first performed, London 1900.
12. Shaw, 'Rules for Directors' in *The Strand*, cxvii, London 1949.
13. ibid.
14. See *Shaw* by A.M. Gibbs, Edinburgh 1969.
15. Shaw, *Mrs. Warren's Profession*, published, London 1898.
16. Shaw, *Back to Methuselah*, first performed as sequence of five plays, New York 1922. First British performance, Birmingham 1923.

CHAPTER 4: John Galsworthy and the Language of Man and Society
1. Shaw, letter to the editor of *The Saturday Review*, cx, 2 July 1910. Quoted in West (ed) *Shaw on Theatre*, New York 1958, p.114.

2. J. Gassner, *Masters of the Drama*, New York (3rd edn) 1954, p.616.
3. J. Galsworthy, 'Some Platitudes Concerning Drama', quoted in R.H. Coats, *John Galsworthy as a Dramatic Artist*, London 1926, p.11 and passim.
4. See, for example, *Loyalties*, first performed, London 1922.
5. Galsworthy, *Strife*, first performed, London 1909.
6. See Galsworthy's essay, 'Some Platitudes', quoted in Coates, op.cit.
7. Galsworthy, *The Silver Box*, first performed, London 1906.
8. Coats, op.cit., p.261.
9. See, for example, *The Silver Box*, op.cit.
10. Galsworthy's writing span extends from *The Silver Box* (1906) to *Escape* (1926). His two best plays—*Strife* and *Justice*—were written in 1909 and 1910 respectively.
11. Coats, op.cit., p.149.
12. Quoted in Coats, op.cit., p.199. The passage comes from the preface to the Manaton edn of the plays.
13. Galsworthy, quoted in Coats, op.cit.

CHAPTER 5: Naturalism, Wesker and Osborne
1. S. Hall in *The Encore Reader*, London 1965, pp.114-15.
2. L. Anderson, *The Encore Reader*, op.cit., p.78.
3. L. Kitchin, *Mid Century Drama*, London 1960, p.113.
4. A. Wesker, *The Wesker Trilogy*, London 1960. It consists of three plays—*Chicken Soup with Barley, Roots, I'm Talking about Jerusalem.*
5. St John Ervine, *Mixed Marriage*, first performed in England, 1911.
6. Wesker, *Chicken Soup with Barley,* first produced as part of the Trilogy, London 1960.
7. The published version of *The Kitchen* derives from a play written before the Trilogy. How much changed it is from the original is not known.
8. J.R. Taylor, *Anger and After*, London 1963 (revised edn), p.144.
9. Taylor, op.cit., p.146.
10. *Theatre Quarterly*, vol.i, no. 2, London 1971, p.16 and passim.
11. ibid.
12. Taylor, op.cit., p.147.
13. Wesker, quoted in Taylor, op.cit., p.146.
14. *Theatre Quarterly*, op.cit.
15. See Chapter 11 for a fuller discussion of Edward Bond.
16. J. Osborne, *The Entertainer*, first performed, London 1957.

CHAPTER 6: W.B. Yeats—the Poet in the Theatre
1. L. MacNeice, *The Poetry of W.B. Yeats,* Oxford 1941, p.191.

2. A. Symons, 'At the Stage-Door', in *Poems*, vol.i, London 1924, p.182.
3. T.S. Eliot, 'Morning at the Window', from *Prufrock*, London 1917.
4. Symons, from preface to *London Nights* (2nd edn), London 1897.
5. Symons 'Mr W.B. Yeats' in *Studies in Prose and Verse*, London 1904, p.235.
6. E. Gordon Craig, *The Art of the Theatre*, London 1911. Quoted in Bentley, op.cit.
7. Yeats subjected his plays to so much rewriting and revision that it is a bewildering task to attempt conclusions about their dating or the extent to which we can be sure that printed texts are to be regarded as the final version. See S.B. Bushrui, *Yeats's Verse Plays: The Revisions 1900-1910*, Oxford 1965.
8. Bushrui, op.cit., p.14.
9. See Ernest Rhys, *Everyman Remembers*, London 1931.
10. W.B. Yeats, *Autobiographies*, London 1965, pp.434-5.
11. T.R. Henn, *The Lonely Tower*, London 1965 (2nd edn).
12. Yeats, op.cit., p.468.
13. Yeats, ibid.
14. A. Wade, *The Letters of W.B. Yeats*, London 1954, p.510.
15. Yeats, *The Green Helmet and other Poems*, 1910.
16. See introduction to *W.B. Yeats, Selected Plays* (ed. Jeffares), London 1964.
17. Bushrui, op.cit., p.226.

CHAPTER 7: The Interlude of the 1930s—the Poet in Society
1. W.H. Auden, 'The Composer' in *Collected Shorter Poems—1927-1957*, London 1950, p.21.
2. Auden, 'Gare du Midi', op.cit., p.25.
3. Auden, 'Lay Your Sleeping Head . . .' op.cit., p.238.
4. J. Lehmann, *New Writing in Europe*, London 1940.
5. S. Spender, *Trial of a Judge*, London 1938.
6. Auden and C. Isherwood, *The Dog Beneath the Skin*, first performed, London 1935.

CHAPTER 8: T.S. Eliot – the Dramatist in Search of a Language
1. Eliot, *The Waste Land*, New York 1922. All quotations from Eliot's poems and plays are, unless otherwise stated, taken from *The Complete Poems and Plays of T.S. Eliot*, London 1969. In the notes, however, the first publication or performance is stated.
2. See T.S. Eliot, *The Waste Land—a facsimile of the original drafts including the annotations of Ezra Pound*, ed. Valerie Eliot, London 1971.

3. D. Thomas, *Under Milk Wood*, first performed and published, London 1954.
4. Eliot, *Poetry and Drama*, op.cit.
5. Eliot, *Sweeney Agonistes, Fragments of an Aristophanic Melodrama*, London 1932.
6. N. Coghill, in *T.S. Eliot, A Symposium*, compiled by R. March and Tambimuttu, London 1948, p.86.
7. E.M. Browne, ibid., p.197.
8. Auden and Isherwood, *The Ascent of F6*, first performed, London 1936.
9. Auden and Isherwood, *The Dog Beneath the Skin*, op.cit.
10. Eliot, *The Rock*. A pageant play written for performance at Sadlers Wells Theatre, London 1934.
11. Eliot, *Murder in the Cathedral*, Canterbury 1935—first acting edition. First complete edition, London 1935.
12. Eliot, *The Family Reunion*, London 1939.
13. E.M. Browne, *The Making of T.S. Eliot's Plays*, London 1969, pp.37-8.
14. Eliot, *The Cocktail Party*, London 1951; *The Confidential Clerk,* London 1954; *The Elder Statesman*, London 1959.
15. In *The Daily Telegraph*, 23 August 1949.

CHAPTER 9: Harold Pinter – the Deceptive Poet
1. E. Bentley, *The Modern Theatre*, London 1948, pp.xxii-iii.
2. See C. Fry, *A Phoenix Too Frequent*, London 1946; *The Lady's Not For Burning*, London 1948; *Venus Observed*, London 1949; *A Sleep of Prisoners*, London 1951.
3. P. Hall in *Theatre Quarterly*, vol.ii, no.7, 1972.
4. Pinter, *The Birthday Party*, op.cit.
5. *The Caretaker*, op.cit.
6. Pinter, *The Room,* first performed, Bristol 1957; published London 1960.
7. Pinter, *The Birthday Party*, London 1960. First performed, Cambridge 1958.
8. Pinter, *The Homecoming*, op.cit.
9. Pinter, *The Room*, op.cit.
10. Pinter, *A Slight Ache,* London 1961.

CHAPTER 10: American Connections—O'Neill, Miller, Williams and Albee
1. H. Miller, *Death of a Salesman*, first performed, 1949.
2. E. O'Neill, *Mourning Becomes Electra*, first performed, 1931.
3. For an appraisal of all three as poets and dramatists see M.

Cunliffe, *The Literature of the United States*, London 1954.
4. Quoted in A.H. Quinn, *A History of the American Drama from the Civil War to the Present Day*, New York 1936 (rev. edn), vol.ii, p.258.
5. See *Waiting for Lefty* and *Awake and Sing*, both produced 1935.
6. K. Tynan, *Tynan on Theatre,* London 1964, p.144.
7. Miller, *A View from the Bridge*, New York 1955, pp.1-2.
8. Miller, *Death of a Salesman*, op.cit. See introduction to edn, London 1961.
9. T. Williams, *The Glass Menagerie*, first performed, New York 1949.
10. Williams, *A Streetcar Named Desire*, first performed, New York 1949.
11. Williams, *The Seven Descents of Myrtle*, New York 1949.
12. Williams, *Camino Real*, first performed, New York 1953.
13. Williams, *Cat on a Hot Tin Roof*, first performed, New York 1953.
14. E. Albee, *Who's Afraid of Virginia Woolf ?*, first performed, New York 1962.
15. S. Beckett, *Waiting for Godot (En Attendant Godot)*, first performed, Paris 1953.
16. Albee, *The American Dream*, first performed, New York 1961.
17. Albee, *A Delicate Balance*, first performed, New York 1966.
18. C. Morgan (1894-1958). Better known as English novelist than as dramatist, but several plays had a short but large vogue—see *The Flashing Stream*, 1938.
19. For example, see Priestley's *Eden End* (1934) beginning Act III, Sc.i.
20. Albee, *The Zoo Story*, first performed, Berlin 1959.

CHAPTER 11: Drama in Contemporary Britain – Verbal and Non-Verbal
1. J.R. Taylor, *The Second Wave,* London 1971, p.206.
2. Quoted in Taylor, op.cit., p.50.
3. P. Nichols, *The National Health*, London 1970.
4. See introduction to P. Terson, *Zigger Zagger*, London 1970, p.17.
5. Terson, ibid., p.19.
6. H. Ibsen, *The Master Builder*, first performed, Berlin 1893.
7. See the introduction to *Zigger Zagger*, op.cit.
8. E. Bond, *Saved*, London 1965.
9. Taylor, op.cit., p.35.
10. Taylor, op.cit., p.81.
11. Quoted in Taylor, op.cit., p.108.
12. Taylor, op.cit., p.11.

13. M. Duffy, *Rites*, London 1969.
14. D. Halliwell, *K.D. Dufford*, London 1970.
15. Terson, *The Apprentice*, London 1970.
16. Terson, ibid.
17. Bond, *Saved*, op.cit.
18. G. Cooper, *The Object*, first performance on BBC, 1964.
19. T. Stoppard, *Rosencrantz and Guildenstern are Dead*, London 1967; D. Rudkin, *'Afore Night Come,* London 1961; J. Orton, *Entertaining Mr Sloane,* London 1965; P. Shaffer, *Equus,* London 1974; E. Bond, *Narrow Road to the Deep North,* London 1968.
20. J. Orton. See *Loot*, London 1967; *What the Butler Saw*, London 1969.
21. D. Mercer, *Belcher's Luck*, London 1966; F. Marcus, *The Killing of Sister George*, London 1965; P. Terson, *The Mighty Reservoy*, London 1970; P. Nichols, *The Ruling Class,* London 1969.
22. Bond, *Passion*, London 1974.
23. Rudkin's plays almost invariably contain an element of violence, but its communication is highly verbal and cerebral.
24. Osborne, *A Bond Honoured*, London 1966—an adaptation of Lope de Vega's *La Fianza Satisfecha*.
25. Taylor, op.cit., p.125.
26. See W. Pater, conclusion to *The Renaissance*, London 1873.

Select Bibliography

In addition to the books named in the notes the following have been consulted:

1. GENERAL 1900–45
Beerbohm, M. *Around Theatres,* London 1924.
Bentley, E. *The Modern Theatre,* London 1948.
Clark, B. H. *The British and American Drama of Today: Outlines for their Study,* New York 1915.
Darlington, W. A. *Six Thousand and One Nights: Forty Years a Critic,* London 1960.
Dukes, A. *Modern Dramatists,* London 1911.
Nicoll, A. *English Drama 1900-1930: The Beginnings of the Modern Period,* Cambridge 1973.
Reynolds, E. *Modern English Drama: A Survey of Theatre from 1900,* London 1949.
Trewin, J. C. *The Theatre Since 1900,* London 1963.

2. GENERAL 1945–76
Armstrong, W. A. (ed.) *Experimental Drama,* London 1963.
Brown, J. R. *Theatre Language: A Study of Arden, Osborne, Pinter and Wesker,* London 1972.
Brown, J. R. and Harris, B. *Contemporary Theatre* (Stratford upon Avon Studies 4), London 1962.
Esslin, M. *The Theatre of the Absurd,* London 1961.
Gascoigne, B. *Twentieth Century Drama,* London 1962.
Nicoll, A. *English Drama: A Modern Viewpoint,* London 1968.
Nicoll, A. *World Drama* (rev. edn). London 1976.
Palmer, D. and Bradbury, M. (eds.) *American Theatre* (Stratford upon Avon Studies 10).

3. BOOKS ON AMERICAN DRAMA PUBLISHED IN THE USA
Bentley, E. *The Dramatic Event: An American Chronicle,* 1954.

Brown, J. M. *The American Theatre as Seen by Its Critics, 1752–1934,* 1934.

Clurman, H. *The Fervent Years,* 1957.

Downer, A. S. *Fifty Years of American Drama, 1900–1950,* 1957.

Rice, E. *The Living Theatre,* 1959.

4. INDIVIDUAL AUTHORS
G. B. Shaw
Bentley, E. *Bernard Shaw,* Norfolk, Connecticut 1947; London 1967.

Chesterton, G. K. *George Bernard Shaw,* London 1909.

Dukore, B. F. *Bernard Shaw, Director,* London and Washington, 1971.

Kaufman, R. J. (ed.) *G. B. Shaw. A Collection of Critical Essays* (20th Century Views), London and Englewood Cliffs, N.J., 1965.

Mills, J. A. *Language and Laughter: Comic Diction in the Plays of Bernard Shaw,* Tucson 1969.

W. B. Yeats
Moore, J. R. *Masks of Love and Death: Yeats as a Dramatist,* Ithaca 1971.

Nathan, L. E. *The Tragic Drama of William Butler Yeats: Figures in a Dance,* New York 1965.

Ure, P. *Yeats the Playwright: A Commentary on Character and Design in the Major Plays,* London and New York 1963.

John Galsworthy
Choudhuri, C. *Galsworthy's Plays. A Critical Survey,* Bombay 1961.

Dupont, V. *John Galsworthy: The Dramatic Artist,* Toulouse and Montpellier 1946.

T. S. Eliot
Donoghue, D. *The Third Voice: Modern British and American Verse Drama,* Princeton 1959.

Gardner, H. *The Art of T. S. Eliot,* London 1949.

Peacock, R. *The Poet in the Theatre,* London 1946.

Smith, C. H. *T. S. Eliot's Dramatic Theory and Practice,* Princeton 1963.

John Osborne
Trussler, S. *The Plays of John Osborne: An Assessment,* London 1969.
Harold Pinter
Esslin, M. *The Peopled Wound: The Work of Harold Pinter,* London 1970.

Arnold Wesker
Leeming, G. and Trussler, S. *The Plays of Arnold Wesker: An Assessment,* London 1971.

Acknowledgments

The author and publisher wish to thank the following for permission to reproduce copyright material:

Edward Albee: to Jonathan Cape Ltd and Atheneum Publishers for extracts from *Who's Afraid of Virginia Woolf?*

W. H. Auden: extract from *Collected Shorter Poems 1927–1957* reprinted by permission of Faber and Faber Ltd

W. H. Auden and **C. Isherwood:** extract from *The Dog Beneath the Skin* reprinted by permission of Faber and Faber Ltd

Edward Bond: to Eyre Methuen and Margaret Ramsay Ltd for extracts from *Passion* and *Saved*

Peter Brook: to MacGibbon and Kee Ltd Z/Granada Publishing Co. Ltd for extracts from *The Empty Space*

Robert Brustein: to Little, Brown and Co. in association with Atlantic Monthly Press for an extract from *The Theatre of Revolt*

R. Bushrui: extract from *Yeats's Verse Plays: The Revisions 1900–1910* by permission of the Oxford University Press

T. S. Eliot: to Faber and Faber Ltd for poetry and play extracts from *The Collected Works of T. S. Eliot* and from *On Poetry and Poets*. To Harcourt Brace Jovanovich, Inc. for the extract on p. 156 from *Murder in the Cathedral,* copyright, 1935, by Harcourt Brace Jovanovich, Inc.; copyright, 1963 by T. S. Eliot. Reprinted by permission of the publisher

John Galsworthy: excerpts from *The Plays of John Galsworthy* are reprinted with the permission of G. Duckworth and Co. Ltd and Charles Scribner's Sons, copyright 1909, 1926, Charles Scribner's Sons

L. Kitchin: extract from *Mid Century Drama* reprinted by permission of Faber and Faber Ltd

Marowitz, Milne and **Hale** (eds.): to Methuen and Co. Ltd for extracts from *The Encore Reader*

Arthur Miller: to Elaine Greene Ltd and The Viking Press, Inc. for extracts from *Death of a Salesman,* copyright © 1949 by Arthur Miller, and *The Crucible,* copyright © 1952, 1953 by Arthur Miller

John Osborne: to Faber and Faber Ltd and David Higham Associates for extracts from *Look Back in Anger* and to David Higham Associates for an extract from *The Entertainer*

J. B. Priestley: to the author and Heinemann and Co. Ltd for an extract from *Dangerous Corner*

G. B. Shaw: to the Society of Authors on behalf of the Bernard Shaw Estate for extracts from *The Plays of G. B. Shaw* and *The Collected Letters of G. B. Shaw 1889–1910* (ed. Dan T. Lawrence)

R. C. Sherriff: to the R. C. Sherriff Estate for an extract from *Journey's End*

Arthur Symons: to Martin Secker and Warburg Ltd for extracts from *The Works of Arthur Symons*

John Russell Taylor: to A. D. Peters and Co. Ltd for extracts from *The Second Wave*

Dylan Thomas: extract from *Under Milk Wood* reprinted by permission of J. M. Dent and Sons Ltd and New Directions Publishing Corporation. Copyright 1954 New Directions Publishing Corporation, New York

Arnold Wesker: to Jonathan Cape Ltd and Harper and Row Publishers for extracts from *The Trilogy* and *The Kitchen.* © Harper and Row, Publishers, Inc., 1959, 1960

Tennessee Williams: to Elaine Greene Ltd and International Creative Management for extracts from *A Streetcar Named Desire* © copyright 1947 by Tennessee Williams

Virginia Woolf: to the Literary Estate of Virginia Woolf and the Hogarth Press, and to Harcourt Brace Jovanovich, Inc. for an extract from 'Modern Fiction' in *The Common Reader*

W. B. Yeats: to M. B. Yeats, Miss Anne Yeats and the Macmillan Co. of London and Basingstoke, and to Macmillan, Inc., New York, for extracts from *Autobiographies* (copyright 1916, 1935 by Macmillan Publishing Co., Inc., renewed 1944, 1963 by Bertha Georgie Yeats) and from *The Letters of W. B. Yeats,* edited by Allan Wade (copyright 1953, 1954 by Anne Butler Yeats)

Index

249